A DISEQUILIBRIUM MACROECONOMETRIC MODEL FOR THE INDIAN ECONOMY

T0347296

*To Dhamayanthi Kalirajan
and Sushma Bhide*

A Disequilibrium Macroeconometric Model for the Indian Economy

KALIAPPA KALIRAJAN

Foundation for Advanced Studies on International Development, Tokyo and Australian National University, Canberra

SHASHANKA BHIDE

Institute for Social and Economic Change, Bangalore and National Council of Applied Economic Research, New Delhi

Routledge
Taylor & Francis Group

LONDON AND NEW YORK

First published 2003 by Ashgate Publishing

Reissued 2018 by Routledge
2 Park Square, Milton Park, Abingdon, Oxon OX14 4RN
711 Third Avenue, New York, NY 10017, USA

Routledge is an imprint of the Taylor & Francis Group, an informa business

Copyright © Kaliappa Kalirajan and Shashanka Bhide 2003

Kaliappa Kalirajan and Shashanka Bhide have asserted their right under the Copyright, Designs and Patents Act, 1988, to be identified as the authors of this work.

Notice:
Product or corporate names may be trademarks or registered trademarks, and are used only for identification and explanation without intent to infringe.

Publisher's Note
The publisher has gone to great lengths to ensure the quality of this reprint but points out that some imperfections in the original copies may be apparent.

Disclaimer
The publisher has made every effort to trace copyright holders and welcomes correspondence from those they have been unable to contact.

A Library of Congress record exists under LC control number: 2003056034

ISBN 13: 978-1-138-70988-1 (hbk)
ISBN 13: 978-1-138-70985-0 (pbk)
ISBN 13: 978-1-315-19906-1 (ebk)

Contents

List of Figures

List of Tables

Preface

Economic reforms in India are now slightly more than a decade old. The results in terms of economic growth and other macro economic parameters have been encouraging. Many research studies have pointed to the benefits and costs of the reform process. However, there is one lacuna in these research efforts in terms of assessment of the impact at the state level. The regional dimension is often not captured in such analyses of reforms. This study is an attempt to fill this lacuna by presenting a framework for incorporating a regional dimension in macro economic analysis.

For this application, we focus on the agricultural sector of the Indian economy. Agriculture has been a crucial sector in the Indian economy because of its implications to food security and as a source of employment to the poor in the rural areas. India's economic reforms of the 1990s held promise of an accelerated growth of agriculture as they sought to remove many of the indirect impediments to growth, for example, by correcting the large tariff protection given to the industrial sector. The trade reforms, under the umbrella of WTO negotiations have also touched Indian agriculture by affecting agricultural trade. Such changes can be expected to be more intense in the future for agriculture. Further, agriculture is an area of policy at the state level in India's federal structure. In this sense, an attempt to examine the impact of various policy changes that are implemented at the national level on the performance of agriculture at the state level would provide important insights to policy makers at the state level.

The issues addressed in the present model relate to the impact of alternative policy scenarios on the agricultural sector. The issues that are central to the debate on economic reforms as they relate to agriculture are the issues of the existing differences in technical efficiencies across and within states, pricing the inputs, pricing and marketing of the output including tariffs and restrictions on international trade, exchange rate variations and generally the role of government in relation to agriculture. The economic reforms at the macro level, such as the exchange rate policy, monetary policy and fiscal policy, also affect agriculture. Thus, policies may relate to the agricultural sector directly or indirectly. While sectoral models can incorporate some of the features necessary for the analysis of the impact of policy changes on agriculture, an economy-wide framework that incorporates the behavioural and structural differences within and across states is more appropriate as the linkages between agriculture and the other sectors can be captured more effectively.

This book emanates from the research project on *Accelerating Growth Through Globalization of Indian Agriculture*, which was jointly carried out by the Australian National University, Canberra, Australia, under the coordination of Professor Kaliappa Kalirajan and the Madras School of Economics, Chennai, India, under the coordination of the Honorary Professor U. Sankar. We are grateful to members of the Advisory Committee, Dr. R. Radhakrishna, Dr. G. Thimmiah, Dr. A. Vaidyanathan and Dr. V.N. Mishra for their comments and suggestions. We thank Dr. U. Sankar, Dr. Ric Shand, Dr. G.S. Bhalla, Dr. K.L. Krishna, Dr. M. Govinda Rao and Dr. Nirvikar Singh for many fruitful discussions. The authors would like to thank Prof. Peter Pauly, University of Toronto for providing them with an opportunity to present the model at the Fall Meetings of the *LINK Project* in September 2001. Some of the results were also presented at the Conference on *Second Generation Economic Reforms in India* held in Chennai in December 1999 and a *Workshop on Rural Infrastructure* organized by the National Council of Applied Economic Research, New Delhi in December 2001. The authors would like to thank the participants for comments and suggestions, which were helpful in organizing this volume.

We are grateful to the National Council of Applied Economic Research in New Delhi for giving access to various data sets on the Indian economy. The financial support provided by the Australia Centre for International Agricultural Research (ACIAR) in Canberra is acknowledged with thanks. The cooperation provided by the ACIAR coordinators, Dr. Padma Lal and Dr. Donna Brennan is greatly appreciated. We are grateful to Ashgate for helping us in bringing out this volume to our satisfaction. We also would like to thank Mr. Raj Gupta for preparing our manuscript for publication.

Kaliappa Kalirajan
Shashanka Bhide

Chapter I

Economic Reforms and Agriculture: Context for the Study

I.1 Introduction

India, the second most populous nation in the world today is also among the largest economies of the world. It is, however, also among the poorest nations in terms of per capita income. It is estimated that one out of every third poor person in the world lives in India. The challenge for policy makers at the national and international level continues to be the design policies that will eradicate poverty. The development strategies that were followed in India since the beginning of the five-year plans in the early 1950s aimed at achieving higher standards of living for the population with equity and speed. Although some distinctions could be made in terms of emphasis and choice of instruments, over the period of four decades since 1950, the overall strategy of achieving economic growth through rapid industrialization is evident. Prominence to public sector enterprises and import substitution were partly a result of poor state of institutional infrastructure for mobilization of resources for industrialization and the experience of colonial rule, which preceded the post-independence development effort. The outcome of overall development effort does not compare favorably with the experience of several other economies, which in general followed an export-oriented strategy. The differences in outcome are not merely in terms of per capita income, but also in terms of other indicators of human development. The comparative experience of different economies provides a yet another basis for reforms in policies to pursue the original goals of achieving higher standards of living for the population as rapidly as possible.[1]

I.1.1 India's Economic Reforms of the 1990s

Economic policies of India changed dramatically in the 1990s providing a greater role for the markets and the private sector in economic activities. The mechanisms of discretionary control were liberalized or abandoned. There was progress in reducing and rationalizing of tax rates. Fiscal deficit was sought to be reduced and financed in ways that are more sustainable. There were major changes in trade

---

[1] A number of good comprehensive accounts of economic development strategies followed in India and elsewhere are available in the literature.

policy, fiscal policy, industrial policy, policy relating to foreign exchange transactions and the policies in the financial sector. The effort was to alter the economic policy environment to transform the economy into one where efficiency and technology could be upgraded to achieve higher levels of economic performance and keep pace with the improvements taking place elsewhere around the world.[2] There was a clear recognition that the policies of import substitution and reliance on public sector were not adequate to achieve sustained economic growth. The macroeconomic crisis of 1991 provided the opportunity for beginning the wide-ranging economic reforms.

In comparison to the economies that were more successful in promoting exports and attracting foreign capital, India's performance in economic growth was poor. As shown in Table I.1, the average annual growth rate of real GDP was

Table I.1   Annual Average Growth Rates (%) of Real GDP in Selected Countries

Country	1970-74	1975-79	1980-84	1985-89	1990-94	1995-99
A. Newly Industrializing Countries						
Hong Kong	8.5	10.2	7.8	6.9	5.3	2.2
Republic of Korea	8.6	8.9	6.1	9.0	7.5	5.0
Singapore	11.5	7.6	8.0	6.3	9.4	6.2
Taiwan	10.3	10.2	7.2	9.1	6.9	5.8
B. South-East Asian Countries						
Indonesia	8.4	7.0	5.0	5.6	8.0	1.7
Malaysia	8.3	7.2	6.9	4.9	9.3	5.2
Philippines	5.7	6.2	1.3	2.7	1.8	3.7
Thailand	6.2	7.8	5.7	9.0	9.0	1.5
C. South Asian Countries						
Bangladesh	0.3	3.9	3.7	4.3	4.5	5.1
India	2.2	4.1	5.1	6.1	4.8	6.5
Pakistan	2.2	5.4	6.3	6.1	4.6	3.4
Sri Lanka	6.2	5.0	5.3	3.2	5.5	4.9
D. China	8.9	5.4	9.7	9.9	10.7	8.8

Source of data: IMF Economic Outlook Data Base (September 2002).

substantially lower than the record of either the Newly Industrializing Economies of East Asia or the major South-east Asian economies, for the entire period of 1970s. In the 1980s India's growth performance began to match some of the South-East Asian country performances. The second half of the 1990s saw India grow faster than the crisis struck Asian economies. However, throughout the period of the 1970s and 1980s, China's growth outpaced India's. The divergence in

---

[2] Cassen and Joshi (1995) and Joshi and Little (1996), provide comprehensive discussion of economic reforms in India in the 1990s.

the levels of living between India and some other countries, which were not so far behind even in the 1970s, is striking (Table I.2). For instance India, Indonesia and Thailand were roughly at the same level of per capita income in the 1950s. But by 1990, Thailand's per capita income (PPP adjusted GNP) was three and a half times the level of India's and Indonesia had a per capita income that was nearly double of India's. China had actually lower per capita income than India, up to 1980. But by 1990, China's per capita GNP was 40% higher than India. Although by her own standards, India's economic growth accelerated during the 1980s, it was still lower than the some of the better performing East and South-East Asian economies. The annual average growth of per capita real national income increased by 3.5% during the decade of 1980s and in the 1990s the increase at a slightly higher rate of 3.8%. This compares impressively with the average increase of 1% during the previous three decades.

Table I.2   Other Countries Move Ahead of India: Ratio of Per Capita GDP (PPP Adjusted US$) of Selected Countries to India

Country	1950	1960	1970	1980	1990	1998
A. Newly Industrializing Countries						
Hong Kong	3.6	4.2	6.6	11.2	13.4	11.6
South Korea	1.2	1.5	2.3	4.4	6.6	7.0
Singapore	3.6	3.1	5.1	9.7	10.9	13.0
Taiwan	1.5	2.0	3.4	6.3	7.6	8.6
B. South-East Asian Countries						
Indonesia	1.4	1.4	1.4	2.0	1.9	1.8
Malaysia	2.5	2.0	2.4	3.9	3.9	4.1
Philippines	1.7	2.0	2.0	2.5	1.7	1.3
Thailand	1.3	1.4	2.0	2.7	3.5	3.6
C. South Asian Countries						
Bangladesh	0.9	0.7	0.7	0.6	0.5	0.5
India	1.0	1.0	1.0	1.0	1.0	1.0
Pakistan	1.0	0.9	1.1	1.2	1.2	1.1
Sri Lanka	1.6	1.4	1.6	2.0	1.9	1.9
D. China	0.7	0.9	0.9	1.1	1.4	1.8

Source of data: Maddison (2001).

The rise in the pace of economic growth, however, has not been uniform either across the sectors or across the regions within the country. While growth has been accompanied by reduction in the percentage of the poor in the population, the decline has also been uneven across the regions and between rural and urban segments of the population. The acceleration of growth witnessed during the 1980s turned out to be unsustainable with respect to fiscal and the balance of payments position. The economic reforms of the 1990s were in response to the developments that resulted from the unsustainable fiscal and balance of payments position of the economy. The reforms, which were initially of a macro nature, have now begun to affect specific sectors of the economy. In the financial sector, policy changes have led to the emergence of new agents, instruments and institutions leading to the expansion of this sector. In the case of infrastructure comprising of power, transportation and communications, policy changes have led to investments by the private sector – domestic and foreign – in ways that were not possible before the reforms. The de-licensing of industries and liberalization of the import regime has led to expansion of capacities and upgrading of technology. There are a number of areas, however, where policy reforms are yet to be effected. Even in areas where there is progress, the agenda for policy reforms is hardly completed.[3]

I.1.2 Agriculture and Economic Reforms

One of the major segments of the economy, where economic reforms have had only an indirect impact is agriculture. While the reforms in the other sectors and at the macro level have an indirect impact on agriculture, reforms relating to international trade in agricultural commodities, role of the public sector agencies in agricultural markets, investments by non-farm entities in agriculture, input subsidies and the land ownership/tenure are still being debated.[4] The lack of any major policy initiatives is also evident in the relatively slow growth of the sector as compared to the non-agricultural sectors. In Figure I.1, the trends in output of agriculture, industry and service sectors are compared for the period 1950-51 to 2000-01.[5] Although the growth of agriculture was slower than the other sectors throughout the five decades (almost), the divergence is more conspicuous in the 1990s. The relatively slower growth of agriculture has also resulted in the transition of the economy from a primarily agrarian to the point where the non-agricultural sectors have begun to play a greater role.

Another aspect of the growth scenario in agriculture, which is overlooked by several earlier studies, concerns the existing gap between the country's potential and realized agricultural outputs. This means that the agricultural sector is in disequilibrium and that output can be increased without having to increase current input levels.

---

[3] NCAER (2001) provides an overview of the course of the economic reforms of the 1990s. The more recent reform efforts are documented in Economic Survey, an annual publication of Ministry of Finance, Government of India.

[4] Reforms relating to trade in agriculture have led to reduction in non-tariff barriers to some extent also eliminating government monopoly in trading. On the domestic front, reform of input subsidies (irrigation, power and fertilizer) remains non-tractable. Government's policies on food grain procurement both to provide market support to the farmers and subsidized food to the poor is causing fiscal strain. Restriction on internal movement of agricultural commodities and related restrictions on storage are now sought to be eliminated (Government of India, 2002).

[5] The reference to years in Indian data is for fiscal or financial year of April-March, unless stated otherwise.

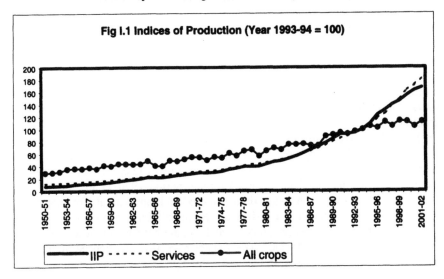

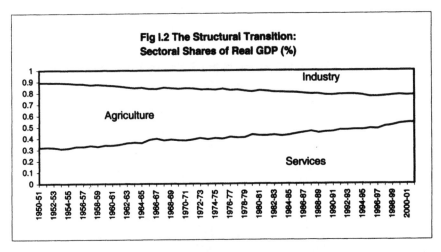

Figure I.2 illustrates the decline in the share of agriculture in the total output of the economy. The declining output share is, however, not matched by the trends in the share of employment of agriculture.

Regional Dimension of Economic Performance

The regional dimension of economic performance is reflected in the variation across different states in India.[6] A brief review of the variations in economic

---

[6] Shand and Bhide (2000) and Ahluwalia (2000) provide a discussion of the trends in the performance of India's states.

performance is presented in this section. Figure I.3 presents the relative position of the 15 major states, in the overall output of the economy. The data relate to net state domestic product (NSDP) in constant prices. Although the data are not strictly comparable across the states, they are a proxy for the level of output at the state level. Two states, Uttar Pradesh and Maharashtra are the largest among the major states considered. Andhra Pradesh, West Bengal, Tamilnadu and Gujarat each account for 7-8% of the combined NSDP of all the 17 states considered. Madhya Pradesh, Karnataka, Rajasthan and Punjab are of a similar order each accounting for 5-6% of combined NSDP. The remaining six states account for less than 5% each, of the combined NSDP. Average annual growth rates of NSDP across 15 major states are presented in Table I.3 for the period 1970-71 to 1995-96. The variation in the growth of net state domestic product is substantial. Over the period of 30 years, some states have consistently registered higher growth rates than the rest. For instance, Maharashtra, Haryana and Gujarat have the highest average rate of growth over the entire 30 years. These states have also experienced high growth states in the 1970s and 1980s. In the 1990s, the rate of growth has been slower in Haryana but yet close to the average of all the states. The states that have lagged behind in growth are: Orissa, Bihar, Assam and Kerala, when we consider the entire 30 year period.

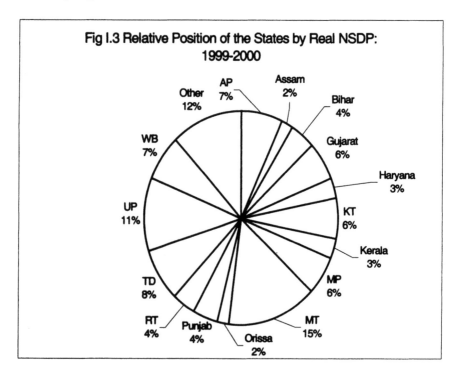

Fig I.3 Relative Position of the States by Real NSDP: 1999-2000

Table I.3   Annual Average Growth Rates (%) of Real NSDP

State	1970s	1980s	1990s	70-71/99-00
Andhra Pradesh	4.20	6.59	5.05	5.28
Assam	2.40	5.30	2.84	3.51
Bihar	3.22	5.16	2.80	3.72
Gujarat	5.53	6.13	6.37	6.01
Haryana	4.08	7.09	5.13	5.43
Karnataka	4.19	4.68	6.77	5.21
Kerala	2.61	2.92	5.89	3.81
Maharashtra	4.89	5.60	6.32	5.61
Madhya Pradesh	1.26	6.37	5.24	4.29
Orissa	2.13	5.90	2.17	3.40
Punjab	4.60	5.29	4.19	4.70
Rajasthan	1.10	7.27	5.94	4.90
TamilNadu	3.82	3.71	6.64	4.72
Uttar Pradesh	1.73	6.76	4.34	4.28
West Bengal	2.07	4.82	6.74	4.54
All-India	2.76	5.78	5.66	4.73

Note: In the case of Rajasthan, the year 1970-71 growth rate was excluded in calculating the averages as this was a year of unusually large positive growth for the state.

Table I.4   Per Capita NSDP for the Major States

State	Per Capita NSDP for Major States (Rs. At 1980-81 Prices)					Per Capita NSDP for Major States (US $)				
	1970-71	1980-81	1990-91	1995-96	1999-00	1970-71	1980-81	1990-91	1995-96	1999-00
AP	1267	1380	2060	2407	2787	160	174	253	277	316
ASSAM	1280	1284	1544	1606	1681	162	162	239	198	214
BIHAR	876	917	1197	983	1219	111	116	148	106	128
GUJARAT	1846	1940	2641	3517	3899	233	245	328	386	404
Haryana	1985	2370	3509	3679	4310	251	300	418	406	469
Karnataka	1469	1520	2039	2558	3292	186	192	256	280	340
Kerala	1459	1508	1815	2200	2558	184	191	234	269	333
Maharashtra	2027	2435	3483	4635	5352	256	308	415	471	522
MP	1315	1358	1696	1854	2069	166	172	226	203	218
Orissa	1330	1314	1383	1634	1761	168	166	171	186	195
Punjab	2159	2674	3730	4176	4719	273	338	464	480	551
Rajasthan	1505	1222	1942	1974	2229	190	155	234	225	252
TamilNadu	1533	1498	2237	2820	3417	194	189	278	306	375
UP	1220	1278	1652	1654	1863	154	162	200	176	195
West Bengal	1619	1773	2145	2704	3370	205	224	260	254	334
All-India	1520	1630	2222	2608	3131	182	206	278	286	349
Minimum	876	917	1197	983	1219	111	116	148	106	128
Maximum	2159	2674	3730	4635	5352	273	338	464	480	551
Range %	246	292	312	472	439	246	292	313	454	430
Mean	1526	1631	2205	2567	2968	193	206	275	281	323
SD	349.32	507.18	793.61	1043.47	1219.89	44.13	64.12	92.22	110.48	125.74
CV %	22.89	31.09	35.99	40.76	41.10	22.88	31.08	33.54	39.25	38.92

However, Kerala's performance improved significantly in the 1990s. There are, thus, some states whose performance in terms of growth has been uniformly better or uniformly poor, and some states whose performance has varied over the years. Put alternatively, there are states that constrain the growth performance of the national economy as a whole just as there are the slow growing sectors that constrain the overall growth. The divergence in per capita output resulting from the differences in output growth rates is shown in Table I.4. While the mean per capita NSDP has increased over the years, the disparity across the states has also increased. Both the standard deviation (SD) and coefficient of variation have increased between 1970 and 1999.

I.2 Objectives of the Study

A number of explanations have been offered in the development economics literature for the slow growth of India's economy. The constraint imposed by the low levels of per capita income that prevailed in the initial stages of development, the lagging levels of technology and technical efficiency that are a result of relatively low levels of integration of the domestic markets with the international markets are among the many explanations. The development strategies have not overcome these constraints so far. The reforms seek to redress these weaknesses by increasing market opportunities through opening up of the economy to international markets as well as increasing competition among the players to improve technical efficiency and productivity. Would there be a difference in the response of different sectors or different regions to the changes in different policies? The differences in performance across sectors and across regions imply that overall policy measures may produce varied impacts across the sectors and regions. An understanding of such differential impacts would be important in designing policies to improve the performance of the lagging sectors or regions. In this study, we focus on the agricultural sector, which is vital for India's overall economic growth. With the adoption of a methodology that captures variation in productivity across producers, we attempt to examine the impact of various policy measures affecting agriculture at the state level.

Performance of agricultural sector is important for the success of the economic reforms in India for a number of reasons. First, it provides livelihood for more than 60% of India's labour force. Second, majority of India's poor live in rural areas where agriculture is the mainstay of economic activities. Third, a number of studies point to the comparative advantage India possesses in agriculture and when there is trade liberalization in economies around the world, Indian agriculture is expected to benefit significantly. Fourth, a few studies have shown that there are significant variations in agricultural productivity across and within states. Finally, consumption of agricultural commodities takes place substantially at lower level of processing and value addition and considerable scope for expansion of agro-based activities exists leading to economic growth based on agricultural growth.

There have been various attempts to analyze the impact of different policy measures on the economy at the sectoral level and also at the overall economy level. Parikh et al (1995) for example, provide an analysis of selected measures of liberalization of agricultural policies at the national level using a Computable General Equilibrium (CGE) Model. Subramaniam (1993) provides a similar analysis for India. Chadha et al (1998) provide an analysis of various trade liberalization measures in a global setting for Indian economy. At the macro economic level there are a number of studies that have attempted to assess the impact of economic reforms in India. But in all these studies, the implications of regional dimension and inter- and intra-state productivity differences are not captured.

The present study focuses on the impact of selected policy reform measures on agriculture. As there are significant variations in agricultural productivity performance across the states, the study also examines the impact of policies on agriculture at the state level. The present study is an attempt at developing an economy-wide model for India incorporating inter- and intra-state productivity differences to assess the impact of selected policy scenarios on agriculture in terms of the impact on output, input use and overall productivity at the national and state levels. In this sense, the study is a distinctive approach to incorporating regional level details in a national economic model.

Two main objectives of the study are:

- Development of an economy wide model of India incorporating inter- and intra-state productivity differences in a disequilibrium framework to assess the impact of selected economic policy changes on Indian agriculture at the national and state level.
- Demonstrating the use of the model through assessment of the impact of selected policy measures relating to a number of variables covering agricultural output and input prices, import tariffs, exchange rate and government expenditures in general.

I.3 An Overview of the Trends in Indian Agriculture

As the focus of the study is on agriculture, we briefly review the broad trends in agricultural sector over time and across the states. Agricultural sector defined as comprising of the crop, livestock and allied activities, makes up about 25% of the real GDP of the Indian economy. Within the agricultural sector, the crop sub-sector accounts for 70% of the value of output and the livestock sector accounting for the remaining 30%. As pointed out earlier, the share of agriculture and allied activities has declined steadily over time from about 50% in 1950-51. The rate of growth of the sector has been slower than the growth of manufacturing and services on the long-term basis since the early 1950s. In a detailed study of the relative growth performance of different sectors, Bhide et al (1998) show that in terms of the growth rate of real GDP, agriculture and allied sub-sectors as a single group shows no structural break during the period 1950-51 to 1993-94 either taken as a whole or in terms of sub-periods. In the case of agriculture alone, a structural break in the growth pattern is noted in the early 1990s when the sub-period 1960-61 to 1993-94 was considered. In contrast, growth in manufacturing shows varying patterns during the period of the four decades. Even at the aggregate level, for the overall real GDP, breaks in growth rate pattern are noted for the sub-periods 1960-61 to 1993-94 and 1970-71 to 1993-94. There were no breaks when we consider the entire period of 1950-51 to 1993-94 or the sub-period 1980-81 to 1993-94. In terms of output per hectare, either as agricultural sub-sector by itself or inclusive of allied activities, the growth rates show a break in the pattern during the periods 1950-51 to 1992-93, 1960-61 to 1992-93 and 1980-81 to 1992-93, but not during 1970-71 to 1992-93. The lack of breaks in the growth pattern at the aggregate level and their presence in the pattern for per hectare output suggests productivity improvements due to the adoption of new technology of production and the declining potential for extensive cultivation of land. The pattern of growth as measured by the annual average rates of growth for different sub-sectors is summarized in Table I.5.

Table I.5   Annual Average Growth Rates of Real GDP by Sectors of Origin

Sector	1951-60	1961-70	1971-80	1981-90	1991-00
Agriculture	3.43	2.54	2.13	3.75	2.72
Agriculture and Allied	3.13	2.55	1.84	3.55	2.70
Mining & Quarrying	5.69	4.03	4.97	8.45	3.98
Manufacturing	6.08	5.31	4.13	7.62	6.06
Electricity gas & water supply	10.35	11.21	6.93	9.13	6.54
Construction	6.76	5.61	3.31	4.70	5.13
Trade, Hotels & Restaurant	5.29	4.82	4.31	5.93	7.29
Transport, Storage & Communication	5.70	5.52	6.18	5.57	7.96
Financing, insurance, real estate & business services	2.99	3.44	4.11	9.87	8.45
Community, social & personal services	3.67	5.31	4.01	6.10	6.77
Public Administration & Defence	5.15	7.91	5.41	6.50	6.31
Other Services	3.06	3.93	2.99	5.78	7.17
Gross domestic product at factor cost	3.94	3.75	3.16	5.64	5.61

Source of data: Central Statistical Organisation (2000).

I.3.1 Crop Output Composition

The pattern of growth of agricultural output has not been uniform across the states. Bhide et al (1998) find that although growth rates of agricultural output (real NSDP) of 15 major states showed a tendency to converge, there was also evidence of higher growth rates being associated with higher proportion of irrigated area in total crop area. The pattern of growth across states in the agricultural sector is summarized in Table I.6. The states of Maharashtra, Gujarat, West Bengal, Punjab and Haryana performed consistently better than average during the period of 1970s, and 1980s. In the case of Tamilnadu and Rajasthan the growth rate was lower than the average during the 1970s but improved to above average during 1980s, whereas in Karnataka and Kerala, although growth rate improved, it was still below the average experienced during the 1980s.

Table I.6 Annual Average Growth Rates (%) of Real NSDP: Agriculture and Allied Activities

State	1970s	1980s	1990s	70-71/99-00
AP	3.53	4.24	2.20	3.32
Assam	1.96	4.40	1.51	2.62
Bihar	1.33	4.22	0.31	1.95
Gujarat	7.98	11.19	2.96	7.38
Haryana	1.08	6.73	2.91	3.57
Karnataka	3.03	2.47	4.40	3.30
Kerala	-0.06	1.14	3.62	1.57
Maharashtra	4.63	5.12	3.42	4.39
MP	-1.62	6.47	4.28	3.04
Orissa	1.31	6.23	-0.18	2.45
Punjab	3.20	5.24	2.69	3.71
Rajasthan	-1.26	9.24	4.06	4.19
TamilNadu	2.18	3.55	3.63	3.12
UP	-0.25	6.08	3.01	2.94
West Bengal	1.75	6.21	5.13	4.36

Source of data: Central Statistical Organization.

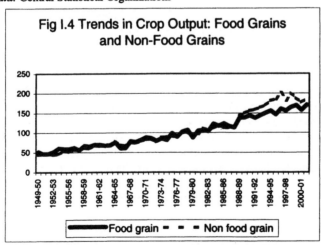

Fig I.4 Trends in Crop Output: Food Grains and Non-Food Grains

There is also variation in the composition of output within the crop sector. In terms of real value of gross output, the non-food grain output increased at a faster rate than the food grain output especially since the mid-1980s (Figure I.4). The share of non-food grains in the growth of crop output increased steadily since the 1960s except for the period of 1980s. Within the food grains, however, the share of rice and wheat has increased relative to the other grains (Figure I.5).

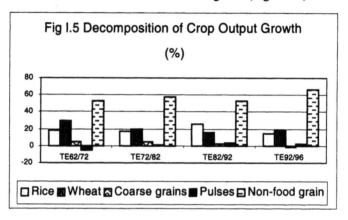

Fig I.5 Decomposition of Crop Output Growth (%)

Note: TE = Three years ending in.

The relative shares of major states in the growth of crop output were obtained from a decomposition of output growth for major crop groups and states. In this analysis, the prominence of non-food grains in their contribution to growth becomes even more conspicuous. Even for the period of 1980s, the share of selected non-food grains in the output growth increases sharply in comparison to the contribution of food grains (Tables I.7a-I.7b). Food grains contributed 54% of the output growth during the 1970s, but accounted for only 47% of the output growth during 1980s. During the 1970s, the states of Uttar Pradesh (UP), Maharashtra (MT), Punjab and Andhra Pradesh (AP) accounted for 65% of the increase in crop output. But in the 1980s, the shares of AP and MT declined and the shares of West Bengal (WB) and Rajasthan increased dramatically as compared to the performance in the 1970s. UP and Punjab continued to be the source of major output gains during the 1980s as well. In the case of Punjab and UP the gains were greater in food grain output than the non food grain output. But the gains in non-food grain output exceeded the gains in food grain output in a large number of states, namely, in Rajasthan, MP, TN, AP, KT, MT, KL and GT. Thus, there are some important changes taking place within agriculture that need to be taken into account while assessing the impact of changes in policies.

I.3.2 Trends in Crop Productivity, Input Use and Prices

The crop productivity measured in terms of output per hectare of land, either as gross output or value added, has increased over time. Conceptually, rise in gross output is on account of the increase in inputs per hectare as well as the increase in 'total factor productivity'. The rise in value added per unit of land includes the effect of increased application of labour and capital inputs per hectare of crop area as well as the improvements in total factor productivity.

Table I.7a   Decomposition of Change in the Value of Crop Output by States and Crops: TE1972 to TE1982 (% Contribution)

State	Cereals	Pulses	Food grain	Non-food grain	Total
Kerala	-0.08	0.03	-0.05	-1.23	-1.28
TN	-2.28	0.10	-2.18	1.24	-0.93
Bihar	-0.38	-0.29	-0.67	-0.02	-0.69
WB	-0.74	-0.41	-1.15	2.67	1.52
Rajasthan	0.97	0.23	1.21	1.32	2.53
Assam	0.95	0.05	1.00	1.81	2.81
MP	2.57	0.64	3.21	0.80	4.01
Haryana	4.16	-1.19	2.97	1.43	4.40
Orissa	0.06	1.81	1.88	2.66	4.54
Karnataka	1.38	0.64	2.02	3.78	5.80
Gujarat	1.63	0.84	2.47	5.47	7.94
AP	7.17	0.43	7.60	3.73	11.33
Punjab	11.17	-0.55	10.62	0.93	11.55
MT	9.91	1.24	11.15	10.01	21.16
UP	14.47	-2.04	12.43	9.19	21.61
Select15	50.96	1.54	52.50	43.79	96.29
Other	3.27	-1.75	1.52	2.19	3.71
India	54.23	-0.22	54.02	45.98	100.00

The trends in variables relating to the value of agricultural output and inputs are shown in Figures I.6a-I.6e. The per hectare value of output and value added, both in constant prices (Figure I.6a), increase together up to the end of 1970s and begin to diverge. The growth of gross output is faster than the growth of value added suggesting the acceleration in the growth of intermediate inputs such as fertilizer beginning in the 1980s.

The rise in the growth of intermediate inputs is also seen in the trend in this variable (Figure I.6b). The nominal input cost increases sharply starting in late 1970s as compared to the previous period.

Table I.7b   **Decomposition of Change in the Value of Crop Output by States and Crops: TE1982 to TE1992 (% Contribution)**

State	Cereals	Pulses	Food grain	Non-food grain	Total
Assam	0.84	0.00	0.84	0.74	1.58
Gujarat	-0.32	0.40	0.08	1.92	2.00
Kerala	-0.24	-0.01	-0.25	2.96	2.71
Orissa	1.67	0.41	2.09	1.01	3.10
Bihar	2.25	0.13	2.38	0.74	3.12
MT	1.31	0.95	2.26	2.50	4.76
Haryana	3.62	-0.02	3.61	2.90	6.51
Karnataka	1.24	0.10	1.33	5.70	7.03
AP	0.82	0.56	1.38	5.75	7.12
TN	2.05	0.39	2.44	5.10	7.54
MP	5.59	-2.00	3.59	4.81	8.40
WB	5.59	0.08	5.67	3.06	8.72
Punjab	7.02	-0.15	6.87	2.02	8.89
Rajasthan	3.05	-0.12	2.93	7.29	10.23
UP	11.12	0.31	11.43	6.22	17.65
Select15	45.62	1.03	46.65	52.72	99.36
Other	1.04	-0.59	0.44	0.19	0.64
India	46.66	0.44	47.09	52.91	100.00

The pattern of rise in output value and input cost (both in nominal terms) in Figure I.6b also points to the faster rise in output value as compared to the input cost.

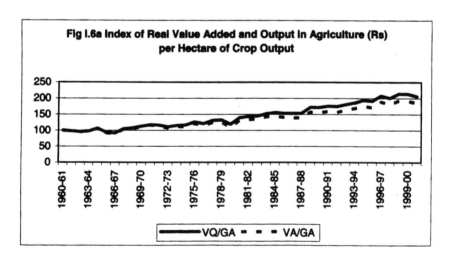

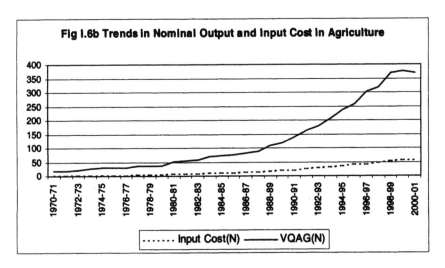

Fig I.6b Trends in Nominal Output and Input Cost in Agriculture

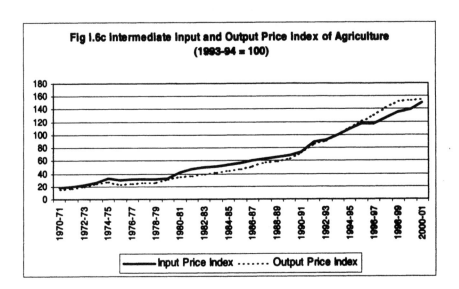

Fig I.6c Intermediate Input and Output Price Index of Agriculture (1993-94 = 100)

As the rise in value added in real terms is slower than the rise in real output, the differential trend in nominal terms is due to the divergent trends in input and output prices (Figure I.6c). The output price index (deflator for crop output) increases at a faster rate than the index of price of intermediate inputs (deflator for intermediates) starting from around the mid-1980s. Thus, beginning in the early to mid 1980s, there was a sharp rise in overall crop price relative to the input prices. This rise in relative price has led to increased application of inputs on per hectare basis. The increased application of intermediate inputs has increased both gross output. But there was also growth in value added per hectare.

Value added has increased with the application of inputs per hectare of crop land (Figure I.6d). This can occur when there is also an increase in the application of labour and/or capital per hectare with improvements in the productivity of inputs. There is a rise in output (value added) per unit of capital stock only towards the end of 1980s (Figure I.6e). Until the end of 1980s, there appears to be a decline in real value added per unit of capital stock in agriculture. Thus, the rise in value added per hectare is associated with the increased application of capital per hectare. In two studies reported by Kalirajan and Shand (1997) and Kalirajan, Shand and Bhide (1998), input growth accounted for about 60% of the crop output growth during the period 1985-90, the rise in input use efficiency accounted for another 25% and the total factor productivity growth the balance 15%. The crop output growth, therefore, is largely influenced by input use.

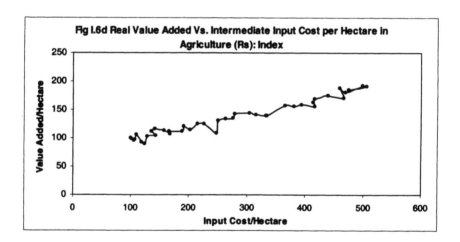

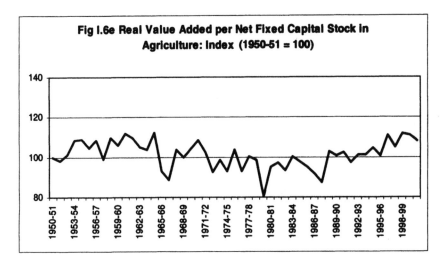

Fig I.6e Real Value Added per Net Fixed Capital Stock in Agriculture: Index (1950-51 = 100)

This suggests that technology changes have been embodied in the inputs. The results, however, indicate a significant role for input use efficiency in influencing output growth that is not emphasized so far in the past studies.

I.3.3 Trends in Investment and Labour Use in Agriculture

The crop output growth, as noted above, has been mainly due to the increasing intensity of application of inputs on a per unit of land. It is not only the intermediate inputs but also labour and capital whose application has increased on per hectare basis. A notable feature of investment in fixed capital stock is the acceleration in the private investment in agriculture as compared to the stagnant public investment (Figure I.7). Rise in the growth of private investment since the mid 1980s coincides with the rise in the relative price of crop output relative to the input prices, referred to earlier. Thus, although public investment stagnated in real terms, private investment rose with favorable trends in output to input price ratio. Net fixed capital stock (NFCS/ha) rose on a per hectare basis throughout the period from 1950-51 to 2000-2001 (Figure I.8).

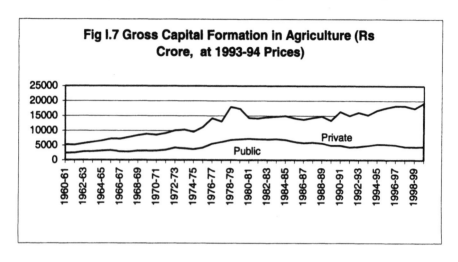

Fig I.7 Gross Capital Formation in Agriculture (Rs Crore, at 1993-94 Prices)

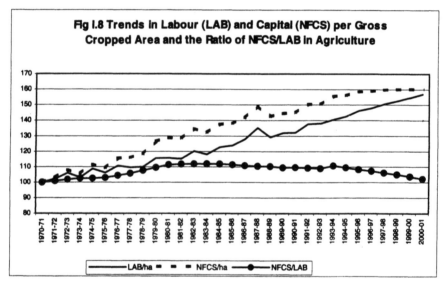

Fig I.8 Trends in Labour (LAB) and Capital (NFCS) per Gross Cropped Area and the Ratio of NFCS/LAB in Agriculture

The trends in labour use per hectare (Lab/ha) of crop area can be inferred only from the decennial Census data at the aggregate level. Figure I.8 indicates the rise in labour force per hectare of crop area over the period from 1970-71 to 2000-01, for the 15 major states combined. At the state level, the labour force per hectare varies from a low of 0.38 persons in Haryana (in TE1992) to 1.46 persons in Tamilnadu. In 11 of the 15 states considered, there is an increase in the labour force per hectare of crop area over the period considered (Table I.8). In the case of four states of Tamilnadu, Kerala, Punjab and Rajasthan, there is a decline in the labour force per hectare of crop area in the 1990s. At the aggregate level capital stock per unit of labour (NFCS/Lab) has declined from the mid 1980s due to slow down in investment.

Table I.8   Agricultural Labour per Hectare of Gross Cropped Area (Number of Agricultural Workers plus Cultivators)

States	TE1975	TE1980	TE1985	TE1990	TE1995	TE2000
Haryana	0.3835	0.4355	0.4691	0.5352	0.6755	1.0980
Rajasthan	0.3956	0.4440	0.4634	0.5128	0.4936	0.3999
Punjab	0.4860	0.4733	0.4815	0.5095	0.5198	0.5087
MP	0.6398	0.7172	0.7518	0.8202	0.8860	0.9501
Gujarat	0.6699	0.7100	0.7743	0.8719	1.1173	1.6918
Maharashtra	0.6823	0.7482	0.8066	0.8633	0.9470	0.8910
Karnataka	0.7060	0.8228	0.8797	0.9328	1.0737	1.3591
Orissa	0.7933	0.7947	0.8474	0.8620	0.9489	1.1346
UP	0.9174	0.8939	1.0393	1.1654	1.2674	1.3122
West Bengal	1.0124	1.1433	1.2589	1.3524	1.4874	1.6747
Assam	1.0475	1.1271	1.1326	1.2649	1.3641	1.5232
AP	1.0494	1.2478	1.4044	1.5001	1.8432	2.4074
Kerala	1.0714	1.3325	1.4318	1.5361	1.3641	1.1075
Bihar	1.3909	1.4976	1.7438	1.9329	3.0538	5.6832
TamilNadu	1.4570	1.6457	1.8369	2.1343	2.0217	1.8111
ALL 15	0.8113	0.8800	0.9584	1.0452	1.1493	1.1975

Note: States are arranged in ascending order of labour per hectare in TE1975. Three-year average ending in a specified year is presented to smooth out year-to-year fluctuations in crop area. Agricultural labour is estimated as number of cultivators plus agricultural workers based on Census data. For years other than Census, estimates are based on interpolation of Census data.

I.4 Organization of the Chapters

The subsequent chapters of this volume provide details of development, estimation and application of the model developed in this study. In Chapter II we present the overall conceptual framework for the model developed in this study. Estimation of the equations relating to agricultural sector is contained in Chapter III. Estimation of the relationships in the non-agricultural sectors is discussed in Chapter IV. The macro or over-arching relationships are developed in Chapter V. Model applications are presented in Chapter VI and a summary of the findings is provided in Chapter VII. Appendix 1 provides some details of data. Appendix 2 provides an algebraic documentation of the model and Appendix 3 contains details regarding estimated equations used in the model.

Chapter II

A Disequilibrium Framework

Diverse nature of the economy across regions of India points to the possibility of different regions responding in a different manner to policy changes. The differences may arise not only due to differences in economic behavior but also because of differences in the structure of the economy in various regions. In this study, we attempt to build a macro econometric model that incorporates these behavioural and regional differences in the economy. Unlike in other studies, these differences are not summed up with the conventional residual term. Realizing their importance, they are directly incorporated in the model in a disequillibrium framework. There have been several ways of analysing disequilibrium from both the theoretical and empirical points of view. A majority of studies have used partial-adjustment models as tools for representing disequilibrium. In such models, the term disequilibrium refers to a state that is not the optimum (Bergstran and Wymer, 1976; and Jonson and Taylor, 1977). However, these disequilibrium models are imperfectly specified models because optimum values are first derived without consideration of adjustments, and then the adjustment costs are superimposed using the partial-adjustment specification. If the costs of adjustments are taken into account while deriving the optimum, then the concept of disequilibrium vanishes. In this study, a different type of disequilibrium model is proposed.

Disequilibrium is defined as a state when a firm is not able or willing to follow the best practice techniques of a given technology and is unable to achieve the maximum possible or potential output from a chosen set of inputs due to certain non-price and organisational factors that do not influence the output directly. The consequence of these behavioural differences will reflect in technical efficiency differences across observations. Such a production environment is modelled by allowing the production coefficients to vary across observations and over time for the same observation with the assumption that the behavioural and structural differences across observations would be entering the model as determinants of the magnitude of the production coefficient of the model. Empirical estimation draws heavily on the methods suggested for estimating the varying coefficients frontier production functions. The attempt is focused on the agricultural sector. We have modeled the manufacturing sector in some detail as compared to the other non-agricultural sectors mainly because of the greater interaction between manufacturing and agriculture. The non-agricultural sectors of the economy are modeled only at the national level. The fiscal, monetary and external sector inter-relationships are specified following the earlier macro econometric models for India.

In this chapter, we present a brief overview of the macroeconomic modelling efforts in India in order to highlight the important contribution of the present study in the context of earlier macro modelling studies. After a brief overview of the past models, we develop the main structure of the present model.

II.1 Macroeconomic Modelling in India: An Overview

Macroeconomic modeling defined to include econometric as well as planning models that incorporated input-output linkages across sectors has a long tradition in Indian economics literature. The planning models have focused on greater desegregation of the sectors of the economy. A review of the planing models can be found in Dahiya (1990). The Planning Commission's Technical Note on the Eigth Five Year Plan provides a documentation of the official plan model for the country at the time. Major reviews of macro econometric modeling efforts for the Indian economy are available in Desai (1973), Krishna et al (1991), Marwah (1991) and Krishnamurty (2001). There is another stream of economy-wide empirical modelling in the form of Computable General Equilibrium (CGE) models for India, which is reviewed in Chadha et al (1998). Three notable examples of analysis of agriculture related policy in an economy-wide CGE framework are those of Storm (1993), Subramanian (1993), and Parikh et al (1995). Krishnamurty in his broad sweep of the macro econometric modelling work in India notes, since the first of such models was published in 1956, a total of over 60 such models have been built. Dividing the work over the five decades into five generations of models, Krishnamurty describes that the fifth generation models of the latter half of the 1990s are large, dynamic and incorporate inter-sectoral dependence of the sectors better than the previous models. Three other macro modelling efforts which have not been noted by Krishnamurty are the work of researchers at the Reserve Bank of India (RBI, 2002) NCAER (2002) and Reynolds (2001). The macro models developed in the RBI and by Reynolds focus on the fiscal and monetary issues of policy. Both the models focus on modeling debt dynamics, an issue that has not been generally incorporated in the other models satisfactorily with some exceptions as in Bhattacharya (1984). The NCAER (2002) study in an attempt to capture two-way link between social sector expending and economic growth.

The basic framework for the macro econometric models has remained the Keynesian income-expenditure accounting framework. The distinguishing structural features of the economy have necessitated specification of sectors and their markets. The prominent role of public sector in markets for goods and services and in investment activity (planning process) also meant that disaggregation in terms of public sector- private sector was important. Some of these features require specification of production relationships in the model. While production functions are generally not incorporated in an explicit form in the macro econometric models, output supply has been related to some inputs and other variables in the case of agriculture and manufacturing. In the planning models, production functions are implicitly the fixed coefficients Leontief type for inter-industry transactions and fixed coefficient type for primary resources. In the CGE models, explicit production functions with fixed coefficients are common.

But in none of the above cited studies, either regional variations in output response or variations in production coefficients across producers and over time for the same producer has been considered. The objective of this study is to fill up this gap in macro econometric modelling.

Before we proceed to the discussion of how the regional and behavioural variations across states are introduced in modelling the production process, we also note that there are some key areas in which the specification of some of the key variables of the macro models has changed since the economic reforms of the 1990s. One is the financial market: the specification of interest rates and the exchange rate. The second is the liberalization of the trade regime. Finally there is the manner in which fiscal deficit of the government is financed by minimizing the monetisation of the deficit. The macro models developed in the latter half of the 1990s, which Krishnamurty (2001) refers to as the fifth generation models, in many ways address these issues. The specification of interest rate has changed from one of 'exogenous policy variables' to one that is sensitive to inflationary pressures, external account pressures, global interest rates and policies. The exchange rate specification has been modified to include the possibility of its endogenous determination in the framework of purchasing power parity principle: exchange rate variation brings about equality between domestic and world prices in the long run in the case of tradable goods and services. By allowing financing of fiscal deficit through domestic borrowing and letting interest rates be affected by market pressures, the new models capture the new features of the economic policy. In the present model, we have not incorporated some of the new features of the economy as the purpose of the present study has been to introduce regional and behavioural variations in production processes in a macro modeling framework. The new features can be introduced relatively easily along the lines of IEG-DSE Team (1999) and NCAER (2002).

II.2 Development of the Present Model

II.2.1 The Overall Framework

The basic macro economic framework that is adopted in the various studies is to begin with modeling the components of aggregate demand such as consumption, investment, government expenditures, exports and imports. On the supply side, agricultural output is specified as a function of inputs such as land, fertilizer and irrigation, and rainfall. Input use in agriculture is made responsive to 'administered input and output prices' as relevant, lagged output prices and other features of agriculture. In some cases, in times of foreign exchange constraints, output supply of certain infrastructure services is constrained and this affects the output of the other sectors, especially the manufacturing output.

The general description of the output determination has been one of 'supply determined output' in the case of agriculture and 'demand determined output' in the case of non-agricultural sectors. In a sense, the output and prices in the non-agricultural sectors are one of 'reduced form' type of specification. The imbalance between supply and demand is captured in some cases by price sensitivity to inventory changes, or inventory changes adjust to prices and then bring about supply-demand imbalance in the longer run through their impact on investment. The macro variables such as government revenues are impacted by tax rates, output and prices, and the government expenditures by policy and prices. The monetary policy is 'accommodative' to finance government's fiscal deficit by holding the interest rates fixed, directing the credit to alternative uses and taking recourse to monetization of deficit if needed.

II.2.2 Approach to Modelling Production

Taking this broad stylized specification, we begin with a discussion of the disequilibrium approach to modelling the production process in the present study. If the production process were simply the engineering relationship between a set of inputs x_{it} and observed output Q_t, then a well-defined production function would describe the process accurately and any variation in inputs would result in a corresponding change in output. The assumption here is that firms are technically efficient in producing the output following the best practice techniques of the technology. However, in reality, observed output is often the result of a series of producers' decisions, which influence the method of application of inputs, and so the variables associated with the relevant production environment (or institution) will also play an important part in an enterprise's decisions and consequently on the output. For this reason alone, some enterprises may be producing not on but inside the frontiers with consequent gap between 'best practice' techniques and 'realized' methods of production. This disequilibrium or the gap, thus, facilitates to development of a measure of technical efficiency. This gap may arise owing to the negative effects of non-price and/or organizational factors such as lack of human capital endowment, and insufficient infrastructure, which are the results of the existing production environment emerging from the existing institutions. For example, lack of incentives, both Centre's and States' soft budget constraints, inefficient transmission of information about production processes to producers, and the ineffectiveness of government control over enterprises could all cause deviation of realized production methods from the 'best practice' techniques. It is very difficult to model the influence of each of the above non-price and organizational factors on output. Nevertheless, the combined influence of all factors can be introduced into the production function in several ways.

One method concerns representing such non-price and institutional variables in the model in an additive fashion, and the effects of changes in these variables on outputs are analyzed within the framework of the model. One advantage of such model is that it is possible to find out whether the deviation of a firm's actual output from its maximum possible output is mainly because it did not use the best practice technique or it is due to external random factors. Thus, one can say whether the difference between the actual output obtained and the frontier output, if any, occurred accidentally or not. The above model is called 'the conventional frontier production function approach' in this study. Several reviews have been published on various aspects of measuring technical efficiency using different forms of conventional frontier production functions. Of these, the very recent one is by Kumbhakar and Lovell (2000).

The Underlying assumptions in these conventional frontier production models, regardless of whether their estimation is based on (i) special distributional assumption for the variable representing the combined influence of the non-price and organizational factors on output (Greene, 1990); (ii) cross-sectional data (Aigner, Lovell and Schmidt, 1977; and Meeusen and van den Broeck, 1977); (iii) time series of cross section data (Kalirajan and Shand, 1992), time-invariant panel (Schmidt and Sickles, 1984) or time-varing panel data (Battese and Coelli, 1992; Kumbhakar, 1990; and Cornwell, Schmidt and Sickles, 1990) are that (1) technical efficiency can be estimated from the residual, and (2) the frontier production function is a neutral shift from the realized production function. In other words, the above model specifications imply that the production response coefficients of the conventional stochastic frontier production function will be the same with the exception of the intercept term for both efficient and inefficient producers. There is no logic behind this reasoning because the aspect which distinguishes the efficient producer from the inefficient producer is that the former, based on the definition, uses the best practice techniques of the technology, while the latter does not.

It is therefore, not rational to argue that the observation-specific production behaviour which varies across observations, would result in the same input response coefficients across observations and that would shift the frontier function neutrally from the realized production function. A neutral shift could well be a special case. A more general case is a non-neutral shift of the frontier from the realized production function. To be more specific, the literature indicates that a firm obtains its full technical efficiency by following the best practice techniques, given the technology. In other words, technical efficiency is determined by the method of application of inputs regardless of the levels of inputs (that is, scale of operation). Method of application of inputs is determined by various non-price and organizational factors which are themselves influenced by factors arising from socio-cultural and government policy measures. This implies that different methods of applying various inputs will influence the output differently. That is, the slope coefficients will vary from firm to firm. Certainly, from the same levels of inputs, the best practice firm will receive higher output response from each input than the firm which does not follow the best practice methods of application of inputs. In this context, the above discussed conventional constant-slope-residual based approach of measuring technical efficiency is not quite helpful. This warrants an alternative approach of modelling observation-specific characteristics and estimating technical efficiency, distinguishing the best firms from the non-best firms, which is discussed below.

As Maddala (1977, p.403) pointed out, '...if economic agents are indeed maximizing, they would be taking these non-price and organizational variables into account in their decisions and thus the variables would be entering the model not in an additive fashion but as determinants of the parameters of the model'. Therefore, a varying parameters model or a varying coefficients model (VCM) is appropriate in evaluating the effects of regional and behavioural differences on outputs across firms (states). Whether such variations in parameters can be restricted only to intercepts terms?

There is no reason to believe that the regional and behavioural differences would have influenced each firm's (State's) production behaviour equally, so different levels of output may be obtained by different firms, albeit using the same set of inputs. In other words, firms' maximum output varies regardless of input levels because the response from each input varies from firm to firm. Hence, the conventional varying intercept and fixed slope production frontier may not be appropriate for measuring a firm's performance, and particularly for measuring firm specific productive efficiency, as has been pointed out by Kalirajan and Obwona (1994). Rather, while modelling firms' behaviour, the slope coefficients should be allowed to vary in the production function to take into account of different input responses to output. Lucas (1981) provides further justification for using the full varying coefficients frontier production function model. In his critique of econometric policy evaluation, Lucas argued, "the standard stable parameter view of econometric theory and quantitative policy evaluation appears not to match several important characteristics of econometric practice. For example, fixed coefficient econometric models may not be consistent with the dynamic theory of optimizing behaviour (of firms); that is, changes in economic or policy variables will result in a new environment that may, in turn, lead to new optimal decisions and new economic structures" (pp. 109-110).

How does the estimation of the varying coefficients frontier production function differ from the estimation of a conventional production function? Production function is traditionally estimated as an average output response to a given level of inputs and technology, though theoretically it is defined as the maximum possible or potential output. The assumption in the conventional estimation of a production function of a firm is that the 'average' response is indeed the 'maximum' possible with the given technology, and that the difference between the estimated and realized outputs is due to factors beyond the firm's control. On the other hand, in the estimation of the varying coefficients frontier production function, it is argued that the difference between the estimated and realized outputs is due to both factors within the firm's control and factors beyond the firm's control.

Let the Cobb-Douglas stochastic varying coefficients frontier production function for a given time period, t be:

$$Q_i = \beta_{0i} \prod_{j=1}^{k} \chi_{ij}^{\beta} \qquad\qquad i = 1, 2, 3, ...n \qquad\qquad (\text{II}.1)$$

where Q_i and x_{ij} are the ith firm's output and jth input respectively. It can be seen from equation (II.1) that the output response coefficients with respect to different inputs vary across firms. It is rational to argue that the institutional and organizational factors, which vary across states, would influence outputs indirectly through the method of application of inputs. When firms follow the best method of application of inputs required by the selected technology to effectively utilize the chosen inputs, they obtain the maximum possible outputs for the given set of inputs because the production response coefficients will be the maximum indicating that the firms are technically efficient. As firms cannot produce more than a theoretically possible level of output, the above model is consistent with the production theory. If due to adverse effects of some institutional and organizational factors (e.g. poor management) firms are not able to follow the best method of application of inputs, the output response coefficients with respect to inputs will be at levels lower than the maximum that the firms would have obtained, had they followed the best method of application of inputs. In this situation, firms are called technically inefficient. Further, any other firm-specific intrinsic characteristics that are not explicitly included may produce a combined contribution over and above the individual contributions. This 'lump sum' contribution, if any, can be measured by the varying intercept term.

The specification of the above model implies that firms could be technically efficient fully, if and only if, the chosen inputs are effectively utilized by following the best method of application. This means that institutional and organizational factors, which influence the method of application of inputs, do not exert any adverse effects on production. This can be interpreted as the State's reform policies being able to eliminate the adverse effects that constrain the firms from realizing fully their productive efficiency realization. On the other hand, if reform measures are not effective fully, firms would not be able to follow the best method of application of inputs and so there will be a significant gap between firms' realized outputs and their maximum possible outputs. One advantage of this methodology is that it is possible to identify which input application is more influenced by differences in States' characteristics over time.

Taking logarithms on both sides of equation (II.1), the stochastic varying coefficients frontier production function, as explained above can be written as:

$$\mathrm{Ln}Q_i = \beta_{0j} + \sum_{j=1}^{k} \beta_{ij} \, \mathrm{Ln}\,\chi_{ij} \qquad\qquad i=1, 2, 3,...n \qquad\qquad (\text{II}.2)$$

For simplicity, it is assumed that Ln $\beta = \beta_0$. The above model requires nk + n coefficients to be estimated with the help of only n observations. Since intercept and slope coefficients vary across firms, we can write:

$$\beta_{ij} = \bar{\beta}_j + u_{ij} \tag{II.3a}$$

$$\beta_{0i} = \bar{\beta}_0 + v_i \tag{II.3b}$$

where $\bar{\beta}_j$ is the mean response coefficient of output with respect to jth input and u_{ij} and v_i are random disturbance terms which satisfy all the classical assumptions. In addition to the classical assumptions the following assumptions are also made:

$$E(\beta_{ij}) = \bar{\beta}_j$$

$\text{Var}(\beta_{ij}) = \sigma_j^2 > 0 \qquad$ for i=0 to k, j=1 to m and

$\text{Cov}(\beta_{ij}, \beta_{im}) = 0 \qquad$ for $j \neq m$

These imply that the random coefficients β_{ij} are independently and identically distributed with fixed mean $\bar{\beta}_j$ and variance σ_j^2. Combining equations (II.2) and (II.3a-II.3b) in a matrix format (Kalirajan and Shand, 1994),

$$Q = X\beta + D_x u + v \tag{II.4}$$

where Q is a (nx1) vector, X is a (nxk) matrix with stacked x_i', Dx is a (nxnk) block diagonal matrix of the x_i', u is a (nkx1) vector of u_i' s and v is (nx1) vector. It can easily be verified that disturbance terms v_i and u_{ij} have zero means and $E(v_i^2) = \sigma_i^2$, $E(v_i v_j) = 0$ for $i \neq j$, $E(u_i u_j') = \Gamma_u$, a diagonal matrix with σ_u^2 for $i = j$ and $E(u_i u_j') = 0$ for $i \neq j$.

Given these assumptions, the composite disturbance vector,

$$w = D_x u + v$$

will have a mean vector of zero and covariance matrix: $\Delta = x_i' \Gamma_u x_i + \sigma_i^2$. It may be noted that this type of Hildreth-Houck random coefficient model belongs to the class of heteroscedastic error models where error variances are proportional to the squares of a set of exogenous variables x. So the random coefficient regression model reduces to a model with fixed coefficients, but with heteroscedastic variances. This heteroscedasticity will remain even if $\sigma_j^2 = \sigma^2$ for all j values so long as the square of the explanatory variables are present in the composite disturbance vector. So, the ordinary least squares (OLS) method yields unbiased but inefficient estimates of mean response coefficients.

Since, the elements of Γ_u are not known, they have to be estimated. Hildreth and Houck (1968) suggest several methods of estimating the elements of Γ. In this study, we used the Aitken's generalized least squares (GLS) to estimate β s following the arguments of Swamy (1970).

Following the above discussion about the method of application of inputs and institutional factors, the highest magnitude of each response coefficient, and the intercept term from the production coefficients of equation (II.4), together constitute the production coefficients of the frontier function, providing the maximum possible output. To elaborate, let β^*_0, β^*_1, β^*_2, β^*_3, ... β^*_K be the estimates of the parameters of the frontier production function yielding the maximum possible output for any given levels of inputs. The frontier coefficients β^* s are chosen to reflect the condition that they represent the production response by following the 'best practice' method of application of inputs. These are obtained from among the individual response coefficients, which vary across observations as

$$\beta^*_j = max \ \{\beta_{ij}\} over \ i= 1, 2...n. \quad for \ j=0 \ to \ k \tag{II.5}$$

When the response coefficients are selected by using (II.5), then the maximum possible output for the ith firm can be worked out as:

$$Ln \ Q_i^* = \beta^*_0 + \sum_j \beta^*_j \ Ln \ X_{ij} \tag{II.6}$$

where x_{ij}'s refer to actual levels of inputs used by the ith firm. In special cases of the production process in which constant returns to scale are imposed on the individual response coefficient β_{ij}, the estimation of β^*_j's would be complicated and intractable. Even when the condition of constant returns to scale is imposed on the mean response coefficients, β^*_j's, then due to the relationship

$$\beta^*_j = \max_i \left(\overline{\beta}_j + \hat{v}_{ij} \right)$$

the possibility that $\Sigma\beta^*_j > 1$ cannot be ruled out. In either case, the problem that remains is that the best practice production outcome might not be feasible if all production processes had to have constant returns to scale by some strict technical rule. Nevertheless drawing on the endogenous technological change long-run growth model proposed by Romer (1986) it may be argued here that it is possible to enjoy increasing returns to scale mainly due to increasing marginal productivity of the intangible capital from good knowledge of the best practice techniques. Subsequently, a measure of overall general technical efficiency can be defined as follows:

$$E_i = \frac{realized\;\;Output}{potential\;\;Output}$$

$$= Q_i / Q_i^* \tag{II.7}$$

E_i varies between 0 and 1 and the above estimation procedure uses only cross-section data.

Following this notion, technical efficiency in the use of input 1 by the i th producer, for example, can be defined as,

$$IEFF1_i = (\beta_{1i} / \beta_1^*) \tag{II.8}$$

with,

$$\beta_1^* = \max (\beta_{1i}) \text{ over } i = 1 \text{ to } n \tag{II.9}$$

where IEFF1 is the technical efficiency of i th producer with respect to input 1; and β_1^* is the coefficient of the most efficient producer with respect to the use of input 1. We term efficiencies with respect to the use of specific inputs as 'embodied or input specific' efficiencies and the efficiency implied by variations in the intercept of the ith producer (MEFFi = β_{0i} / β_0^*) is termed as 'disembodied efficiency'. Embodied (or input specific) efficiency refers to efficiency arising from following the best practice production technique of applying the specific inputs. Disembodied efficiency refers to efficiency that is independent of any inputs appearing in the production function. For example, in crop production where fertilizer and irrigation are two inputs, 'embodied' efficiency is specific to the use of these two inputs whereas the 'disembodied' efficiency is a more general concept that may reflect organizational or such efficiencies of combining these core inputs. The terminology is similar to the one used in the case of technical progress in economics literature.

The production process expressed at the producer level for a group of producers and specifically for the ith producer with respect to the frontier respectively can now be formulated in terms of production frontier and the jth producer's technical efficiencies as follows:

$$Ln\;Q^* = \beta_0^* + \beta_1^* Ln\;X1 + \beta_2^* Ln\;X2 \tag{II.10}$$
$$Ln\;Q_j = \beta_0^* . MEFF_j + \beta_1^* . IEFF1_j\;Ln\;X1_j + \beta_2^* . IEFF2_j\;Ln\;X2_j \tag{II.11}$$

Output now can be influenced by variations in input levels as well as in technical efficiencies. The efficiency concepts discussed in this section correspond to the 'static case' where production during only one period has been considered. Three cases can be distinguished depending upon the availability of data for analysis. First as discussed above, there is the case of 'cross-section data' where we have observations on a set of producers for one period of time. Then there is 'time-series data' where we have data on a single producer (or all producers as one group) for a number of time periods. Third, there is the 'panel data' case where there are observations on a set of producers over a period of time. We discuss the latter two cases below as the 'panel data' case and the 'time series data' cases are finally applied in the present study.

II.2.2a   The Panel Data Case   In the context of panel data, variations in production function coefficients can occur not only across the producing units but also over time for the same (individual) units. Variations across the producing units during a specific time period reflect static efficiency variations whereas variations over time reflect changes in efficiency over time when compared with a given production frontier, as well as technical progress when different production frontiers are compared. To illustrate the concepts, we consider the VCM frontier production model in its Cobb-Douglas functional form

$$\text{Ln } Q^{**}_t = \beta_0^{**}{}_t + \beta_1^{**}{}_t \text{Ln } X1 + \beta_2^{**}{}_t \text{Ln } X2 \tag{II.12}$$
$$\text{Ln } Q_{it} = \beta_0^{**}{}_t \cdot MEFF_{it} + \beta_1^{**}{}_t \cdot IEFF1_{it}$$
$$\text{Ln } X1_{it} + \beta_2^{**}{}_t \cdot IEFF2_{it} \text{ Ln } X2_{it} \tag{II.13}$$

where Q^{**}_t is the output from the frontier production function or the 'maximum possible' output from the technologies so far available to the firms. The equation (II.12) can be called 'technical frontier' to indicate possible slippage in the year-to-year performance of the producers. To distinguish production frontier in a dynamic context from the static one defined earlier, we distinguish its coefficients with ** rather than '*'. The frontier coefficients applicable at time 't' are defined as,

$$\beta_j^{**}{}_t = \max (\beta_{jy}) \text{ over } j = 1 \text{ to } n, \text{ and } y = 1 \text{ to } T \tag{II.14}$$

Technical efficiencies, embodied (*IEFF*) and disembodied (*MEFF*) are defined as,

$$IEFFi_{jt} = (\beta_{jt} / \beta^{**}_t) \text{ for } i= 1 \text{ and } 2, j=1 \text{ to } n; \text{ and } t= 1 \text{ to } T \tag{II.15a}$$
$$MEFF_{jt} = (\beta_{0jt} / \beta_0^{**}_t) \text{ for } j=1 \text{ to } n; \text{ and } t=1 \text{ to } T \tag{II.15b}$$

The shifts in production frontier over time, indicated by increases in the frontier coefficients β^{**}_{it}, reflect technical progress (Kalirajan and Shand, 1997). The estimation techniques outlined in Kalirajan and Shand (1994) can be used to estimate the frontier function coefficients as well as the efficiency estimates for the case of panel data where we have observations for a set of producers (states) over time. Taking the case of 'disembodied' efficiency or the efficiency associated with the intercept, we can now proceed to specify the factors affecting efficiency. In equation (II.16) below, the disembodied efficiency is specified as a function of a number of variables.

$$MEFF_{jt} = f(Z1_{jt}, Z2_{jt}, Z3_{jt}, \ldots)$$ (II.16)

where Zi_{jt} are the factors affecting efficiency of jth producer in time period t. This equation allows us to introduce producer-level characteristics in explaining variations in output responses. In the models explaining economic growth factors affecting human capital such as health status of the population and level of education are used to explain a part of the growth that is not explained by the growth of inputs alone. In the same manner, similar factors can be introduced in equation (II.16) above as explanatory factors for explaining variations in efficiency.

The advantage of using the varying coefficients production frontier approach relative to the conventional production function approach is that it captures the impact of producer-specific characteristics on production in a systematic manner. In other words, we now have a production function applicable to individual producer. In the context of using a State as a producer, the approach allows us to define a production function for each state individually.

II.2.2b The Time-Series Data Case The VCM in the time-series models for a producer is also interpreted as 'time varying coefficients model'. We discuss the model in the context of an application to production modelling. The production function in equation (II.2) is re-written for two inputs as,

$$\text{Ln } Q_t = \beta_0 + \beta_1 \text{ Ln } X1_t + \beta_2 \text{ Ln } X2_t + e_t$$ (II.17)

where the subscript t now replaces 'i' in the original equation. The VCM formulation of the model is,

$$\text{Ln } Q_t = \beta_{0t} + \beta_{1t} \text{ Ln } X1_t + \beta_{2t} \text{ Ln } X2_t + e_t$$ (II.18)

with,

$$\beta_{it} = \beta_i + v_{it}$$ (II.19)

The year-to-year variability in output response may arise due to a number of factors that may not be captured in the variations in inputs alone. Improvement in output response over time to inputs is also a reflection of technical progress. Once we have estimates of v_{it} the production frontier can be defined as,

$$\text{Ln } Q^{**}_t = \beta_0^{**}_t + \beta_1^{**}_t \text{ Ln } X1_t + \beta_2^{**}_t \text{ Ln } X2_t$$ (II.20)
$$\text{Ln } Q_t = \beta_0^{**}_t . MEFF_t + \beta_1^{**}_t . IEFF1_t \text{ Ln } X1_t + \beta_2^{**}_t . IEFF2_t \text{ Ln } X2_t$$ (II.21)

where Q^{**}_t is the output from the production frontier or the 'maximum possible' output from the technologies available over time so far. The equation (II.20) is now termed a 'technical frontier' to indicate possible slippage in the year-to-year performance of the producers. The frontier coefficients applicable at time 't' are defined as,

$$\beta^{**}_{it} = \max (\beta_{iy}) \text{ over } y = 1,2, \ldots n, \text{ for } i=0 \text{ to } 2 \text{ and } t= 1 \text{ to } T \qquad (II.22)$$

Technical efficiencies, embodied (IEFF) and disembodied (MEFF), are defined as,

$$IEFFi_t = (\beta_{it} / \beta^{*}_{it}) \text{ for } i= 1 \text{ and } 2 \text{ and } t= 1,2, \ldots T \qquad (II.23a)$$
$$MEFF_t = (\beta_{0t} / \beta_0^{**}_t) \text{ for } t= 1,2, \ldots T \qquad (II.23b)$$

The variations in $MEFF_t$ and $IEFF_t$ can be modeled as a function of factors that influence year-to-year variations in output response. In the case of manufacturing, year-to-year variations in output response are reflected in changes in capacity utilization. Factors influencing capacity utilization, therefore, can be among the factors influencing variations in efficiency.

II.2.2c A Digression on Taxonomy of Technical Efficiency   In the previous three sections, we presented embodied and disembodied technical efficiencies in the static and dynamic situations. We define the overall general efficiency noted as E_i in equation (II.7) in the static case as,

$$EFFG_j = Q_j / Q_j^{*} \qquad (II.24)$$

where Q_j is the actual level of output for the jth producer and Q_j^{*} is the potential output for the jth producer using the same level of inputs that the producer actually applies but based on the 'frontier' coefficients. Such overall efficiency can also be defined for the dynamic cases (panel and time-series) also. The overall efficiency defined in equation (II.24) depends on the level of inputs as well as the input coefficients. In other words, the overall efficiency depends on embodied efficiency, disembodied efficiency and input mix. We provide below a decomposition of the overall efficiency into these three factors. The decomposition is based on a monotonic transformation of the efficiencies defined earlier. The transformation lends itself to a decomposition such that values of the transformed efficiencies also remain within the logical limits of 0 and 1.

To assess overall efficiency reflected by technical efficiencies alone, taking the case of two inputs as before, transformed efficiency measures are defined as follows:

$$IEFF2_{ijt} = \text{Exp}(\beta_{ijt} - \beta_j^{**}_t) \text{ for } i= 1 \text{ and } 2; j=1 \text{ to } n; \text{ and } t= 1 \text{ to } T \qquad (III.25a)$$

$$MEFF2_{jt} = Exp(\beta_{ojt} - \beta_o^{**}{}_t) \text{ for } j=1 \text{ to n and } t= 1 \text{ to T} \qquad \text{(III.25b)}$$

where, Exp is the exponent to the natural base (e) and it is a monotonic transformation of the earlier definition of efficiencies, $IEFF_{ijt}$ and $MEFF_{jit}$. The overall firm-level technical efficiency can now be defined as,

$$EFFG2_{jt} = MEFF2_{jt} * \pi_{i=1 \text{ to } 2} (IEFF2_{ijt}) \qquad \text{(III.26)}$$

where, π indicates multiplication or product of all the arguments. The overall firm level efficiency (including the effect of input levels) can now be expressed as,

$$EFFG_{jt} = EFFTG2_{jt} \cdot \{ \pi_{i=0 \text{ to } 2} (X_{ijt} / e)^{\beta_{jt}-\beta_{t}^{**}} \} \cdot Exp(u_{jt}) \qquad \text{(III.27)}$$

where, the term within { } on the right hand side of equation (III.27) is the effect of specific levels of inputs used by the firm on overall efficiency, which can be termed the 'input-mix effect' on firm's efficiency. The variable $X0$ takes the value of '1' in all the observations. The term $Exp(u_{jt})$ reflects the impact of the conventional stochastic residual. If we use predicted values of Q_{jt} in defining $EFFG_{jt}$, in equation (III.24), then the residual effect in (III.27) vanishes and the overall firm level efficiency can be interpreted as the feasible output as a proportion of potential output. There are, thus, two measures of overall efficiency, viz. 'input level invariant overall efficiency' (*EFFG2*) and the 'overall efficiency' (*EFFG*). A schematic presentation of the various technical efficiency measures is provided in Figure II.1. The simple time-series case is not specified in the figure, as it is a special case of the panel data.

II.2.3 Production in Agriculture and Manufacturing

Keeping in view the availability of data, we have adopted the panel data approach to modelling agricultural output in the present study. State level data on inputs and crop output over time are the basis for the estimation of production frontier and production efficiencies. In the case of manufacturing, systematic data are available on inputs, output and prices only in the case of 'registered' manufacturing or manufacturing in the organized sector.

II.2.4 Other Sectors and Model Components

Besides the production in agriculture and manufacturing, the model consists of other inter-relationships as noted previously. As these inter-relationships are formulated in standard ways, we present them along with their estimates in subsequent chapters.

Fig II.1 Taxonomy of Technical Efficiency Terms

Major Types
1. Static
2. Dynamic

Further sub-types
Static
  1.1 Embodied ($IEFF_i$: β_{ji}/β_j^* for j≠0)
  1.2 Disembodied ($MEFF_j$: β_{0i}/β_0^*)
  1.3 Overall
        1.3a Input level Invariant ($EFFG2$: $\Pi_{j=0,k}(e^{\beta_{ji}-\beta_j^*})$
        1.3b General ($EFFG$: Q_i/Q^*)
Dynamic
  2.1 Time Variant Frontier
  2.1a Embodied ($IEFF_{ijt}$: $\beta_{jit}/\beta_{jt}^{**}$ for j≠0)
  2.1b Disembodied ($MEFF_{it}$: $\beta_{0it}/\beta_{0t}^{**}$)
  2.1c Overall
        2.1ci Input level Invariant ($EFFG2$: $\Pi_{j=0,k}(e^{\beta_{jit}-\beta_{jt}^{**}})$
        2.1cii General ($EFFG$: Q_{it}/Q_{it}^{**})
  2.2 Time Invariant Frontier
  2.2a Embodied ($IEFF_{ijt}$: β_{jit}/β_j^{**} for j≠0)
  2.2b Disembodied ($MEFF_{jt}$: β_{0it}/β_0^{**})
  2.2c Overall
        2.2ci Input level Invariant ($IEFFG2$: $\Pi_{j=0,k}(e^{\beta_{jit}-\beta_j^{**}})$)
        2.2cii General ($EFFG$: Q_{it}/Q_i^{**})

Note:
The expressions for various efficiency measures given in the boxes above relate to the following production function for the jth producer, Ln $Q_i = \beta_{0i} + \Sigma_{j=1,k} \beta_{ji}$ Ln $X_{ji} + u_{ij}$. In the dynamic case, time subscript is added. The frontier coefficients (β_j^*, β_{jt}^{**} and β_j^{**} for j=0,1, 2,..k) are defined in each case as outlined in the text.

II.2.5 Estimation Techniques and Model Solution

There are basically two sets of estimation techniques used in the present study. The VCM methods outlined in Kalirajan and Shand (1994) are used to estimate production relationships in agriculture and registered manufacturing sectors. In the estimation of equations using panel data as in the case of 'efficiency' equations, pooled data estimators are utilized. For the remaining model equations, either the

Autoregressive Distributed Lag (ARDL) model or the Ordinary Least Squares (OLS) estimators have been used. The standard model diagnostic tests were carried out. All the equations were estimated in a 'single equation' framework. While a case for using one of the suitable simultaneous equation methods can be made, we have attempted to address the problem of interdependence of the independent variables in the regression models by careful diagnostic tests. As can be noted from Appendix 3 results, problems do remain in some of the equations. However, in majority of the cases, the estimated equations 'pass' the diagnostic tests. Besides SHAZAM 7.0 and Microfit 3.0, a software package called 'TERAN' developed by the authors to estimate VCM has been used in this study.

The model comprising of system of simultaneous equations was solved in EVIEWS 3.1. The model has been solved for in-sample simulations.

Chapter III

Model Development:
The Agricultural Sector

The share of agricultural sector in real GDP has declined from about 58% in the early 1950s to 25% by the end of 1990s. The decline in the share has come about as the non-agricultural sectors have increased at a faster pace than agriculture. The differences between agriculture and non-agricultural sectors in output performances follow the development experience of many economies and are a result of technological development, consumer preferences as well as economic policies. Inter-sectoral linkages also influence the relative growth of one sector as compared to another, resulting in either divergent or complementary pattern of growth of different sectors. In this sense, quantification of the growth process of each sector requires capturing not only the relationships within the sector but also inter-relationships among the sectors. In this chapter we develop a part of the overall model, focusing on the determination of output and prices in the agricultural sector. As international trade provides a further link between production and prices, the equations linking output, prices and trade in the agricultural sector are also developed in this chapter.

III.1 Agricultural Production and Input Use

Output of agriculture consists of crops and livestock products. The crop sector accounts for 65% of the combined output of these two segments. In this study, we have focused on crop output in greater detail given the limitations of the available data. Generally, agricultural output has been modelled in the empirical studies in two ways: (1) direct estimation of a production function that relates agricultural output to core input levels and (2) through a production function that is implicit in the optimizing behaviour of the producers. In the latter approach, the profit maximizing or cost-minimizing framework provides the basis for deriving the output response to variations in input levels. The second approach typically requires information on net returns or profits from crops, cost shares of inputs and prices for estimation. Such detailed information is more likely to be found in the surveys of farm households than in the aggregate provincial or national level data sets. As the present study is based on state and national level data, and consistent information on net revenues and cost shares and prices is not available for the entire crop sector at both these levels, we have adopted the direct estimation of the production function for the crop sector in this study. A further advantage of the 'optimizing producer' framework is the desirable property of the likely independence of input prices which enter the regression model as independent variables and the random error associated with per unit profit from crops or the cost shares of inputs. However, input decisions are made prior to the harvest of crops when crop yield or output is obtained, and hence, the simultaneous estimation of input use and production function is not essential. Direct estimation of production function also allows us to examine the issues relating to technical efficiency of input use which can be a source of output growth in addition to the policies influencing input and output prices.

With these considerations, we have adopted direct estimation of the production function for the crop sector of Indian agriculture in the present study. Traditionally, production function has been estimated as an average response function relating output level to a set of input levels. The underlying assumption is that the output level indicated by the production function is the maximum possible from the given levels of inputs and available production technology. The deviations from the 'average' response are assumed to be random deviations. However, variability in the output response across producers can also be thought of as arising from variations in the methods of application of inputs, 'technical efficiency', of the producers. This approach has led to the specification of a 'production frontier' in the literature and technical efficiencies relate actual production response at the producer level to the production frontier. The systematic differences in technical efficiency at the producer level that is the basis for the disequilibrium approach adopted in this study provide the additional source of output growth, to be exploited from a policy perspective.

III.1.1 Production Frontier, Technical Efficiency and Production Functions

In Chapter II, three approaches to the estimation of production frontier and technical efficiencies were discussed depending on the availability of data on time-series, cross-section or panel basis. In the case of agriculture, as data on some of the key inputs and outputs can be compiled at the state level on annual basis over a period of time, the approach relevant to the 'panel data' can be adopted. To recapitulate from Chapter II, the production function at the producer (state) level can be formulated in terms of a production frontier and technical efficiencies as follows.

$$\text{Ln } Q^{**}{}_t = a0^{**}{}_t + a1^{**}{}_t \text{ Ln } X1 + a2^{**}{}_t \text{ Ln } X2 \tag{III.1}$$

$$\text{Ln } Q_{jt} = a0^{**}{}_t. \text{ } IEFF0_{jt} + a1^{**}{}_t. \text{ } IEFF1_{jt} \text{ Ln } X1_{jt} + a2^{**}{}_t. \text{ } IEFF2_{jt} \text{ Ln } X2_{jt} \tag{III.2}$$

where $Q^{**}{}_t$ is the output from the frontier production function or the 'maximum possible' output from the technologies available among the firms and over time upto period t. It was pointed out previously that the frontier coefficients applicable at time 't' can be defined as,

$ai^{**}{}_t = \max (ai_{jq})$ over $j = 1$ to m and $q=1$ to t for $i =0$ to 2
and $t=1$ to T $\hspace{5cm}$ (III.3)

Taking the 'panel data case' presented in Chapter II, efficiency measures relevant here are:

(a) Embodied input specific efficiency

$\hspace{1cm} IEFFi_{jt} = (ai_{jt}/ai^{**}{}_t)$ for $i=1,2$ $j=1$ to m and $t =1$ to T $\hspace{2cm}$ (III.4)

(b) Disembodied technical efficiency

$\hspace{1cm} MEFF_{jt} = (a0_{jt}/a0^{**}{}_t)$ for $j=1$ to m and $t =1,T$ $\hspace{2.5cm}$ (III.5)

(c) Overall input level invariant efficiency (dynamic, time varying frontier)

$\hspace{1cm} EFFG2_{jt} = \prod_{i=0\ to\ 2} (IEFF2i_{jt})$ $\hspace{5cm}$ (III.6)

where $\prod$ is a multiplication or product operator and $IEFF2i_{jt} = \mathrm{Exp}\ (ai_{jt}-ai^{**}{}_t)$ for $i=0$ to 2 $j=1$ to m and $t=1$ to T.

(d) Overall general efficiency (dynamic, time varying frontier)

$\hspace{1cm} EFFG_{jt} = (Q_{jt}/Q_{jt}^{**})$ $\hspace{6cm}$ (III.7)

We note that by substituting the estimated Q_{jt} from the producer-specific production function, we can derive the 'input mix effect' on overall general efficiency as,

$\hspace{1cm} INPMIX_{jt} = \mathrm{Ln}\ EFFG_{jt} - \mathrm{Ln}\ EFFG2_{jt}$ $\hspace{4cm}$ (III.8)

The input-mix effect can be positive or negative. If the jth producer uses more than the 'common' level of input (e in the present case) in which she is inefficient, then the input-mix effect is negative. If the jth producer reduces his use of any input below the 'common' level (value of 'e'), in which her efficiency is less than 100%, then input-mix effect can be positive. We use these measures of efficiency to compare the overall efficiency, related to the 'best practices' application of inputs across all producers.

III.1.2 Estimation of Crop Output Response Crop output is a function of a number of inputs applied in the production process. Among the major inputs are irrigation, fertilizer, labor and machinery. While information is available at the state level and over time on the output of individual crops, measures of aggregate crop output such as 'value of total crop output' or 'index of total crop production' are available only at the national level. Information on the quantum of inputs is available over time and at the state level only at the aggregate level, i.e. crop level information on input use is not available on a consistent basis at the state level. Thus, it is necessary to aggregate crop output at the state level so that we have consistent data series on crop output and inputs over time. The individual crop output data are aggregated to a single measure of crop output at the state level after converting physical output to value in constant 1980-81 prices. The crops included at the state level are listed in Appendix 1. A second measure of crop output (agricultural output) that could be considered in the output response analysis is the real *NSDP* from agriculture. This measure of value added from agriculture includes value added from livestock production. However, as data on inputs used in livestock production is not available at the state level, the analysis would be far weaker.

The variables used to reflect the quantity of inputs at the state level are, (1) amount of total nutrients or sum of nitrogen (N), phosphates (P_2O_5) and Potash (K_2O), (2) irrigated area and un-irrigated crop area, (3) number of cultivators and agricultural workers and (4) number of tractors in operation. In each of the cases, there are factors that limit the accuracy of the chosen measures of inputs in reflecting their actual usage.

In the case of fertilizers, it is not merely the total quantity of major nutrients that is relevant in determining the output response but also the ratio of N to P_2O_5 to K_2O. Timing and method of application of fertilizers also influence crop output. But such information is of limited value at the aggregate level of all crops. In the case of irrigation, coverage of crop area under irrigation does not indicate the intensity of irrigation or quality of irrigation. For example, the area irrigated only once would have different impact on crop output as compared to the crop area irrigated more frequently depending on the agronomic requirements.

In the case of labour, the number of cultivators and agricultural labourers does not reflect either the actual utilization of labour or the quality of labour. Moreover, data on the number of workers actually employed in agriculture is not available on an annual basis. Census data were used to interpolate the number of agricultural workers for the inter-census period. For the years beyond the last Census, the growth rates of the previous inter-Census period were used as the basis for projection of labour force. This does pose a problem in terms of the use of 'migrant labour' in some states and the under employment of labour in the off-season. Secondly, although the numbers of 'cultivators' and 'agricultural labour' were projected separately in each state based on the Census data, distinction between male and female labour was not possible. A difference in the type of labour employed may have a different impact on the crop output. Given the data constraints, no adjustments are made to reflect the variations in the rates of utilization of labour, quality of labour or inter-state migration of labour during certain periods of the year in this study.

The measure of usage of 'tractors' adopted here also has drawbacks. There is no correction for the type of tractors (say, in terms of horse-power of the tractors) or the actual utilization of the existing number of tractors, again due to lack of adequate data. Tractors are used for field operations in crop cultivation as well as for transportation in rural areas. A break-up of the overall usage of tractors for farming and non-farming activities over the years is not available. Data on the sale of tractors at the state level and the number of registered tractors in a base year were used to estimate the number of tractors at the state level over time. The data on sales in a state do not accurately reflect the actual usage of those tractors in that particular state.

The main reasons for persisting with the simplistic measures of inputs in this study are two. One is, as pointed out above, lack of sufficient data for improving the input measures. Second, given the level of aggregation in the output measure which comprises of output of all the crops, the aggregate measures of inputs that are available may be adequate to reflect the trends in variations in input usage. The data on crop output and inputs used in the present study are also presented in Appendix 1.

Besides the inputs noted above, two other factors should be considered. One relates to the agro-climatic conditions and the second relates to the composition of output. Rainfall during the monsoon period (June-September) is taken as the variable reflecting the agro-climatic conditions influencing crop production. The impact of variations in rainfall in the monsoon season on crop output in India has been modelled in this fashion in a number of previous studies of the economy. The second factor that influences output is the composition of output itself. The proportion of rice and wheat in total food grain output is used to reflect the composition of crop output. The use of proportion of rice and wheat in food grain output to capture the variations in crop output reflects the differences in crop yields: the yield per hectare in the case of rice and wheat is significantly greater than in the case of other food grains. Thus, as the output of rice and wheat increases relative to total food grains (comprising of rice, wheat, other cereals, millets and pulses), total crop output would increase for the same level of input application. This effect of crop output composition is likely to be more prominent in the case of crop yield per hectare than total crop output. However, differences in crop prices also would lead to variations in total crop output and hence output composition can be a source of variation in total crop output.

Two specifications of the output variable were examined. One specification involved total crop output (value in 1980-81 prices) as the output measure and secondly, as crop yield (value in 1980-81 prices) per hectare of crop area. In both the cases, the logarithmic functional form was utilized.

The alternative formulations to estimate the mean response of the varying coefficients model (VCM) defined in Chapter II are,

$$\text{Ln } VQ = a0 + a1 \text{ Ln } R + a2 \text{ Ln } UA + a3 \text{ Ln } IA + a4 \text{ Ln } LAB + a5 \text{ Ln } F$$
$$+ a6 \text{ Ln } TR + \text{Ln } RWFG \tag{III.9}$$

$$\text{Ln } (VQ/GA) = a0 + a1 \text{ Ln } R + a2 \text{ Ln } (IA/GA) + a3 \text{ Ln } (LAB/GA)$$
$$+ a4 \text{ Ln } (F/GA)$$
$$+ a6 \text{ Ln } (TR/GA) + \text{Ln } RWFG \tag{III.10}$$

where *VQ* is the value of crop output in constant prices, *R* is the index rainfall, *UA* is the unirrigated crop area, *IA* is the irrigated crop area, *LAB* is the number of workers (agricultural labour plus cultivators) in agriculture, *F* is the consumption of fertilizer nutrients ($N+P_2O_5+K_2O$), *TR* is the number of tractors, *RWFG* is the ratio of output of rice and wheat to total food grain output and *GA* is the gross cropped area.

The equations were first estimated without the term '*RWFG*'. The results showed that in the case of total output as the dependent variable, the coefficient of Ln *UA* was not statistically significant even at 10% level whereas in the case of Ln (*VQ/GA*) as the dependent variable, all the coefficients were significant. In both the cases, random coefficients model (RCM) could not be rejected. The sum of aj coefficients relating to inputs, *IA, LAB, F* and *TR* turn out to be less than 1.0 in the case of Ln *VQ* indicating diseconomies of scale in crop production. As this result is less acceptable as compared to the case of constant returns to scale, we adopt the formulation in (III.10) for further analysis. In the case of yield function such as (III.10), the constant returns to scale condition is implicit. The estimated 'mean response function' with the details of estimation is reported in Appendix 3.

For convenience, the estimated coefficients are presented below in equation form,

$$Ln\ (VQ/GA) = 1.3008 + 0.2489\ Ln\ R + 0.1215\ Ln\ (IA/GA)$$
$$+ 0.2178\ Ln\ (F/GA) + 0.1244\ Ln\ (LAB/GA)$$
$$+ 0.0731\ Ln\ (TR/GA) + 0.2276\ Ln\ RWFG \qquad \text{(III.11)}$$

III.1.3 Technical Efficiency and Technical Progress

III.1.3a Technical Efficiency The divergence of a producer-level production function from the potential technical production frontier, is a measure of technical inefficiency. Defined in a 'positive' sense, technical efficiency indicates how close a firm is to the 'best practices' in production. Based on the estimates of state level crop yield function derived from the VCM model of crop output, the input specific and overall efficiency measures described in the earlier section were estimated. The efficiency measures were estimated for each state and each of the years from 1970-71 to 1992-93. The trends in various efficiency measures in terms of mean, minimum and maximum of the efficiency estimates for each of the states over the 23- year period are shown in Tables III.1a-III.1d. For convenience, the efficiency estimates are presented as percentages. The states are arranged in the ascending order of their mean level efficiency.

The estimated efficiencies at the state-level point to the significant differences across the states in the case of 'intercept' or 'disembodied' efficiency of the producers. For instance, in Table III.1a, the lowest mean disembodied efficiency estimate for the state of Bihar is 62 and the highest for Kerala is 92. The state-level input specific and overall efficiency estimates also vary considerably among the states as well as over time as indicated by the difference between the maximum and minimum levels of efficiency. The variation in efficiency for the individual or specific inputs is negligible in the case of irrigation, tractors and fertilizers. In the case of labour the variation in efficiency between the most efficient state and the least efficient state on the average is less than 3 percentage points. Even in the case of rainfall and RWFG, the state level differences are relatively minor. In comparison, the 'disembodied' and overall state-level efficiencies vary substantially across the states and over time.

Although differences in individual input-specific efficiencies across the states are relatively small, the combined input-specific efficiencies (Table III.1d) are significantly less than 100% for all the states. A major part of the combined input-specific efficiency comes from the 'disembodied' (intercept) efficiency. The combined input-specific efficiency is indicative of the divergence of actual output from the potential output if the input levels were to be held 'fixed' across all the states. These efficiencies are comparable across the states. Thus, Bihar, MP, West Bengal, Maharashtra and UP are the states with the lowest technical efficiency. The top five states in ascending order of average technical efficiency are Haryana, Karnataka, Punjab, Assam, Tamilnadu and Kerala. Thus, in Bihar, if technical efficiencies were to increase to the most efficient level, there would be a gain of about 85% in crop yields in this state. The gains from higher technical efficiency in the states of Assam, Tamilnadu and Kerala are relatively small.

Table III.1a   Variation in Efficiencies across States and over Time: Intercept and Irrigation

State	Intercept				State	Irrigation			
	Mean	Min	Max	Difference		Mean	Min	Max	Difference
Bihar	62.75	58.10	71.10	13.00	Kerala	95.91	95.67	96.28	0.60
MP	67.24	61.34	76.53	15.19	Assam	96.18	95.65	96.49	0.84
WB	71.92	67.95	74.04	6.09	Tamilnadu	96.54	96.39	96.77	0.38
MT	72.52	69.76	77.40	7.64	Karnataka	96.81	96.33	97.05	0.71
UP	73.15	69.75	78.80	9.05	Punjab	97.04	96.88	97.38	0.50
Rajasthan	73.86	71.40	78.32	6.92	Haryana	97.12	96.97	97.32	0.36
AP	74.57	70.65	82.77	12.12	Gujarat	97.25	96.77	97.64	0.87
Orissa	74.64	71.00	76.37	5.37	UP	97.29	97.20	97.42	0.21
Gujarat	76.05	71.47	80.75	9.28	AP	97.32	97.26	97.42	0.16
Haryana	79.41	75.51	83.57	8.06	Orissa	97.40	97.14	97.74	0.60
Karnataka	81.13	77.50	85.32	7.82	Rajasthan	97.45	97.24	97.54	0.30
Punjab	82.95	80.14	86.26	6.13	WB	97.59	97.33	97.93	0.61
Assam	89.28	84.90	94.43	9.53	MT	97.77	97.04	98.78	1.73
Tamilnadu	90.99	85.89	94.87	8.98	Bihar	98.08	97.94	98.17	0.23
Kerala	92.69	90.66	94.44	3.79	MP	98.29	97.74	98.59	0.85

Notes:
(1) The state name abbreviations are: AP = Andhra Pradesh, MP= Madhya Pradesh, MT = Maharashtra, UP = Uttar Pradesh and WB = West Bengal, (2) Min/max/mean/diff = minimum/maximum/ mean and difference between minimum and maximum, respectively, of efficiency over the sample period 1970-71 to 1992-93.

Table III.1b **Variation in Efficiencies across States and over Time: Fertilizer and Tractors**

State	Fertilizer				State	Tractors			
	Mean	Min	Max	Difference		Mean	Min	Max	Difference
Bihar	99.90	99.88	99.93	0.05	Bihar	99.60	99.50	99.74	0.24
MP	99.91	99.89	99.93	0.04	MP	99.65	99.54	99.78	0.25
MT	99.92	99.91	99.94	0.03	UP	99.72	99.67	99.80	0.13
WB	99.93	99.91	99.93	0.02	WB	99.72	99.67	99.76	0.09
UP	99.93	99.91	99.94	0.03	MT	99.72	99.66	99.79	0.13
AP	99.93	99.92	99.95	0.03	Rajasthan	99.73	99.68	99.79	0.11
Orissa	99.93	99.93	99.93	0.01	AP	99.74	99.69	99.83	0.14
Rajasthan	99.93	99.93	99.94	0.01	Gujarat	99.75	99.66	99.83	0.17
Gujarat	99.94	99.92	99.95	0.03	Orissa	99.76	99.71	99.78	0.08
Haryana	99.95	99.93	99.96	0.03	Haryana	99.81	99.75	99.85	0.10
Karnataka	99.95	99.94	99.96	0.01	Karnataka	99.82	99.78	99.87	0.10
Assam	99.96	99.95	99.96	0.00	Punjab	99.88	99.83	99.93	0.10
Punjab	99.96	99.95	99.97	0.02	Assam	99.91	99.86	99.96	0.10
Kerala	99.98	99.98	99.99	0.01	Tamilnadu	99.93	99.88	99.97	0.09
Tamilnadu	99.98	99.97	99.99	0.02	Kerala	99.94	99.93	99.96	0.03

Table III.1c Variation in Efficiencies across States and over Time: Labour, Rainfall and Output Composition

State	Labour				State	Rainfall				State	RWFG			
	Mean	Min	Max	Difference		Mean	Min	Max	Difference		Mean	Min	Max	Difference
Bihar	95.92	94.11	98.14	4.03	Bihar	99.23	99.11	99.45	0.35	Bihar	92.86	91.62	95.10	3.48
Punjab	96.85	96.01	97.73	1.72	MP	99.34	99.18	99.58	0.39	MP	93.97	92.65	96.18	3.53
Haryana	97.20	96.55	97.52	0.97	WB	99.45	99.35	99.52	0.18	WB	94.84	93.87	95.67	1.80
AP	97.34	96.57	98.56	1.99	MT	99.46	99.39	99.57	0.18	MT	95.11	94.52	95.90	1.38
WB	97.36	96.68	98.55	1.87	UP	99.48	99.40	99.62	0.22	UP	95.11	94.40	96.47	2.07
Karnataka	97.37	96.97	98.07	1.10	Rajasthan	99.50	99.45	99.61	0.16	Rajasthan	95.25	94.64	96.28	1.65
Gujarat	97.44	96.69	98.56	1.87	Orissa	99.51	99.42	99.57	0.15	Orissa	95.36	94.50	96.06	1.55
UP	97.47	96.91	98.19	1.28	AP	99.51	99.43	99.69	0.26	AP	95.40	94.57	97.28	2.71
Orissa	97.62	97.04	98.62	1.58	Gujarat	99.54	99.43	99.64	0.21	Gujarat	95.51	94.26	96.33	2.08
MT	97.75	97.13	99.20	2.08	Haryana	99.61	99.53	99.71	0.18	Haryana	96.30	95.50	97.37	1.88
Assam	97.80	97.35	98.55	1.21	Karnataka	99.64	99.57	99.73	0.16	Karnataka	96.51	95.84	97.40	1.56
Rajasthan	98.00	97.27	98.70	1.44	Punjab	99.68	99.62	99.73	0.11	Punjab	97.02	96.39	97.66	1.27
MP	98.05	97.61	98.71	1.10	Tamilnadu	99.80	99.71	99.89	0.18	Assam	98.19	97.32	99.03	1.71
Kerala	98.31	97.80	98.74	0.94	Assam	99.82	99.73	99.91	0.18	Tamilnadu	98.35	97.41	99.37	1.96
Tamilnadu	98.84	98.02	99.35	1.33	Kerala	99.89	99.84	99.95	0.11	Kerala	98.81	98.35	99.47	1.12

Table III.1d Variation in Efficiencies and the Input-mix Effect across States and over Time: Input Specific, Overall and Input-mix Effect

	State level Input Specific					State Level Overall					Input-mix Effect			
State	Mean	Min	Max	Diffe-rence	State	Mean	Min	Max	Diffe-rence	State	Mean	Min	Max	Diffe-rence
Bihar	54.26	48.43	64.51	16.08	Bihar	40.36	32.47	53.95	21.48	Bihar	-30.72	-39.98	-17.89	22.10
MP	60.30	53.91	70.47	16.56	MP	49.72	40.04	65.63	25.60	MP	-20.35	-29.76	-7.12	22.64
WB	64.25	59.66	67.82	8.16	WB	53.29	47.03	58.19	11.16	WB	-18.88	-23.80	-15.32	8.47
MT	65.34	62.05	70.12	8.07	UP	55.46	50.24	66.45	16.21	UP	-16.90	-20.46	-8.13	12.34
UP	65.44	61.65	72.08	10.43	AP	58.01	51.16	73.18	22.02	AP	-14.82	-19.62	-4.80	14.82
Rajasthan	66.64	63.76	71.99	8.23	Orissa	59.08	52.46	62.28	9.82	Orissa	-12.94	-18.35	-9.92	8.43
AP	66.91	62.25	76.77	14.53	Rajasthan	59.20	56.38	61.38	5.00	Rajasthan	-11.80	-15.93	-9.12	6.81
Orissa	67.16	63.02	69.92	6.90	MT	59.59	55.01	67.29	12.28	MT	-9.39	-13.71	-4.12	9.58
Gujarat	68.33	62.79	73.19	10.39	Gujarat	63.27	55.69	71.18	15.50	Haryana	-8.78	-14.67	-1.58	13.08
Haryana	71.76	67.57	76.85	9.29	Haryana	65.97	58.42	75.65	17.22	Gujarat	-8.00	-13.36	-2.78	10.58
Karnataka	73.40	69.45	77.83	8.38	Punjab	71.76	66.62	77.36	10.74	Punjab	-4.88	-7.71	-0.82	6.89
Punjab	75.28	71.96	78.21	6.26	Karnataka	71.92	65.42	79.34	13.92	Karnataka	-2.28	-6.09	1.93	8.01
Assam	82.22	77.31	87.79	10.48	Assam	83.07	74.97	91.67	16.70	Tamilnadu	-0.54	-5.23	3.70	8.94
Tamilnadu	85.18	78.94	90.46	11.52	Tamilnadu	84.87	74.92	93.87	18.96	Assam	0.86	-3.08	4.48	7.56
Kerala	86.21	83.44	89.04	5.60	Kerala	91.02	87.25	96.74	9.50	Kerala	5.38	2.77	8.30	5.53

In addition, there are gains from the particular levels of inputs used, as efficiency improves. The input-mix effect is significant for several states. As shown in Table III.1d, it decreases the overall state-level efficiency by more than 10 percent in seven out of 15 states, in comparison to the case if all the states were using the same level of inputs. In other words, because of the larger levels of inputs combined with inefficiency of the input use, the divergence of actual output from the potential output increases. The potential gains from improving technical efficiency, therefore, are higher in states where inefficiencies exist and the quantum of inputs (per hectare in the present case) used is also great. There is considerable change in the order or ranking of the states when the basis of ranking changes from 'input-specific' efficiency to 'overall efficiency' indicating the importance of improving the efficiency in specific inputs in specific states. In the case of Assam and Kerala, the 'input-mix effect' is positive due to the relatively high levels of technical efficiency and lower levels of input use per hectare of land. The large negative input-mix effect is indicative of the potential gains in crop yield through changes in the input levels on top of the gains indicated by input-specific efficiency.

While there are substantial benefits to improvements in efficiency in the case of individual inputs, these benefits are smaller as compared to the gains from improving the efficiency indicated by the magnitude of the disembodied efficiency. For this reason, we have attempted to explain only the 'disembodied efficiency' in terms of selected non-price and organizational explanatory variables and incorporate it in the present model.

III.1.3b Technical Progress Changes in input growth and technical efficiency provide an explanation for a part of output growth. The production function provides an approach to the decomposition of growth in output in terms of input growth and traditionally, technical progress or a shift in production function. The production frontier approach, however, provides an alternative explanation for the shifts in production function across the producing units. The shifts in production frontier over time can be viewed as a reflection of technical progress (Kalirajan and Shand, 1997). The changes in production technology, embodied in the 'green revolution' of the late 1960s and late 1970s, is one possible source of technical progress in Indian agriculture. The estimates of 'production frontier coefficients' for the 'intercept' are shown in Figure III.1 for the period 1970-71 to 1992-93. In the present study, the data period does not include the years of late 1960s and hence the impact of technological progress of this period is not captured.

The estimated intercept coefficient of the production frontier shows an increase in 1976-77 and again in 1977-78 but remains stable for the entire period afterwards. The pattern of technical progress in the crop sector as a whole, captured in the estimated crop yield production frontier, is one of a major shift in the second half of 1970s and then no change since then. The result does not imply that there are no technological changes in the production process, but imply that there are no significant changes in crop yield that can not be explained by the changes in input growth and changes in the efficiency of input use. The technical progress is 'embodied' in the inputs. In the context of modelling agricultural production, explanation of changes in input use and technical efficiency would be more important as the shifts in technical frontier appear to be less frequent and hence could be assumed to be exogenous.

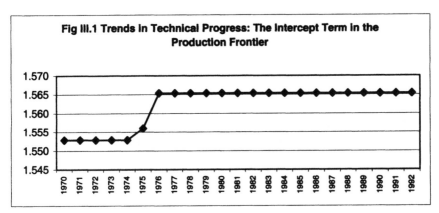

Note: 1970 = 1970-71.

III.1.3c Modelling General Efficiency The disembodied efficiency represented by the magnitude of the intercept term relative to the intercept of the frontier has been interpreted as the contribution of various 'firm-level' or 'producer-level' characteristics to production efficiency (Kalirajan and Shand, 1994). Deviation of firm-level output from the frontier output for the same input level arises for a number of non-price and organizational factors: lack of knowledge of the 'best practices' in production, differences in access to fixed factors such as roads, electricity, credit institutions and also a suitable natural endowment or agro-climatic conditions in the case of agricultural production. The range in the estimated input-specific efficiencies was indicated in terms of mean, minimum and maximum for each of the states over the estimation period in Tables III.1a-III.1c. As our focus in this study would be on the general efficiency (indicated by the variations in intercept from its frontier), a review of the trends in disembodied efficiency at the state level is presented through Figures III.2a-III.2d.

The disembodied efficiency exhibits no uniform trend across the 15 states considered in this analysis. Among the four southern states (Figure III.2a), Kerala and Tamilnadu have a higher level of efficiency and show a slight positive trend from the mid 1980s onward whereas in the case of AP and Karnataka there is a downward trend generally, ending with an upturn in 1991-92 and 1992-93. Among the three western states, MP exhibits a declining pattern of general efficiency whereas Maharashtra and Gujarat show no uniform pattern (Figure III.2c). In all the three states, disembodied efficiency rises in 1991-92 and 1992-93 over the level of 1990-91. Among the four northern states, in Punjab and Haryana the trend is less conspicuous whereas Rajasthan and UP show an upward trend during the 1980s (Figure III.2d). In the case of four eastern states, Bihar and

Assam exhibit a declining pattern of general efficiency whereas Orissa and West Bengal show a mixed pattern of change over the period 1970-71 to 1992-93 (Figure III.2b).

Fig III.2   Trends in Disembodied Efficiency:
           Across States in Different Regions

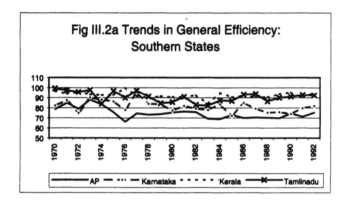

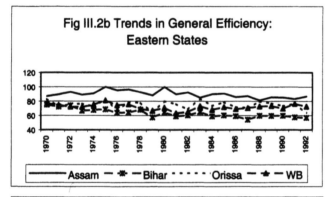

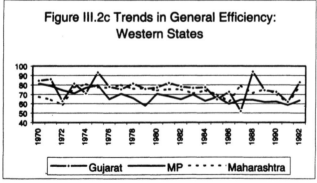

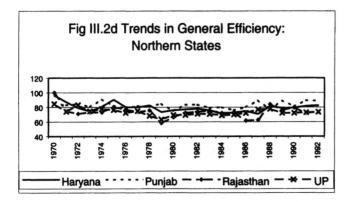

Fig III.2d Trends in General Efficiency: Northern States

The general pattern that emerges is one of a decrease in the level of efficiency in 1970s followed by an improvement in the 1980s that has continued into the 1990s. The pattern is more discernible for the southern and northern states (Fig III.3a and III.3d) than for the other two regions (Fig III.3b and III.3c). At the national level, the decline in the 1970s is striking, but there is no clear increasing trend in the 1980s (Figure III.4). Thus, there is a lower level of efficiency in the 1980s as compared to 1970s which together with the result of no further shifts in the frontier production since 1976 imply declining trend in the efficiency of the use of inputs.

The pattern at the aggregate level for all the 15 states shown in Figure III.4 shows that the general efficiency declined during the period from 1970-71 to 1980-81 and then has remained stable or shown a slightly increasing trend. The aggregate efficiency measure was derived using value of crop output in each state as the weights. In general the pattern suggests significant variations in efficiency from one state to another and varying trend in different states over time.

**Fig III.3   Trends in Disembodied Efficiency: Regional Level
(State Level Efficiencies Weighted by Crop Output)**

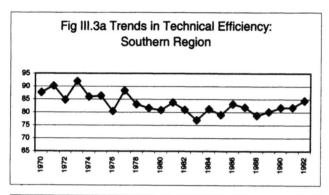

Fig III.3a Trends in Technical Efficiency:
Southern Region

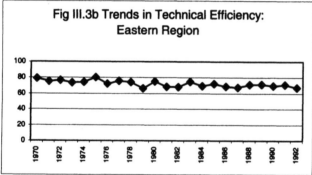

Fig III.3b Trends in Technical Efficiency:
Eastern Region

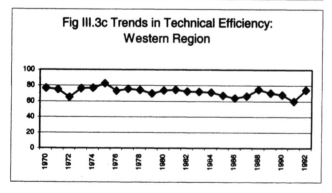

Fig III.3c Trends in Technical Efficiency:
Western Region

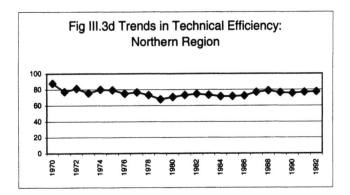

A number of variables can be hypothesized to have influence on technical efficiency. These factors may relate to infrastructure in rural areas (such as roads, communication facilities) and ability of the farmers to absorb new technology or practices (literacy, health status). Improved infrastructure reduces the transaction costs involved in getting access to new technologies and their adoption at the farm level. This in turn would reduce the gap between actual output and the potential output. Improvement in access to new technology can come about not only from the direct effects of improved infrastructure but also through the inter-linkages between farm and non-farm sectors.

The inter-sectoral linkages increase the potential for improved communication and hence the potential for knowledge gains at the producer level. Transaction costs are also reduced when agricultural sector is relatively large so that there are some economies of scale in the development of input supply network. As we are using aggregate crop production as the output variable, it is necessary to account for the effects of shifts in the composition of output also. At one level, the output composition was reflected in the ratio *RWFG*. However, another important distinction in the crop output that is relevant from a policy perspective is the distinction between food grain and non-food grain output. We have used the ratio of food grain to non food grain output (real gross value of output) as an indicator of the change in the composition of crop output.

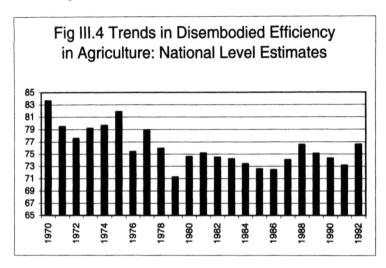

Fig III.4 Trends in Disembodied Efficiency in Agriculture: National Level Estimates

Factors influencing the disembodied efficiency of the producers in a state, thus, vary from physical characteristics such as agro-climatic conditions, variables that can be influenced by policy such as the level of education of the producers, level of infrastructure facilities to the variables reflecting the development of the economy as indicated by the inter-sectoral relationships. An appropriate framework of analysis to quantify the impact of the various explanatory variables on the disembodied efficiency of the states in crop production is the regression analysis. Using state level disembodied efficiency as the dependent variable and a number of explanatory variables as the independent variables, for 15 states over the period 1970-71 to 1992-93, alternative regression models were estimated. The explanatory variables included in the analysis were,

1. Ratio of food grain to non-food grain output,
2. Ratio of agricultural net state domestic product (NSDP) to total NSDP,
3. Ratio of agricultural NSDP to population,
4. Ratio of NSDP from agriculture to total manufacturing,
5. Ratio of NSDP from agriculture to unregistered manufacturing,
6. Rural literacy rate,
7. Average farm size of the operational holdings,
8. Ratio of real NSDP from transport, storage and communications to total NSDP from all the sectors
9. Ratio of real NSDP from transport, storage and communications to total population in the state.

The general formulation of the regression model is,

$$MEFF_{jt} = f(X1_{jt}, X2_{jt}, X2_{jt}, ...t)$$ (III.12)

where $X1$, $X2$ etc are the explanatory variables noted above. $MEFF2_{jt}$ is the disembodied efficiency of jth state in tth year. As the formulation represents panel data framework, the generalized least squares procedure which utilizes the cross-section and temporal data taking into account the variance-covariance matrix of the equation errors is an appropriate estimation procedure.

Specification of the functional form for equation (III.12) should take into account the need to restrict the projected values of $MEFF_{jt}$ to between zero and 1. A transformation of the dependent variable in equation (III.12) that imposes such a restriction is provided in equation below:

$$\{MEFF_{jt} / (1- MEFF_{jt})\} = f(X1_{jt}, X2_{jt}, X2_{jt}, ...t) \qquad (III.13)$$

While the dependent variable in equation (III.13) may take any real values, the implicit value of $MEFF_{jt}$ ranges between zero and 1. The transformation also implies that the elasticity of $MEFF_{jt}$ with respect to the explanatory variables may not be constant but depends on the level of $MEFF_{jt}$ also.

Equations for disembodied efficiency in agricultural production were estimated in both forms of the dependent variable. In the equations that were estimated, rural literacy ($RURLIT$) and infrastructure ($TSCPOP$) are significantly and positively related to disembodied efficiency. Thus, improvements in human resources (represented by literacy) and physical infrastructure (represented by transportation, storage and communication output) improve production efficiency, leading to an increase in crop output. The 'crop-mix effect' represented by the ratio of non- food grain output to food grain output has a positive impact on efficiency. As the composition of output changes in favour of non-food grains, production efficiency improves. As the share of agriculture in the total economy of the state rises (the ratio, $AG/NSDP$) disembodied efficiency is estimated to increase also. While this result would imply the potential sources of economies of scale in delivering inputs and services to agriculture by other agents, it is also suggestive of weak inter-sectoral linkages.

In the estimated equations farm size and efficiency are negatively associated. However, when rural literacy improves, the gain in efficiency is greater when farm size is larger. Equations with the transformed dependent variable provide broadly similar results as the original specification of the efficiency (equation (III.13)).

Farm size has the same effect in the transformed model as in the original specification of disembodied efficiency: negative relationship with efficiency, but a positive interaction term with rural literacy. The disembodied result of positive relationship between rural literacy, infrastructure and disembodied efficiency is captured in the transformed equation. Although there are no independent effects of rural literacy and infrastructure, both have positive effect on disembodied efficiency. Since the equation also captures the positive interaction and all the estimates of regression coefficients are significant, we have retained the equation using the transformed dependent variable for inclusion in the present model.

The selected equation for further analysis is,

$$\text{Ln } \{MEFF_{jt} / (1 - MEFF_{jt})\} = 139.98 - 0.5215 \text{ Ln } (FGQ/NFGQ) + 0.5514 \, DUMAG$$
$$-0.7596 \text{ Ln } FSZ + 0.0072 \text{ Ln } FSZ * RURLIT$$
$$+ 0.00004 \, RURLIT * (TSC/POP) - 0.0687 \, T \quad \text{(III.14)}$$

where $(FGQ/NFGQ)$ is the ratio of output of food grain to non-food grain; $DUMAG$ is a dummy variable with value of 1 if the ratio of NSDP from agriculture to overall NSDP (both in real terms) is 0.4 or greater and zero otherwise; FSZ is the average farm holding size; $RURLIT$ is the rate of rural literacy; (TSC/POP) is the per capita real NSDP from transportation, storage and communication and T is a trend variable. Ln is the logarithmic operator as defined previously. Estimation details are in Appendix 3.

III.1.4 The Input Demand Equations

From the estimated production frontier (based on equation (III.1) and the production efficiencies associated with different states, the yield function (in logarithmic form) that is specific to a state can be derived as,

$$\text{Ln } Y_{jt} = (a0^{**}_t + \text{Ln } MEFF_{jt}) + a1 \text{ Ln } (IA/GA)_{jt} + a2 \text{ Ln } (F/GA)_{jt}$$
$$+ a3 \text{ Ln } (TR/GA)_{jt} + a4 \text{ Ln } LAB_{jt} + a5 \text{ Ln } R_{jt}$$
$$+ a6 \text{ Ln } RWFG_{jt} \quad \text{(III.15)}$$

where we have removed the subscripts for the coefficients other than intercept a0 to indicate that only intercept or the disembodied efficiency variations are incorporated into the production model. The production function (as against the yield function) in the logarithmic form can be written as,

$$\text{Ln } VQ_{jt} = \text{Ln } GA_{jt} + (a0^{**}_t + \text{Ln } MEFF_{jt}) + a1 \text{ Ln } (IA/GA)_{jt} + a2 \text{ Ln } (F/GA)_{jt}$$
$$+ a3 \text{ Ln } (TR/GA)_{jt} + a4. \text{ Ln } LAB_{jt} + a5 \text{ Ln } R_{jt}$$
$$+ a6 \text{ Ln } RWFG_{jt} \quad \text{(III.16)}$$

where VQ is the real gross crop output and all the other expressions are as defined earlier.

In terms of absolute values the production function is,

$$VQ_{ijt} = \text{Exp}(a0^{**}_t) . MEFF_{jt} . GA_{jt}^{(1-a1-a2-a3-a4-a5-a6)} . IA^{a1}_{jt} . F^{a2}_{jt} TR^{a3}_{jt} . LAB^{a4}_{jt}.$$
$$R^{a5}_{jt} . RWFG^{a6}_{jt} \quad \text{(III.17)}$$

The basic optimization problem of the individual farmer is to choose the levels of inputs that maximize the present value of the net revenues subject to a number of constraints. The level of general efficiency is assumed fixed at any given point in time, as the factors influencing efficiency are primarily external to the producer. A direct specification of the optimization problem at the aggregate or state-level may be possible, but given the level of aggregation in the present study (of all the producers at the state level) it may be more appropriate to specify a statistical model that links the explanatory variables to the input decisions.

Although decisions on the levels of different inputs are inter-dependent, a distinction between decisions on different inputs is possible in a sequential manner. In the case of labour, we assume that all the available labour is utilized in agriculture. In other words, agriculture is the residual sector for labour employment and there is no optimization of labour use in agriculture. While this is an over-simplification, given the prevalence of significant employment of hired labour in agriculture (including migrant labour in some states), it should be noted that such employment is largely 'seasonal'. The decisions relating to variable inputs such as fertilizer are dependent on the existing farm-level conditions such as the extent of crop area that can be irrigated in a farm or type of crops that can be grown given the irrigation facilities and equipment (tractors) available. The decision on the type of crops to be grown also precedes the decision on the amount of fertilizer to be applied. In this sense, all the variables such as *GA, IA, TR* and *LAB* are determined prior to the decision on fertilizers or they are exogenous to the decision on fertilizer application. Fertilizer demand would depend on the level of such exogenous variables.

As we have aggregated the crop production in all types of land and farm level conditions, these inter-linkages need to be explicitly incorporated in the input demand functions. Profit maximization without any constraints would imply that ratios of input price to output would be a major determinant of the input use. In the case of 'fixed' inputs such as tractors, their purchase is influenced by factors affecting farmer's ability to finance the purchase of the fixed inputs as well as by the price ratio and output response over the life period of the fixed input. In evaluating the farmer's access to credit, the type of land and other assets on the farm would be important. In this sense, purchase of tractors would depend on the size of the farm and the extent of irrigation facilities on the farm. In the case of expansion of irrigation facilities, it is not merely the investment decision of the farmer but also the decision of the government on public investment in irrigation that would be relevant. The area cultivated under all crops (*GA*) is determined by an exogenous factor rainfall (*R*) and expansion of irrigated area. Expansion of irrigated area often allows growing of more than crop from the same piece of land in one year, leading to increased *GA*. Inadequate rainfall in the sowing season can result in reduced area under cultivation, thus affecting *GA*. Rainfall is an exogenous variable to the farmer. Gross crop area is primarily a function of rainfall and irrigation.

The ratio of output of rice and wheat to total food grain output, *RWFG*, is determined by the crop-mix the farmer adopts depending upon the relative profitability of growing rice, wheat or other food grains from the same piece of land. Investment decisions such as expansion of irrigation facilities and purchase of tractors are dependent on the potential for a changing the crop-mix to increase net revenue from crops. The potential for change in the crop mix is based on technical or agro-climatic conditions and hence year-to-year changes in investment decisions are more likely to be influenced by the price variations rather than changes in potential for crop-mix variations. In other words, RWFG is influenced by the availability of irrigation (a technical factor) and changes in relative prices of crops, but purchase of tractors and irrigation expansion are less likely to be influenced by the trends in *RWFG*.

The above discussion provides a framework for the specification of input demand functions. A sequential rather than simultaneous approach appears suitable in the specification of input demand functions. In the implicit optimization framework, the disembodied efficiency, although affects level of input use, it does not affect the response of input use to changes in relative prices. The optimal input levels are derived based on expectations of output response as well as prices. Whereas output response may be predicted from the production function, price expectations are more difficult to predict. Among the alternative models, we choose the adaptive expectations model for output prices. We also use the 'partial adjustment' of the actual input use relative to the optimal use which leads us to the use of lagged dependent variable in the input demand equation.

III.1.4a Fertilizer Demand The general specification of fertilizer demand equation which combines adaptive expectations model of (output) price expectations with a partial adjustment to optimal input level, adopted in this study is,

$$(F/GA)_{jt} = f\,[(F/GA)_{j,t\text{-}1}\,(PF_t\,/\,PA_{\,t\text{-}1}),\,(IA/GA)_{\,jt},\,R_{jt}\,] \qquad\qquad \text{(III.18)}$$

where *PA* is the price index of the crop output, *PF* is the price index of fertilizer (paid by the farmer) and all other expressions are as defined previously.

A number of simplifying assumptions are implicit in the above specification. Since *GA* is assumed to be exogenous to the decisions on fertilizer use, fertilizer use per hectare of crop area is estimated rather than the total fertilizer consumption. The expected crop output price *PA* is the previous year's price and the relative prices are the same for all the states. As the production functions are assumed to vary across the states only in terms of the intercept, the coefficients of the demand function with respect to relative price, irrigation and rainfall may not vary across the states. However, price elasticity of demand may vary with the level of fertilizer consumption or irrigation due to the variation in the cost of applying fertilizer. The intercept of the demand function, however, would vary across the states. The intercept varies over time also if the shifts, over time, in production frontier or efficiency are significant. The use of fertilizers is assumed to be independent of the use of labor and tractors. This simplifies the estimation of fertilizer demand equation but it does imply that the impact of increased mechanization of crop production or increased labor use on per hectare basis is captured by the variations in the ratios $(IA/GA)_{jt}$. Increased mechanization leads to more efficient organization of farm operations, changes the composition of output produced on the farm and would allow higher application of fertilizers. Increased mechanization in turn would be influenced by changes in output prices or expansion of irrigation facilities affecting crop yields. In this sense, changes in number of tractors per hectare of crop area are reflected by changes in output price and irrigated area.

Variations in labour use on per hectare basis are related to the cropping pattern and intensity of use of other inputs that also influence the use of labor. Therefore, changes in labor use affect fertilizer consumption only to the extent that the factors causing these changes also directly affect fertilizer consumption. There is, in other words, no direct effect of changes in labor use on fertilizer consumption.

The fertilizer demand equations are estimated using the annual data for the period 1970-71 to 1992-93 relating to the 15 major states. Given the 'panel' nature of the data two estimation procedures are used. First approach is that of Generalized Least Squares (GLS) that takes into account the correlation of random error term across the states and over time. The second approach is that of the Instrumental Variables (IV), which recognizes the potential interdependence of the lagged dependent variable with the random error term associated with the demand equation.

In all the estimated equations, signs of the estimated coefficients of fertilizer demand function follow the expected pattern: positive with respect to irrigation, negative with respect to price of fertilizers and positive with respect to expected output per hectare. The sign with respect to the coefficient of rainfall variable is negative, reflecting the pattern of fertilizer consumption in India: lower fertilizer consumption per hectare in regions with higher rainfall. However, when a dynamic relationship between fertilizer consumption and the above variables was estimated, the impact of fertilizer price and expected productivity per hectare becomes insignificant. The coefficient on the lagged dependent variable is significant and very close to 1.

Based on the alternative estimates available, the equation in the 'first differences' is selected for further analysis.

The selected equation of fertilizer demand is,

$$
\begin{aligned}
D[Ln(F/GA)] = {} & 0.5356 + 1.3206 \, D[IA/GA] + 0.4638 \, D[Ln(PF/PA_{t-1})] \\
& - 0.0996 \, Ln \, RM \, 0.1108 \, Ln \, RM^* \, D[Ln(PF/PA_{t-1})] \\
& + 0.3362 * (IA/GA) * D[Ln(PF/PA_{t-1})]
\end{aligned}
\tag{III.19}
$$

where (F/GA) is fertilizer consumption per hectare of crop area, (IA/GA) is the proportion of crop area under irrigation, RM is the long-term average rainfall during June-September during the period in the state, PF is the fertilizer price index, PA is the aggregate crop price index and Ln is the logarithmic operator. Estimated equation is reported in Appendix 3.

The estimated equation suggests a more price elastic demand for fertilizers in states with higher rainfall and lower area under irrigation. This result appears to be consistent with higher crop output elasticity with respect to fertilizers in regions with greater extent of irrigation. A further explanation for the presence of interaction terms for the price variable in the input demand equation when the production function itself is of Cobb-Douglas type is the pattern of cost of cultivation at higher levels of fertilizer consumption. As the cost per hectare varies, the interaction terms can arise. Hence, the more general model with interaction terms in input demand function for fertilizers is retained.

Intercept of the selected equation is adjusted for each state based on the state-level residuals of the equation over the years. Average deviation of the actual fertilizer consumption per hectare from the estimated fertilizer consumption per hectare over the period 1970-71 to 1992-93 is added to the estimated overall intercept.

III.1.4b Demand for Tractors Tractors are one of the few machineries that some of the Indian farmers own and operate. Demand for tractors thus, reflects an investment demand by the farmers. Tractors are also commonly used for rural transportation. Rural transportation demand is influenced by agricultural output and income from agriculture. Hence, we estimate the demand for tractors as arising from demand derived from crop production. To the extent that rural transportation demand is also linked to crop output, this approach is justified.

As in the case of any investment good, demand for tractors is influenced by expected returns and cost of purchase. Return to addition to tractor stock is affected by the extent of coverage of crop area under irrigation as well as the extent to which tractors are effectively utilized. As the average size of Indian farms is relatively small, a tractor's capacity can be fully utilized only when there is a rental market for tractors. When farm size is larger, the dependence on rental market and the associated cost of renting out tractor-time decreases and the demand for additional tractors would be higher. Thus, besides the coverage under irrigation, average size of farm holdings is a factor influencing demand for tractors. Demand for tractors is also influenced by variations in crop output per hectare as farmers would have to provide a part of the output for payment towards the margin money on tractor's price. With these arguments, demand for tractors is specified as,

$$(TPUR/GA)_{jt} = f \, [(TPUR/GA)_{j,t-1}, \, (IA/GA)_{j,t-1}, \, (PTR_t/ \, PA_{t-1}), \, FSZ_{jt},$$
$$(VQAG/GA)_{j,t-1} \,] \tag{III.20}$$

where *TPUR* is the number of tractors purchased, *GA* is the gross crop area, *IA* is the area under irrigation, *FSZ* is the average size of the farm holdings and *VQAG* is the real gross crop output. As in the case of fertilizer demand, output price expectations are assumed to be 'static' and actual input demand as a partial adjustment to the optimal level.

Data used for estimating the demand function for tractors is the annual data on sales for the period 1970-71 to 1992-93 for the 15 major states. Two estimation procedures followed are GLS and Instrumental Variables method.

The dynamic specification provides better overall fit to the data than the static relationship. Based on the overall performance, the following equation below is retained for further analysis:

$$\text{Ln } TPUR = -1.2357 + 0.0854 \, D1 + 0.7482 \text{ Ln } TPUR_{t-1} + 0.8582 \, (IA/GA)_{t-1}$$
$$-1.6820 \text{ Ln } (PTR/PA_{t-1}) + 0.2517 \text{ Ln } FSZ$$
$$+ .3599 \text{ Ln } VQ_{t-1} \tag{III.21}$$

The estimated price elasticity of demand for tractors is relatively large: exceeds unity in absolute value. The long-term elasticity is even greater. The high elasticity is likely to be the result of the rapid growth in tractor purchases from a low base. Since the level of mechanization is still low in Indian agriculture, we have retained the estimated equation inspite of the large price elasticity. Irrigation has a positive effect on demand for tractors. As irrigation opens up the range of options in terms of type of crops grown, varieties of crops and intensity of land use, demand for tractors is likely to be positively influenced with irrigation. Irrigation also enhances the credit worthiness of the farmer, as purchase of tractors would require recourse to credit. Two further points to be made in connection with the estimated equation for demand for tractors are (1) positive relationship between farm size and (2) tractor demand and lagged value of crop output and tractor demand. Farm size also influences access to credit, keeping all other factors the same and hence the positive relationship with demand for tractors. Lagged crop output is a proxy for the availability of funds with the farmer for at least the margin money on the purchase of tractors.

III.1.4c Irrigated Area Irrigation has been a key element of the agricultural production strategy in the Indian context. It influences crop output both in terms of level of output and variability of crop output from year-to-year. The impact of irrigation on crop output has several dimensions. It increases crop yield even if there is no change in other inputs where rainfall is not adequate in terms of quantity of water supplied by rain and in terms of its timing. It may permit raising of crops in seasons, where cultivation would have been impossible due to lack of water. Irrigation also affects application of other inputs such as the use of high yielding varieties of crops and fertilizers. Access to irrigation also affects choice of crops themselves, thereby raising the potential for output per unit of land. Access to irrigation also raises the credit-worthiness of a farm, thereby, providing access to credit for the purchase of investment goods such as a tractor. Because of these multiple effects, decision on developing irrigation facilities is also influenced by numerous factors.

Expansion of irrigated area results from investments made by both the private or individual farmers as well as by the government. Government investment in agriculture is mainly in irrigation projects. These irrigation projects include major projects such as the dams on rivers and canals to bring the water from reservoirs to the fields, as well as minor projects such as sinking of tube wells and pumping ground water from the aquifers to the fields. Private investment in agriculture is in the form of on-farm irrigation projects such as digging of new wells/tube wells, installation of sprinklers, installation of pump sets and purchase of other machinery. There is no published data on crop area irrigated from privately developed irrigation sources and public projects. However, there is data on public and private investment is agriculture, a large part of it is in irrigation development. Data on investment in agriculture is available only at the national level and not at the state level. Therefore, in order to isolate the effect of government investment in agriculture on irrigation and the impact of other factors influencing private development of irrigation facilities, a combination of both national and state level data is needed.

Trends in real fixed investment in agriculture at the national level, shown in Figure I.7 in the pervious chapter, point to the decline of real public (government) investment in agriculture beginning in the mid-1980s. But real private investment accelerated during this period. As development of irrigation facilities is the major portion of investment expenditures in agriculture, factors explaining agricultural investment would also help explain expansion of irrigated area.

Public investment in agriculture is a policy variable and expansion of irrigated area can be expected to be positively influenced by the former. Development of irrigation facilities by the individual farmers is influenced by expected returns and cost of bringing additional areas under irrigation. Cost of bringing additional area under irrigation is related to the cost of pump set needed to bring irrigation water to the field besides the cost of civil works relating to the cost of digging the wells or laying the field channels. Expected net return on investment in irrigation is related to the expected crop yield, crop prices and the operating cost of irrigation facilities. Crop yield is affected not only due to the direct effect of increased coverage of crop area under irrigation but also by the indirect effect through the increase in the use of other inputs such as fertilizer. Taking previous year's output price and crop yield as the expected yield and price, we specify the following relationship between irrigated area and its explanatory variables,

$$(IA/GA)_t = f\left[\,(PUBINV/GA)_t\,,\,\{(YLD*PA)_{t\text{-}1}/PM_t\}\,,\,t\,\right] \tag{III.22}$$

where *PUBINV* is the government investment in agriculture (real, fixed), *YLD* is the crop yield per hectare of crop area, *PA* is the price index of crop output, *PM* is the price index of manufactured products as a proxy for the price of machinery needed in conjunction with the irrigation source to irrigate the land (pump set, for instance). The time trend variable 't' captures the effect of other factors such as the more intensive use of existing irrigation facilities.

The impact of changes in $\{PUBINV/GA\}$ and $\{(YLD*PA)_{t\text{-}1}/PM_t\}$ on $\{IA/GA\}$ may be felt over a period of time as time lags between the stimulus to new investment and the actual investment is likely to be over one year. Hence we use the Auto Regressive Distributed Lag (*ARDL*) procedure, to allow for the possible lagged effects of the independent variables.

After reviewing alternative estimates, we selected the following equation:

$$\text{Ln}\,(IA/GA)_t = -2.0205 + 0.0178\,t + 0.0584\,\text{Ln}\,(PUBINV/GA)_t$$
$$+ 0.0958\,\text{Ln}\,\{(YLD*PA)_{t\text{-}1}/PM_t\} \tag{III.23}$$

where *IA*, *GA*, *PA* and *YLD* are irrigated area, gross crop area, crop price index and crop yield index, respectively. *PM* is the index of manufactured products to reflect the trends in the cost of development of irrigation facilities, *PUBINV* is the public investment in agriculture and 't' is the trend variable. It may be noted that the

ARDL procedure picked out an equation with no additional lag structures. Details of estimation are in Appendix 3.

The estimated equation provides a model for forecasting irrigated area as a proportion of gross cropped area at the national level. To obtain estimates of irrigated area as a proportion of gross cropped area at the state level, further disaggregation of the national level forecast is needed. We obtain the disaggregation based on the past trends in the proportion of state-level irrigated area out of the national level irrigated area. One reason for this approach is the lack of information on public investment in agriculture at the state level. Expansion of irrigated area in a particular state may be at a higher rate than the national average because of the potential for expansion of irrigated area in the state or because of the greater incentives to increase irrigation. Incentives may differ due to the variations in agro-climatic conditions favouring cultivation of irrigated crops, or due to the presence of markets for crops, which provide adequate returns to new investments. The equation used to estimate the share of state 'j' in national level irrigated area in year 't' is,

$$(IA_j/IA)_t = a0_j + a1_j (1/t) + u_t \tag{III.24}$$

where IA_j is the irrigated area in the 'jth' state, IA is the irrigated area at the national level and u is the random error. The trend is captured by the variable t, taking the values 1, 2, ...T. The equation for each of the 15 states is estimated by OLS. In equation (III.24), if $a1_j$ is <0, the (IA_j/IA) increases as t increases. That is, the share of j th state in total irrigated area increases over time. If $a1_j$ >0, the (IA_j/IA) decreases as t increases. In both the cases, (IA_j/IA) tends towards $a0_j$ over time. The estimated coefficients of $a0_j$ and $a1_j$ for each of the states are summarized in Appendix 3. While the estimated equations do not perform well as an explanation of the pattern of evolution of the irrigated area in each of the states there is consistency in the overall allocation of the national level irrigated area. The estimated intercepts of all the states add up to 100 so that over time when the share of each state converges to its respective intercept, all the national level irrigated area is allocated fully to the states. The coefficients of $(1/T)$ for all the states also add up to nearly zero.

III.1.4d Gross Cropped Area Increase in crop area is one source of the increase in crop output. Larger land area was brought under cultivation as population increased. Increased net cropped area was a major source of increase in crop output in India until the early 1970s. As the potential for bringing additional land under cultivation disappeared over time, the increase in crop area was on account of the rise in gross cropped area. The distinction between net and gross cropped area arises from the possibility of multiple cropping or taking more than one crop from the same land area in one year. The trends in net cropped area and gross cropped area are shown in Figure III.5.

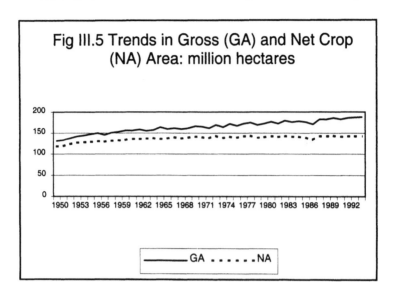

Fig III.5 Trends in Gross (GA) and Net Crop (NA) Area: million hectares

Cropping intensity, or the ratio of gross crop area to the net crop area, is a function of conditions for crop production. One of the key conditions is access to water. Expansion of irrigation facilities has also aided in multiple cropping. A second factor that has enabled multiple cropping in some areas is the development of short duration crop varieties that reduce the time required for crop production thereby enabling raising of more than one crop within a year. Thirdly, use of machinery for certain field operations has also led to reduction in the time needed for pre-sowing farm operations, thus reducing the overall land-time needed for crop production within a year. Rainfall also influences the area under cultivation in any year, especially where irrigation facilities are limited or are also influenced by rainfall. If rainfall is not adequate or not timely during the sowing period, area sown will be smaller than had the rainfall been adequate and timely. During periods of very favorable rainfall conditions, crop area increases as irrigation potential of the existing facilities also improves.

Impact of the various factors reviewed above on the gross cropped area can be represented as,

$$GA_{jt} = f \{ IA_{jt}, (R_{jt}/RM_j), t \}$$ \hfill (III.25)

where R is the level of rainfall during June-September period and RM refers to the mean level of rainfall during the same period. Increase in irrigated area IA is expected to have a positive impact on GA through various effects discussed previously and the deviation of rain fall in a particular year from the mean level (average for the period 1970-71 to 1992-93) is also expected to be related positively to GA. The impact of rising population pressure leading to bringing of larger land area under cultivation is represented by the trend variable. Some exploratory estimates suggest significant impact of irrigation and rainfall on gross crop area. As the estimates also suggest a possible dynamic relationship, estimates based on instrumental variables approach was adopted. FolloOwing equation was selected for further analysis:

$$\text{Ln } GA_{jt} = -0.1981 + 0.9897 \text{ Ln } GA_{j,t-1} + 0.0213 \text{ Ln } IA_{jt}$$
$$+ 0.0284 \text{ Ln } (R_{jt} / RM_j) \tag{III.26}$$

where all the variables are as defined previously. Details of estimation are in Appendix 3.

III.1.5 Crop Output Composition

In the crop yield equation, output is measured as an aggregate over all major crops produced in each state. When output composition changes for the same level of inputs, aggregate output may also vary due to the differences in the aggregation weights attached to various individual crops. Crop output composition is distinguished at two levels in this study. First, we reflect the difference between the main cereals, rice and wheat, and the other food grains. Second, we distinguish between food grains and non- food grain crops. Within food grains, output shares of rice and wheat have increased sharply during the period 1970-71 to 1992-93 (Figure III.6). In the case of rice and wheat both the technological innovations such as the development of high yielding varieties of crops and the market support in the form of procurement network have provided an advantage over the other food grains.

The ratio of food grain output to non-food grain output has moved in favor of non-food grains over the period 1970-71 to 1992-93 (Figure III.7). Shifts in crop area in favor of one crop relative to another are a result of changes in relative profitability and possibility of substitution limited by agro-climatic conditions. Profitability of one crop relative to another is affected by factors such as relative price, relative yield, input cost, post-harvest processing cost and availability of market for the produce. Agro-climatic conditions limiting the range of substitution among crops include requirement of crops in terms of water, sunshine for crop production and suitability of soil for particular crops.

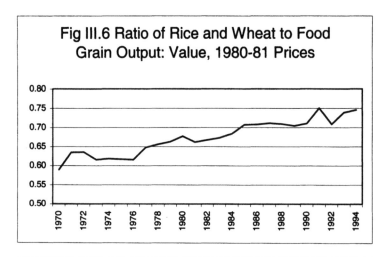

Fig III.6 Ratio of Rice and Wheat to Food Grain Output: Value, 1980-81 Prices

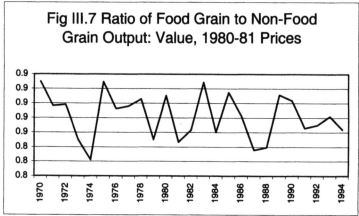

Fig III.7 Ratio of Food Grain to Non-Food Grain Output: Value, 1980-81 Prices

Taking into consideration the factors that influence the choice of a crop-mix by the producers and the availability of data, the following equations were specified for (1) the ratio of rice and wheat output to total food grain output and (2) the ratio of food grain output to non-food grain output:

$$RWFG_{jt} = f1\ [RWFG_{j,t\text{-}1},\ (PRW/PFG)_{t\text{-}1},\ (IA/GA)_{jt},\ R_{jt},\ RM_j\ ] \tag{III.27}$$

$$FGNFG_{jt} = f2\ [\ FGNFG_{j,t\text{-}1},\ (PFG/PNFG)_{t\text{-}1},\ (IA/GA)_{jt},\ R_{jt},\ RM_j,\ DFG_j\ ] \tag{III.28}$$

where $RWFG$ is the ratio of output of rice plus wheat (tonnes) to the total food grain output; PRW is the price index for rice and wheat (based on the wholesale price index for the two crops). PFG is the price index of food grains (wholesale price index). $FGNFG$ is the ratio of output of food grains to the non-food grains (based on gross value of output in constant prices). *PNFG* is the price index of non-food grain crops. *DFG* is a dummy variable taking the value of 1 if the ratio of food grain output to non-food grain output is equal to or is less than 0.4. All other expressions are as defined previously. The dummy variable *DFG* reflects the factors that lead to a high degree of specialization in non-food grain production that may be related to development of market infrastructure for non-food grain crops. Estimated alternative equations suggest positive impact of higher price of rice and wheat on the ratio of output of these crops relative to total food grain output. Irrigation also raises the proportion of rice and wheat in total food grain output. Although year-to-year fluctuations affect *RWFG* negatively, the average rainfall level is positively associated with higher *RWFG*. Attempt to estimate the equation using the 'IV' approach produced estimates with insignificant coefficients and direction of impact not expected from the sample.

In the case of the ratio *FGQ/NFGQ*, six estimated equations suggest a high and significant coefficient on the lagged dependent variable. The results also suggest significant impact of irrigation, rainfall and relative prices. Irrigation affects the ratio (*FGQ/NFGQ*) positively—this result is likely to be a reflection of the impact of irrigation on rice and wheat production. Price of food grain relative to non- food grain crops has a positive association with the output of food grains relative to non-food grains. While the direction of impact indicated in GLS estimates is obtained in the 'IV' estimates also, the level of significance of the coefficients decreases.

We have chosen the following equations for further analysis given the satisfactory overall performance of the explanatory power of the model:

$$\text{Ln } RWFG_{jt} = -3.7255 + 0.2889 \text{ Ln } RWFG_{j,t-1} + 0.3819 \text{ Ln } (PRW/PFG)_{t-1}$$
$$+ 0.3904 \text{ Ln } (IA/GA)_{jt} - 0.3478 \text{ Ln } R_{jt}$$
$$+ 0.7779 \text{ Ln } RM_j \tag{III.29}$$

$$\text{Ln } FGNFG_{jt} = 0.0588 + 0.9709 \text{ Ln } FGNFG_{j,t-1} + 0.1737 \text{ Ln } (PFG/PNFG)_{t-1}$$
$$+ 0.0189 \text{ Ln } (IA/GA)_{jt} + 0.1472 \text{ Ln } (R_{jt}/RM_j)$$
$$- 0.0677 \ DFG_j \tag{III.30}$$

The equations described in this section form the basic equations for estimating crop production in the model.

III.1.6 Output of the Non-crop Agricultural Sub-sectors

Livestock products of milk, eggs and meat, output of the fisheries sub-sector and output of the forestry sub-sector are traditionally considered as part of the agricultural and allied activities. In Figure III.8, the indices of GDP from agriculture (including livestock), fisheries and forestry are shown for the period 1970-71 to 1992-93 at the national level. In Figure III.9, the indices of GDP from agriculture, and agriculture and allied sectors are shown separately. When individual sub-sector output trends are compared, as in Figure III.8, there are distinct patterns for each sector. However, when the aggregate trends are compared

(Figure III.9), trends in agriculture dominate the trends in GDP from agriculture and allied sectors as a whole. At the national level, trends in crop output are a reasonable indicator of the trends in overall agriculture and allied sectors. On this basis, we have estimated equations linking the output (net state domestic product) of livestock, fisheries and forestry to the output (real gross output) of the crop sector at the state level. The estimated equations are summarized in Appendix 3.

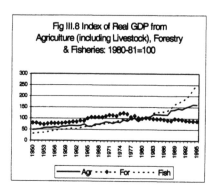

Fig III.8 Index of Real GDP from Agriculture (including Livestock), Forestry & Fisheries: 1980-81=100

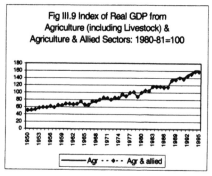

Fig III.9 Index of Real GDP from Agriculture (including Livestock) & Agriculture & Allied Sectors: 1980-81=100

III.2 Agricultural Prices, International Trade and Government Operations in Food Grains

Given the key roles agricultural prices play in affecting agricultural income, investment in agriculture, consumer expenditures on agricultural products and the over all price level via their effect on wage rate and raw materials, government policies have sought to influence them in a number of ways. Agricultural prices are subject to developments that may originate within the agricultural markets or in other markets. These developments may be caused by government policies or by market forces. For instance, government decisions affecting the prices of agricultural inputs produced or supplied by the industry, viz. fertilizers, fuel, power affect cost of agricultural production and hence agricultural prices. These decisions relate to prices themselves, when they are administered by the government or to taxes and subsidies. Tariff policies relating to manufactured products can have an impact on agricultural prices through their impact on agricultural input prices or through their impact on agricultural investment and output. Exchange rate variations, caused by government policies or market forces, affect agricultural prices as they have an impact on the supply and demand for agricultural products as well as inputs. Finally, monetary conditions also influence agricultural prices just as they influence all other prices. The government interventions in the agricultural markets attempt to insulate agricultural prices from the impact of various developments if these developments adversely affect the objectives relating to agricultural production, income and consumption.

There are direct price interventions by the government in the form of minimum support prices and procurement prices; indirect interventions through controls over imports and exports; direct interventions through subsidies and levies; and indirect interventions through buffer stock operations. Thus, agricultural prices are subject to the market conditions as well as a variety of government policy measures within the agricultural markets as well as in other sectors of the economy.

Agricultural prices influence prices in other sectors depending upon the extent of inter-sectoral linkages and the impact of agricultural prices on wage rates in the economy. The inter-sectoral linkages are a result of the input-output linkages between agricultural and other sectors. Thus, agricultural prices are inter-dependent with the prices of other prices in the economy. Any attempt to quantify the agricultural price formation process would have to consider the supply and demand factors for agricultural commodities, government interventions in the domestic and external trade in agricultural commodities as well as the inter-dependence of agricultural prices with the other prices. Importance of the various factors would vary at the commodity level depending on the linkages between different factors and the nature of the markets for specific commodities. In quantifying the price formation process, it is also important to recognize the long-run and short-run relationships. The short-run relationships are those in which crop output can be taken as the exogenous variable and the long-run relationship as the one where crop output responds to price variations, possibly with a lag. In this section we present the price formation equations that were estimated for the agricultural sub-sectors described in the previous section of this chapter.

III.2.1 Agricultural Prices

In the agricultural production block described in the previous section, agricultural output prices entering into either input demand equations or output composition equations are (1) price of the composite commodity, 'rice and wheat', (2) price of food grains (and implicitly price of food grains other than rice and wheat), (3) price of non-food grain crops and (4) price of agriculture or price index of all crops. These are the four agricultural output prices affecting input use and output choice decisions by the farmers in the present model.

At the level of aggregation that we have considered, the mechanism of the government intervention in the pricing of rice and wheat is clearer than in the case of other crops. In the case of rice and wheat, government agencies purchase these commodities from the farmers at prices announced at the beginning of the crop sowing season. These prices are called 'procurement prices'. The government's purchases of rice and wheat are well organized in the 'food grain surplus' areas of the country. The procurement prices often act as the 'minimum' prices for rice and wheat. As procurement prices are based on the recommendations of the Agricultural Prices Commission, they take into account changes in the cost of production of crops and provide a 'reasonable' return to the farm entrepreneur. The recommendations relating to procurement prices are also, therefore, implicitly subject to the assessments of the consumer interests. The consumer interests, particularly of the lower income groups in urban areas, are also protected by the sale of rice and wheat at subsidized prices through the Public Distribution System (PDS). The PDS sales reduce the demand for rice and wheat in the open market and hence affect the market prices. However, at the producer level, procurement prices play a more extensive role than the operation of PDS at the consumer level.

The government also influences the prices of rice and wheat in the domestic market through its controls on international trade. The import of food grains was restricted to government agencies until the liberalization of the 1990s so that the government agencies had adequate stock of food grains to meet the requirement of the PDS. Exports of rice and wheat were also subject to a variety of controls including the requirement that exports be made through the specified government agencies. Exports and imports of rice and wheat were largely used to ensure adequate supplies of food grains in the domestic market. Exports were permitted when stocks of the government agencies were adequate and domestic inflationary pressures were moderate. Exports of high-value or 'superior' variety of rice (Basmati) were generally permitted, subject to restrictions of quantity and price, but exports of other rice varieties were permitted only in years of adequate domestic supplies. Exports and imports of rice and wheat are, thus, determined by the domestic price (supply) scenario rather than the other way around.

In the case food grains other than rice and wheat, both the procurement and PDS sales are relatively small. As the proportion of rice and wheat in food grain output increased over the years, there was a decline in the share of coarse cereals and pulses. The relative decline in other food grains, reflected higher profitability of rice and wheat production relative to other food grains. Increased availability of rice and wheat replaced other cereals and millets in the consumption basket. In the case of pulses, rise in imports was necessary to meet the consumption demand. Imports were, however, on government account. The price of food grains other than rice and wheat (POFG) is thus, influenced by the price of rice and wheat as the two crop groups are substitutes both for the producers as well as consumers. Although procurement and PDS sales of other food grains were relatively small, procurement/or minimum support prices were announced for other food grains also. Thus, a rise in the procurement price of rice and wheat generally also meant an increase in the price of other food grains and consequently their market price as well.

In the case of non-food grain crops, the determinants of prices vary across commodities. For example, in the case of commodities where exports are significant, as in the case of tea, coffee and spices, variations in exchange rate or movements in export demand may be a significant factor affecting prices. In the case of prices of raw materials such as cotton and sugarcane, the demand conditions relating to cotton textiles and sugar are an important determinant. However, government interventions in the form of minimum or procurement/support prices, export quotas and levies can also be important determinants. Oilseed crop prices are influenced by government policies relating to tariffs and controls on the import of edible oils. A large proportion of output in the non-food grain sector, such as fruits and vegetables, is not subject to price interventions. Thus, in the case of price of non-food grain crops as a group, the main determinants can be taken as the broad factors influencing the supply and demand such as income, exchange rate, and monetary conditions, rather than the crop specific factors.

III.2.1a A Review of Trends in Crop Prices The overall agricultural price is shown relative to the price index of manufactured products in Figure III.10. The price ratio, also often termed 'barter terms of trade' between agriculture and manufacturing sectors has fluctuations around a declining trend from the early 1970s up to the beginning of the 1980s and then the trend turns positive up to the beginning of the 1990s. The trend remains stable in the 1990s. In other words, prices of the crop sector as a whole moved slower than the manufacturing sector prices during the 1970s but increased at a faster pace since the beginning of the 1980s. The trends in the price of rice and wheat (PRW), other food grains (POFG) and non-food grain crops (PNFG) show slightly different pattern when compared to each other (Figure III.11). In the case of PRW, the decline in the 1970s, relative to manufactured product prices is sharper and the recovery since the mid 1980s is slower. In the case of POFG, the initial decline in the 1970s is not pronounced and the rise relative to PM is sharper than the other two crop prices. In the case of PNFG, the pattern is similar to PRW but the rising trend since the early 1980s is slightly sharper than PRW. Thus, the terms of trade between agriculture and manufacturing has moved in favour of agriculture since the early 1980s with the increase being most pronounced in the case of POFG followed by PNFG and PRW.

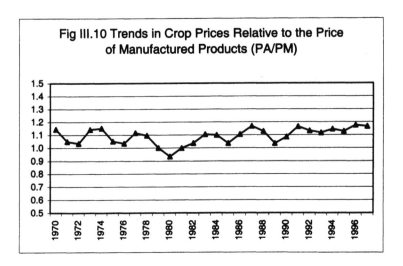

Fig III.10 Trends in Crop Prices Relative to the Price of Manufactured Products (PA/PM)

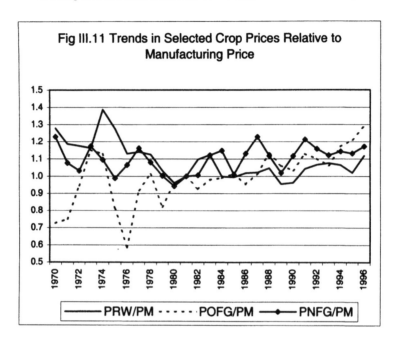

The slower rate of increase in the case of PRW relative to the increase in the other crops can be partly explained by the higher rate of growth of output of rice and wheat relative to the output growth of the other crops. The estimated price sensitivity of rice and wheat output to changes in relative price, presented in the previous section, is also greater than in the case of ratio of food grain to non food grain output. The output growth of rice and wheat may also be linked to the market support provided by the government in the form of assured 'procurement purchases'. In other words, as output of rice and wheat increased faster than the other crops, particularly during the period since 1980, the rise in PRW has been slower. The price changes in the longer run are, thus, influenced by both the supply and demand factors.

III.2.1b The Supply and Demand Framework for Agricultural Price Determination
The set of price formation equations for the agricultural sector can be developed in the framework of supply and demand for agricultural commodities. A general specification for the demand equations is,

$$QRW^d{}_t = f1\ [(PRW/WPI)_t,\ GDPR_t] \tag{III.31}$$

$$QOFG^d\ t = f2\ [(POFG/WPI)_t,\ GDPR_t,\ (POFG/POFG^*)_t] \tag{III.32}$$

$$QNFG^d\ t = f3\ [(PNFG/WPI)_t,\ GDPR_t,\ (PNFG/PNFG^*)_t] \tag{III.33}$$

where *QRW*, *QOFG* and *QNFG* with the superscript 'd' are the total demand for domestic output of the composite commodity, 'rice and wheat', other food grains and non- food grain crops, respectively. The demand, as defined above, includes demand for domestic uses as well as for exports. *PRW*, *POFG* and *PNFG* are the prices of the three commodity groups. Prices are at the wholesale level and this implies that wholesale and consumer prices follow a proportionate relationship. *GDPR* is the real *GDP* and reflects the impact of growth in income as well as the changes in economic activity with the consequent effect on demand for agricultural products through inter-sectoral linkages such as the input-output linkages. *POFG* and *PNFG* with the superscript '*' are the international prices of the respective commodities of 'other food grains' and non-food grains expressed in terms of rupee equivalent indices. Exports of agricultural commodities are influenced by government policies relating to trade, which in turn are influenced by domestic price scenario. In the case of rice and wheat, the export and imports are influenced by government policies not so much with reference to the international prices but the availability of these commodities in the domestic market and domestic prices. When domestic prices increase, exports tend to be discouraged and imports are undertaken even on government account. Hence, in the demand equation for rice and wheat, we have excluded international prices as an explanatory variable. In the case of 'other food grains', exports are limited but imports fill the gap between demand and domestic supply. The demand for domestically produced 'other food grains', therefore, are influenced by international prices as well. In the case of demand for non-food grains also, international prices affect exports and hence the overall demand for domestically produced output.

In the case of rice and wheat, the operation of PDS has an impact on demand as the price at which these commodities are sold through PDS are subsidized. However, this impact is likely to be greater on the choice of sale outlet (PDS vs. market) rather than on overall demand. Hence, we have not included the price of rice and wheat through PDS as a variable affecting total demand for these two commodities.

The domestic supply of agricultural commodities is implicit in the production process described in the previous section. Optimal levels of inputs are a function of input prices, expected prices of output and other exogenous factors affecting the production process and technical efficiency. In deriving input demand functions, presented in the previous section, expected output price is taken as the previous year's price level. In the case of rice and wheat, however, a part of the output is purchased by the government agencies at pre-announced 'procurement price' and hence, the supply of output is also influenced by the procurement price. Further, procurement prices also reflect input costs and hence they are a proxy for input prices as well. In the case of 'other food grains', the procurement price for rice and wheat influences it supply as these crops are substitutes in production. In the case of non-food grain crops, although some of these crops do compete with rice and wheat for the same resources (particularly land), because of the level of aggregation the extent of substitution possibilities would be low. Hence, the procurement price for rice and wheat (PP) is not taken as a factor influencing supply decisions in the case of non-food grain crops.

The set of domestic supply equations can be expressed as,

$$QRW^s_t = g1[(PRW/PFG)_{t-1}, R_t, PP_t] \tag{III.34}$$

$$QOFG^s_t = g2[(POFG/PFG)_{t-1}, R_t, PP_t] \tag{III.35}$$

$$QNFG^s_t = g3[(PNFG/PFG)_{t-1}, R_t] \tag{III.36}$$

where the superscript 's' indicates supply of output.

Together, equations for demand and supply form a set of equations that can be used to estimate the quantities produced and prices of the three commodity groups. The market clearing condition, 'supply equals demand', provides the basis for such a solution. The equations are recursive rather than simultaneous in the sense that supply is determined based on variables that are not dependent on the factors influencing demand. Rather than estimating the structural equations, we estimate the reduced form equations for the crop prices. The reduced form equations would include all the exogenous variables as the explanatory variables. The 'supply quantities' are taken as an exogenous variable in the price equations as production decisions are made before the prices are observed. Rather than estimating equations for relative prices, we specify the price equations individually for each crop group. This requires the use of aggregate money supply among the independent variables. Since crop output is taken as an exogenous variable in the price equation, we have dropped the rainfall variable (R), the effect of which is captured by the crop output.

The specification adopted for the crop prices is as follows,

$$PRW_t = P1[PP_t, QRW_t, GDPR_t, M1_t] \tag{III.37}$$

$$POFG_t = P2[PP_t, QOFG_t, GDPR_t, M1_t, eR_t] \tag{III.38}$$

$$PNFG_t = P3[QNFG_t, GDPR_t, M1_t, eR_t] \tag{III.39}$$

$$PFG_t \equiv w1 * PRW_t + w2 * POFG_t \tag{III.40}$$

$$PA_t \equiv w3 * PFG_t + w4 * PNFG_t \tag{III.41}$$

where *PRW, POFG, PNFG, PFG* and *PA* are the price indices of rice and wheat, 'other food grains', non-food grain crops, food grains and all crops, respectively. *QRW, QOFG* and *QNFG* are the quantities (real output) of rice and wheat, 'other food grains' and non-food grains produced, respectively. *GDPR* is the real *GDP* at factor cost representing real income (or aggregate output), *M1* is the narrow money aggregate, *eR* is the nominal exchange rate of the rupee and w1-w4 are aggregation weights based on wholesale price index weights. The estimated equations together with the details of estimation are summarized in Appendix 3.

The selected estimates of the price equations are also presented below:

$$\text{Ln } PRW = -5.7576 + .0072 \ T + .4867 \text{ Ln } PP + .2841 \text{ Ln } PRW_{t-1}$$
$$- .3234 \text{ Ln } (QRW/GDPR) - .5907 \text{ Ln } (QRW/GDPR)_{t-1} \tag{III.42}$$

$$\text{Ln } PROFG = 3.8924 + .0445 \ T + .7646 \text{ Ln } PP - .2053 \text{ Ln } QOFG$$
$$- .7705 \text{ Ln } QOFG_{t-1} \tag{III.43}$$

$$\text{Ln } PFG \equiv \text{ k1 } PRW + \text{k2 } POFG \tag{III.44}$$

$$\text{Ln } PNFG = 2.5942 + .0815 \ T + .3566 \text{ Ln } ER + .0631 \text{ Ln } PNFG_{t-1}$$
$$- .5697 \text{ Ln } PNFG_{t-2}$$
$$+ .1118 \text{ Ln } (M1/GDPR) - .3720 \text{ Ln } (QNFG/GDPR) \tag{III.45}$$

$$PA \equiv \text{w1 } PRW + \text{w2 } POFG + \text{w3 } PNFG \tag{III.46}$$

III.2.2 International Trade in Agriculture

Although historically, agricultural products have formed a significant portion of India's exports, they have accounted for only about 10% of the value of India's exports since the early 1970s. Imports of agricultural commodities have been mainly food grains. Within the crop sector, agricultural exports have been traditionally, plantation crops such as tea and coffee, spices, and tobacco. High quality rice has also been a traditional export item from India but in recent years, even the lower quality or 'non-Basmati' rice exports have grown so that rice is now the single largest export item of India. Agricultural exports, have seen liberalization from controls such as minimum export price, quotas and canalization through official agencies in the 1990s although, the extent of liberalization varies for different crops.

For the crop groups considered in this study, in the case of rice and wheat, both exports and imports have been subject to strict government controls until the early 1990s. Imports were canalized through the government agencies. Exports were subject to quotas in order to ensure adequate supplies for domestic consumption. In this sense, export and import quantity quotas were assigned to meet the domestic demand without regard to international prices. When the domestic supply-demand balance was favorable, that is domestic prices were not subject to upward pressures, exports were permitted. Under these favorable domestic conditions, if international prices were sufficiently high relative to domestic prices, exports could rise. However, if the international prices were not favorable, exports may not increase even if domestic conditions were favorable.

In general, food grain exports, particularly rice, can be expected to be positively influenced by the ratio of international price to domestic price, even under the restricted export trade regime in which only superior varieties of rice exports were permitted.

In the case of imports, wheat is the dominant item among cereals. Wheat imports were undertaken when domestic supplies fell short of demand due to crop failures resulting from unfavorable weather. The government operated public distribution system (PDS) of food grain depends for its supplies on domestic procurement and when domestic output decreases, imports become necessary. The government also maintains a buffer stock of food grain to meet the needs of PDS. Thus, one indicator of the need for imports is the level of food grain stock with the government. If the food grain stock is low relative to the requirements then the import requirements would be greater. Domestic price conditions are another indicator of the need for imports.

Based on these factors, the rice export supply and wheat import demand functions are specified as,

$$XRICE_t = X1 \left[(PRW/ PRW^*)_t, FGST_t \right] \tag{III.47}$$

$$MWHT_t = M1 \left[PRW_t, FGST_t \right] \tag{III.48}$$

In the case of imports of 'other food grains', they are mainly imports of pulses. While the production of rice and wheat increased in the 1970s, 1980s, 1990s, the production of pulses has declined. The resulting shortfall in domestic supply is met by imports. The year-to-year fluctuations in the output of 'other food grains' and 'rice and wheat' caused by rain fall variations can be expected to be positively correlated. Hence, relatively higher food grain stocks with the government, indicative of a good harvest of rice and wheat in the previous year, would also imply adequate supplies of 'other food grains'. Imports of 'other food grains' are, therefore, likely to be negatively related to food grain stocks with the government. Exchange rate variations affect the domestic price and demand for imported grains and the level of imports would also be adversely affected if there is a depreciation of the exchange rate.

The import equation for 'other food grains', based on the above considerations can be specified as,

$$MOFG_t = M2 \left[POFG_t, eR_t, FGST_t \right] \tag{III.49}$$

In the case of exports of non- food grain crops, the quantum of exports is influenced by relative profitability of exports and growth in world demand. Inclusion of relative profitability or price among the explanatory variables clearly reflects the 'export supply' framework for non-food grain crops. The presence of 'world demand' variable, in an export-supply framework is justified since poor world demand conditions may require additional marketing costs and hence lower export supplies. Under normal demand conditions, marketing costs would be lower and hence, supplies can be increased at the same price level. The export equation for 'non-food grain crops' is specified as,

$$XNFG_t = X2 \left[(PNFG^*/ PNFG)_t , WGDP_t \right] \tag{III.50}$$

The estimated equations of exports and imports of agricultural commodities are presented in Appendix 3. The selected equations are,

$$\text{Ln } XQRICE = 8.1640 + .5346 \text{ Ln } (FGST/POP) - .9670 \text{ Ln } (PRW/UVIXR)_{t-1}$$
$$+ .8465 \text{ Ln } XQRICE_{t-1} \tag{III.51}$$

$$\text{Ln } XQNFG = 5.5898 + .0109 \ T + .9577 \ D80$$
$$- .1778 \text{ Ln } (PNFG/UVIXN)_{t-1} \tag{III.52}$$

$$\text{Ln } MQWHT = -1.8979 - 1.8328 \text{ Ln } (FGST/POP)$$
$$+ .1860 \text{ Ln } (PRW/UVIMW)_{t-1} \tag{III.53}$$

$$\text{Ln } NMPUL = .3041 + .0476 \ T - .1704 \ QOFG_{t-1} \tag{III.54}$$

III.2.3 Procurement, Distribution and Stocks of Food grains with the Government and Procurement Price

III.2.3a Food Grain Stocks As procurement and distribution of food grain by the government agencies is largely in rice and wheat, we consider the procurement, distribution and food grain stock operations of the government as relating only to rice and wheat. In the equations for exports of rice and imports of wheat, the level of stock of rice and wheat (at the beginning of the year) with the government is an explanatory variable. The stock of rice and wheat with the government is a function of previous year's stock, procurement of food grains by the government during the previous year, distribution of food grains through the PDS and imports of rice and wheat. Thus, the identity linking food grain (rice and wheat) stock and other operations by the government in rice and wheat markets is,

$$FGST_t \equiv FGST_{t-1} + PROC_{t-1} - DIST_{t-1} - XRICE_{t-1} + MWHT_{t-1} \tag{III.55}$$

where PROC is the procurement of food grains by the government, *DIST* is the level of distribution of food grains by the government through *PDS* and *XRICE* and *MWHT* are the variables defined previously.

III.2.3b Procurement of Rice and Wheat This identity introduces two additional variables that need to be explained within the model: *PROC* and *DIST*. The level of procurement of rice and wheat is a function of procurement price (*PP*) relative to market price and the level of output of rice and wheat. As *PP* rises relative to market price, the quantum of grains purchased or procured by the government will also increase. Besides the incentives provided by the price differential between the open market and the government offer, farmers also tend to supply to the government agency a higher proportion of their output when the output increases.

This has been explained in the past studies as a result of 'convenience' of selling to the government agencies: cash is given to the seller on the spot; grading and weighing of the produce are standardized and transparent. Accordingly, the equation for procurement of rice and wheat by the government is estimated as,

$$\text{Ln } PROC = 3.2727 + 0.8622 \ T + 2.0097 \ \text{Ln } (PP/PRW) \tag{III.56}$$

Details of the estimation are presented in Appendix 3.

III.2.3c Distribution of Rice and Wheat through PDS Distribution of food grains (rice and wheat) through the PDS is a function of two main factors: (1) price at which the grains are sold through the PDS (*IP* or issue prices) and the open market price (*PRW*) and (2) the level of output of rice and wheat (*QRW*). The impact of (*IP/PRW*) on the level of distribution can be understood in terms of the implications of the relative price to the consumer's budget. The impact of output on distribution has to be understood through the availability of grains in the market. A good harvest would provide greater access to grains in the open market at all levels (rural-urban continuum or across regions) and in terms of different qualities. The estimated equation for *DIST* incorporating these two factors is,

$$\text{Ln } DIST = 3.5000 + .0290 \ T - .1857 \ \text{Ln } QFG - .8154 \ \text{Ln}(IP/PRW) \tag{III.57}$$

Details of the estimation are presented in Appendix 3.

III.2.3d Procurement Prices of Rice and Wheat Procurement prices for food grains are announced by the government, as noted earlier, primarily based on the estimated cost of production of these crops including a 'reasonable' return to the farmer. The reasonable return would imply considerations relating to the profitability of farming as a production activity and the profitability of new investments. A factor that enters into these considerations is the terms of trade between agriculture and other activities. Favorable terms of trade (ratio of agricultural price to non-agricultural prices) would be an objective to encourage new investments in agriculture. The reasonable return would be bounded from above by considerations relating to the overall price situation affecting the consumers. In other words, implications of high procurement price would be higher market price for food grains implying demand for higher wage rates and potential for inflation. There is also the consideration relating to the cost of operating the procurement-distribution operations. A higher procurement price implies an increased level of procurement and without a corresponding increase in distribution, food grain stock with the government would rise leading to higher expenditures without corresponding returns. Increased subsidies to be financed by the general budget can become another source of inflationary pressures. Hence, procurement prices are tempered by the considerations relating to overall price implications. In this sense, procurement prices are not entirely 'exogenous' but influenced by (1) changes in terms of trade between agriculture and other sectors,

(2) the trends in market price of rice and wheat in recent years and (3) the level of food grain stocks with the government. The equation for PP incorporating these considerations is estimated as,

$$\text{Ln } PP = -0.5034 - 0.0864 \text{ Ln } (FGST/POP) - 0.0864 \text{ Ln } (PRW/PM)_{t-1}$$
$$+ 1.0513 \text{ Ln } PP_{t-1} \tag{III.58}$$

Details of the estimation results are presented in Appendix 3.

Chapter IV

The Non-Agricultural Sectors: Output, Prices and Trade

The composition overall output of the Indian economy, in the recent period of 1993-94 to 1997-98, points to the relatively large share of the non-agricultural sectors. The non- agricultural sectors make up 73% of the overall GDP in India. Among the non-agricultural sectors, manufacturing accounts for 22%; electricity, water supply and gas, mining and construction sub-sectors account for 9%, and the service sector, comprising of all other sub-sectors, accounts for the remaining 42%. Manufacturing as a single group of activities, thus, is a major sector in the Indian economy. In this study, we focus on the manufacturing sector within the non-agricultural sector as the linkages between agriculture and the non-agricultural sectors are likely to be more important in this sector. Output of the other sectors of construction and services is linked to the output of agriculture and manufacturing or overall real GDP.

IV.1 The Manufacturing Sector

It is convenient to distinguish two segments of the manufacturing sector from the viewpoint of data availability as well as the nature of the firms. One is the 'organized sector' or more specifically the sector that is covered under Factories Act. Data for this segment is available through the Annual Survey of Industries. Over the years, the share of organized sector in manufacturing GDP has increased in comparison to the unorganized or unregistered sector (Figure IV.1). From the period of early 1950s when the unregistered sector contributed more than the registered sector, there has been a significant change by the beginning of the 1990s when the share of registered sector is 50% higher than the share of unregistered sector. The organized sector is beginning to dominate the manufacturing sector output. In this study, we have estimated the output of organized manufacturing sector as a function of its inputs and linked the output of unorganized sector to the output of organized sector. The approach is justified on the grounds that (1) the share of organized sector is rising and hence the trends in this sector are likely to reflect the overall output trend and (2) more detailed data are available in the case of organized sector and hence a detailed approach in this case is possible.

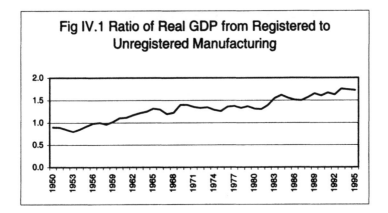

Fig IV.1 Ratio of Real GDP from Registered to Unregistered Manufacturing

IV.1.1 Modelling Manufacturing Output

IV.1.1a The Production Frontier and Production Functions   Output of the manufacturing sector is a product of the transformation of inputs of labour, capital and intermediates through the technological process. Taking out the cost of intermediates from the value of gross output, the resulting value added is often considered as the output and capital and labour as the inputs. This step from gross output to gross value added is based on the assumption of independence of the effects of individual inputs or 'separability' of inputs in the production process. When a Cobb-Douglas form of technology is assumed, the separability assumption is satisfied and a production technology representing gross value added as a function of capital and labour can be specified. While the production process at the firm and product level can be viewed as a single production technology, when we consider a group of products or group of firms, the aggregate production function is an aggregation of the individual technologies. When the aggregation is over firms and products, the aggregate production function would based on the existing structure or composition of output and the firms. Following the traditional approach, manufacturing sector's output over all the product sub-sectors can be specified in the form of a production function as,

$$QMFG\_ASI = f\,[K, L] \qquad\qquad (IV.1)$$

where *QMFG_ASI* is the gross value added in constant prices from the organized manufacturing sector (ASI sector), *K* is the fixed capital stock and *L* is the number of labour days of employment in the sector. For any estimation of the production function, data on output, capital stock and labour are required. The ASI provides information on values of gross output, material inputs, labour days of employment, fixed capital stock (book value) and capital formation (fixed and inventories). Thus, value added and labour input can be estimated from the published data. Balakrishna and Pushpangadan (1996) point out that real output should be calculated based on the value of gross output at constant price and the value of material inputs also at constant price, unless the price ratio of output and inputs is fixed. Secondly, real stock of fixed capital has to be estimated based on the book value of capital stock and the data on capital formation.

Estimation of capital stock at the product level or provincial level requires data on the composition of fixed capital stock for a 'base year' in terms of the 'vintage', rates of depreciation for the fixed assets, and the price indices of capital goods that make up the 'base year' capital stock. As such a procedure would be beyond the scope of the present study, we have carried out the analysis only at the national level using the published data.

Real gross value added has been estimated using the methodology outlined in Balakrishna and Pushpangadan (1996). Capital stock series provided by the same authors has been updated for the period 1988-89 to 1995-96. Data on labour days is obtained from the reports of the Annual Survey of industries (Central Statistical Organization, various issues). The data on labour or capital are not adjusted for variations in quality over time. The data on the three series, value added, capital stock and labour days is illustrated in Figure IV.2. The rise in capital stock is steady and sharper than the growth in labour and output. The rise in average labour productivity and stagnant average productivity of capital are evident in Figure IV.3 where trends in the ratios of gross value added to capital and labour are shown for the period 1970-71 to 1993-94.

The approach used for assessing the productivity growth in manufacturing in India has involved the specification and estimation of a production function and taking the 'residuals' from the estimated production function as a measure of the contribution of 'total factor productivity'. There are variations with respect to the functional form, data periods and the measure of output. Although there are important aspects in the specification and measurement of inputs and output, the basic approach can be illustrated by taking the specific case of Cobb-Douglas functional form in which output (value added) is a function of capital and labour,

$$\text{Ln } GVAD_t = a0 + a1 \text{ Ln } K_t + a2 \text{ Ln } LAB_t + e_t \tag{IV.2}$$

where $GVAD$ is the gross value added, K and LAB are the two inputs of capital and labour, respectively and e is the random error term. The estimated coefficients of 'ai' are used to estimate the residuals as,

$$RES_t = \text{Ln } GVAD_t - (a0 + a1 \text{ Ln } K_t + a2 \text{ Ln } LAB_t) \tag{IV.3}$$

The residuals series '*RES*' is then examined for its pattern of changes over time and in relation to other variables. In the context of macroeconomic models the specification of production relationship has been extended to include the effect of capital formation on output with lags of different order, impact of demand through capacity utilization variations and other factors that affect productivity. Often the production function is not directly estimated but only the consequent relationship between output and the various explanatory variables is modelled. While these alternative approaches lead to models of production, they do not take into account the potential for efficiency improvements in the production process. In this study, we attempt to incorporate explicitly a production function for the manufacturing sector within the framework of varying coefficients model (VCM). In Chapter II we have outlined the approach under the 'time-series' data framework.

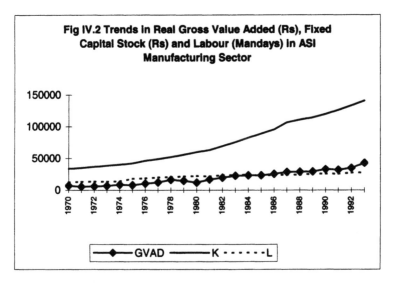

Fig IV.2 Trends in Real Gross Value Added (Rs), Fixed Capital Stock (Rs) and Labour (Mandays) in ASI Manufacturing Sector

Note: Gross value added is derived by deflating gross output and intermediate inputs separately using respective price indices. Gross value added and capital stock estimates are in crores of rupees in 1980-81 prices. Labour is in thousands of mandays of total employed.

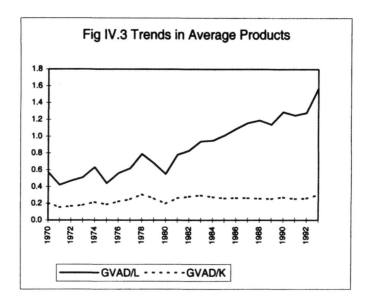

As we are considering the input-output relationship over a period of time, the sources of growth in output include (1) growth in inputs (2) technical progress and (3) changes in technical efficiency in the use of inputs by the firms (Kalirajan and Shand, 1999). In other words, at the micro level, technical efficiency in production may vary from year to year due to factors such as better incentives to the producers as well as workers and better training for the workers in the production process. At the 'average' or aggregate level, the average levels of technical efficiency for the sector as a whole would be affected by growth of more efficient firms relative to less efficient firms. Thus, even at the aggregate level of the sector at the national level, the concepts of technical efficiency in production are meaningful. Incorporating efficiency and technical progress in the production process, the logarithmic Cobb-Douglas production function for the organized manufacturing sector is specified as,

$$\text{Ln } GVAD_t = \text{Ln } (a0_t{}^* . \theta_{0t}) + a1_t{}^* . \theta_{1t} . \text{Ln } K_t + a2_t{}^* . \theta_{2t} . \text{Ln } LAB_t \qquad \text{(IV.4)}$$

where $aj_t{}^*$ are the coefficients of the production frontier, θ_{jt} are the technical efficiency parameters associated with input j (j=1 for K, =2 for L and =0 for the general efficiency).

Following the methodology outlined in Kalirajan and Shand (1997), production function reflecting the average technology for year 't' can now be written as,

$$\text{Ln } GVAD_t = b0_t + b1_t \text{ Ln } K_t + b2_t . \text{Ln } LAB_t \qquad \text{(IV.5a)}$$

$$bj_t = bj_t{}' + e_{jt} \qquad \text{(IV.5b)}$$

where e_{jt} and v_t are the random variables with zero mean, constant variance and independent of each other. Using the methodology proposed for the random varying coefficients model, the estimates of bj_t' and e_{jt} can be estimated. These estimates provide the basis for deriving coefficients of the production frontier. For any given year 't', maximum of the coefficient bj_t (i.e., $bj_t' + e_{jt}$) for each bj_t over all the years up to t, result in the highest level of output and can be given the interpretation of the coefficients of a 'frontier' technology or the 'best practices' technology. More formally,

$$bj_t^* = \max \{ bj_k \} \text{ for k} = 0,1,2, ...t \qquad \text{(IV.5c)}$$

Efficiency with respect to the use of K in year t is defined as,

$$\theta_{1t} = b_{1t} / b_{1t}^* \qquad \text{(IV.6)}$$

Similarly, efficiency with respect to the use of L in year t is defined as,

$$\theta_{2t} = b_{2t} / b_{2t}^* \qquad \text{(IV.7)}$$

The general level of efficiency is defined as,

$$\theta_{0t} = b_{0t} / b_{0t}^* \qquad \text{(IV.8)}$$

The concepts relating to efficiency and technical progress parallel the discussion provided in the previous chapter relating to agriculture. The difference here being, there are no cross-section production units to which the technical efficiency can be related. Hence, comparison of overall efficiency over the years, will require adjustment for the levels of inputs as in the case of agriculture, discussed in the previous chapter. Shifts (upward) in bj_t^* over time represent shifts in 'best practices' technology or 'technological progress'. Factors explaining changes in levels of efficiency may differ from the factors responsible for the shifts in technology frontier or technological progress.

Estimation

Parameters of the production function (IV.5a-IV.5b) obtained using the data for the period 1970-71 to 1993-94 were estimated first. The generalized least squares estimates of the coefficients which take into account the 'heteroscedastic' error in the equation arising from the VCM suggest significant economies of scale in production as the sum of the coefficients of capital and labour at 1.6 exceeds the value of 1.0 by a significant margin. Further, the estimates also indicate no significant variation in the parameters b1 and b2 over time. Economies of scale in the aggregate production function for the manufacturing sector while plausible, are also indicative of technical progress particularly in the context of time-series data on inputs and output over time. One approach to take into account the effect of technical progress as well as impose the condition of constant returns to scale is to represent the production model by the following specification,

$$\text{Ln} \ (GVAD/LAB)_t = b0_t + b1_t \ \text{Ln} \ (K/LAB)_t + b2_t \ . \ t \qquad (\text{IV.9})$$

where the coefficients $b0_t$, $b1_t$ and $b2_t$ are random variables with the associated random errors subject to the assumptions of zero mean, constant variance and independence. The elasticity of output with respect to labour can be derived from the estimate of $b1$ from the assumption of constant returns to scale as ($1-b1$). While the variations in the coefficients $b0$ and $b1$ can be interpreted as being due to variations in technical efficiency, variations in the coefficient b2, associated with the time trend require an explanation.

The variation associated with $b0_t$ has two components. One is related to the 'general efficiency' of the producers and the second, to the impact of 'demand factors' that influence utilization of the existing production capacity. The general efficiency is not associated with any specific input and capacity utilization in the present interpretation also can not be associated with specific inputs. Variations in the coefficient '$b1$' over time would reflect 'efficiency' in the use of capital per unit of labour. The variation in coefficient $b2$ reflects uneven technological progress. While technical progress is generally characterized as 'uniform', variations in the rate of progress are also recognized in the past studies of technical progress. The varying rates of technical progress are often related to changes in policy regimes or expenditures on research and development or imports of technology. However, in such studies, the effect of various factors on technical progress cannot be distinguished from efficiency changes. In the above specification, equation (IV.9), variations in technical progress can be distinguished from efficiency changes as well as changes in 'demand factors'.

The results of estimation of the VCM of the equation are summarized in Appendix 3. The coefficient $b1$ is found to be 'fixed' rather than 'random' or the coefficient has not varied significantly over the years. The elasticity of manufacturing output with respect to capital (or labour) has remained constant through the period 1970-71 to 1993-94. However, the 'intercept' term and the coefficient of time variable show variation over time. For convenience we note the estimated production function for a specific year 't' in the following equation,

$$\text{Ln} \ (GVAD/LAB)_t = 0.3680^* \ \theta0_t + 0.4148 \ \text{Ln} \ (K/LAB)_t$$
$$+ \ 0.4157^* \ \theta2_t \ . \ t \qquad (\text{IV.10})$$

where $\theta1$ and $\theta2$ are the efficiencies associated with intercept and time trend. The coefficient associated with the ratio (K/L) is constant over time.

The estimated intercept coefficient and the coefficient representing technical progress are shown in Figure IV.4. Both the series show very similar patterns. Simple correlation coefficient between the two series works out to 0.81. Thus, the factors influencing general efficiency and capacity utilization also influence technical progress in the same manner. It seems plausible that factors affecting capacity utilization such as a drop in the level of demand for manufactured products, would also influence the ability of the firms to adopt new technologies. Supply side constraints, such as infrastructure bottlenecks, affect capacity utilization as well as ability of firms to adopt new technologies. While adverse demand or supply environment may lead some firms to invest in new and more efficient technologies, the overall results suggest that technical progress and capacity utilization are positively related to each other.

Variation in the intercept term and the rate of technical progress lead us to the 'potential output' from a given level of inputs and given technology. Variation in the intercept term can be used to define the 'frontier production intercept' based on the definition in equation (IV.5c). The frontier function intercept is the level of intercept when the average level of efficiency of the manufacturing firms in any year is the maximum achieved so far, including in that year. In other words, potential output is achieved when the average efficiency and capacity utilization are at the peak level.

In the case of rate of technical progress, definition of a frontier coefficient along the same lines as in the case of intercept, would imply that technical progress could be manipulated just as technical efficiency. The complex nature of technical progress makes this assumption difficult to justify. But the framework of frontier coefficient and efficiency measure allows us to model the two coefficients for the purpose of estimating output of the manufacturing sector in relation to factors such as capacity utilization and technical changes. The estimated efficiencies with respect to the intercept coefficient and coefficient of technical progress are shown in Figure IV.4. The variation with respect to general efficiency is greater than in the case of technical progress, although the two variables are correlated with each other. Both the efficiency measures show fluctuations during the period of 1970s with a decline in 1979-80 and 1980-81 with a recovery in the subsequent year. From 1983-84, there is a decline in efficiency until the beginning of the 1990s. Efficiency estimates decline again in 1991-92 and recover in 1993-94. The pattern of changes in general efficiency and technical progress is suggestive of its strong association with demand factors. For example, the years of 1979-80, 1980-81 and 1991-92 are years of relatively 'poor demand conditions' affected by poor agricultural harvest and in 1991-92 by a severe contraction of aggregate demand. The relatively small variations in the efficiency as compared to technical progress indicate steady levels of technical progress over the years.

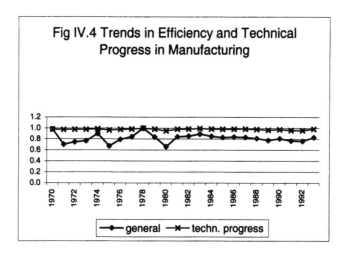

For deriving 'potential output' for the sample period, three alternative assumptions regarding technical progress are possible: (1) technical progress is at the rate observed during the sample period, (2) technical progress is at the maximum rate observed for any year, up to and including a specific year and (3) technical progress is at an 'average' rate observed during the sample period. The potential output from a given level of (K/LAB) can now be defined as,

$$\text{Ln } (GVAD/LAB)^*_t = b0^*_t + b1 \text{ Ln } (K/LAB)_t + b3_t . t \tag{IV.11}$$

where $b0^*_t = \max (b0_t)$ for all the years up to t. The actual output is roughly 20% below the potential output for majority of the years. The estimated ratios are shown in Table IV.1.

Table IV.1   The Impact of Inefficiency in Manufacturing Output

Period	Potential with Maximum Technical Progress		Potential with Actual Technical Progress		Potential with Average Technical Progress	
	Actual/ Potential %	Output Loss %	Actual/ Potential %	Output Loss %	Actual/ Potential %	Output Loss %
1970-1975	80.80	19.20	81.00	19.00	80.92	19.08
1976-1980	82.07	17.93	83.27	16.73	83.37	16.63
1981-1985	83.62	16.38	85.37	14.63	86.41	13.59
1986-1990	77.90	22.10	81.43	18.57	81.45	18.55
1991-1993	73.04	26.96	78.63	21.37	77.11	22.89
1992-1993	74.42	25.58	79.59	20.41	78.65	21.35
1970-1993	80.08	19.92	82.18	17.82	82.21	17.79

Note: Period indicates the starting and ending financial years.

Table IV.2   The Impact of Changes in Efficiency on Output Growth in Manufacturing

Period	Contribution of sources of growth (%)			Actual Annualized Growth %
	Input Growth	Efficiency Change	Technical Progress	
1970-1975	256.57	-315.68	159.11	0.02
1975-1980	55.11	1.11	43.78	0.09
1980-1985	30.08	35.79	34.13	0.13
1985-1990	50.64	-6.48	55.84	0.07
1990-1993	41.65	8.90	49.45	0.09
1970-1993	56.81	-7.92	51.10	0.08

Note:
1. Period indicates the starting and ending financial years.
2. The actual growth rate should be multiplied by 100 to obtain the percentage rate.

This finding points to the potential gains from improved efficiency in the manufacturing sector. The concept of potential output also provides the basis for a decomposition of output growth during a period into contributions due to (1) input growth, (2) changes in efficiency, (3) technical progress and (4) interaction between efficiency and technical progress. The contribution of technical progress is the shift in production frontier or potential output between any two years, contribution of input growth is the movement along a production function and the contribution of efficiency is the difference in output for the same level of inputs between the actual production function and the frontier production function with the balance of contribution being attributed to the interaction term. The input growth and technical progress contributed positively and roughly equally to the output growth for the various sub-periods considered. The changes in efficiency, however, have contributed negatively to output growth when we consider the entire period from 1970-71 to 1993-94. The contribution of efficiency change was positive during the first half of the 1980s but negative during the latter half of 1980s. In the first three years of 1990s, efficiency has improved making a positive contribution to output growth. Generally, efficiency is seen to improve when input growth is relatively lower and deteriorate when input growth is higher. While the efficiency changes have contributed to the decline of output growth rate, the lower level of efficiency itself has meant lower level of output as compared to the potential output. In this sense, attempts to improve general level of efficiency are an important source of output growth.

IV.1.1b General Efficiency and Variations in Technical Progress The random coefficient model of production provides the basis for estimation of manufacturing output from given levels of inputs, capital and labour, general level of efficiency and the rate of technical progress. The input levels are derived from the underlying optimization model for the firms while specification of efficiency and rate of technical progress requires specification of how these parameters are determined. We have estimated the general efficiency primarily in terms of its relation to capacity utilization. A general specification in terms of possible explanatory variables can be summarized as,

$$INTEFF_t = f\left((STK/Q)_{t-1}, (XM/Q)_{t-1}, R_t \right) \tag{IV.12}$$

where *INTEFF* is the estimated general (intercept) efficiency, *STK* is the level of stocks in the manufacturing (ASI) sector at the beginning of the year, Q is the real gross output, *XM* is the sum of exports and imports of the manufacturing sector and R is the level of rainfall during the monsoon season. The level of stocks relative to output reflect the 'demand' factors, with the higher stock reflecting poor demand and lower stock reflecting good demand conditions. As demand conditions improve, capacity utilization is expected to improve and the general efficiency also to improve. Volume of trade relative to output has two effects. One, increased export demand would imply improved demand conditions and hence improved capacity utilization. Increased imports may imply increased competition for some sectors but they may also be associated with increased demand for the domestic output, which leads to higher imports of imported intermediate inputs. Secondly, trade also influences choice of technology and hence efficiency. Rainfall is included as a proxy for a number of supply and demand related factors. Favorable rainfall implies larger crop harvest and farm incomes implying higher demand for manufactured products. Favorable rainfall also implies better availability of raw material inputs to the agro-based industries. Thirdly, favorable rainfall would also reflect improved generation of hydro-electricity, supplementing other sources of power for the economy as a whole. In the case of stocks and trade variables, we have used lagged terms rather than their current levels to indicate the possible lags in adjusting the level of capacity utilization in response to altered conditions in the economy.

In the case of variations in technical progress, factors influencing general efficiency are also expected to have an effect. While average rate of technical progress itself may be a function of a number of factors, its variations are likely to be influenced by factors that reflect short term demand conditions in the economy. For this reason, equations incorporating the same set of variables as in equation (IV. 11) were estimated for variations in technical progress (TEFF) also. Given the close similarities between the two measures of variability in the intercept and time trend, we have also estimated variations in technical progress (TEFF) as a function of INTEFF.

Although rainfall was initially incorporated in the equation, its effect was not significant and hence the variable was dropped from the specification. The selected equations from among those estimated are presented below.

(a)   General efficiency:

$$\Delta \text{Ln } INTEFF_t = -0.1937 + 0.7202 \ \Delta \text{ Ln } INTEFF_{t-1} + 0.5004 \ \Delta \text{ Ln } INTEFF_{t-2}$$
$$+ 3.4321 \ \Delta \ (STQ/Q)_{t-1} + 1.4143 \ \Delta \ (STQ/Q)_{t-2}$$
$$- 1.9721 \ ECM_{t-1} \tag{IV.13a}$$

where

$$ECM_t = \text{Ln } INTEFF_t - 3.4300 \ (STQ/Q)_t - 0.0027 \ t \tag{IV.13b}$$

The equations IV.13a and IV.13b were estimated as a part of the cointegrating relationship between *INTEFF* and *(STQ/Q)*

(b)   Technical progress:

$$\text{Ln } TECEF_t = 0.0012 + 0.1131 \text{ Ln } INTEFF_t \tag{IV.14}$$

IV.1.2 Inputs in Manufacturing

The two inputs in the production function model described in the previous section are fixed capital and labour. At the firm level, optimal levels of capital stock and inputs can be derived from the profit maximizing conditions of a dynamic optimization model, in which capital stock is related to investment as an accumulation identity. Derivation of optimal levels of investment requires assumptions relating to efficiency, technical progress and prices for the life period of capital stock. A second set of variables important in determining the optimal levels of inputs are those relating to policy. For example, monetary and fiscal policies affect interest rate, inflation rate, trade protection and access to credit by the manufacturing sector. There are also government decisions relating to investments in the public sector enterprises of the manufacturing sector. In this study, we do not attempt to derive the optimal capital stock or investment and labour from an explicit optimization model. Instead, the input demand equations are specified as a function of factors suggested by such an optimization model.

IV.1.2a Gross Fixed Capital Stock and Fixed Capital Formation Fixed capital stock at the beginning of the year t, in real terms, is updated using the usual identity,

$$K_t = K_{t-1} + GFCF_{t-1} - DEP_{t-1} \qquad (IV.15)$$

where GFCF is the real gross fixed capital formation in the organized manufacturing sector and DEP is the depreciation of the real fixed capital stock. Based on the data on nominal values of depreciation and book value of fixed capital stock, the rate of depreciation is about 7% of the capital stock. This estimate of the depreciation rate is used in the capital stock identity.

Fixed investment or GFCF has been modelled in the literature in a variety of ways. Besides the traditional models that provide the main role to interest rate, expected inflation rate and returns to investment net of taxes, in the developing economies, the role of credit constraint, public investment and foreign exchange constraints have also been emphasized. Owing to the limited data series available, we have considered only three explanatory variables in the investment function. The general form of investment equation specified in this study is,

$$GFCF_t = I\ [\ (NR_t\text{-}INFLM_{t-1}),\ Q_{t-1}\ ] \qquad (IV.16)$$

where *NR* is the nominal rate of interest at which the manufacturing sector borrows credit (the proxy used is the minimum lending rate of Industrial Development Bank of India), *INFLM* is the inflation rate measured in terms of wholesale price index of manufactured products and *Q* is the gross output of the manufacturing (ASI) sector. The inflation rate variable is used in the lagged form as a proxy for the expected rate of inflation. Lagged output level is used to reflect availability of internal funds for investment by the firms. Larger the output, availability of funds is expected to be greater than otherwise. Improved availability of funds is expected to reduce the overall cost of borrowing and hence have a positive impact on investment. Nominal rate of interest is expected to affect investment negatively due to its effect on the borrowed funds for investment. Price increase in the manufacturing sector affects the real interest rate expectations of the firms and influences investment positively.

The estimated equation is,

$$\begin{aligned} \text{Ln } GFCF_t = {}&\text{-}2.2179 + 0.4756\ \text{Ln } Q_{t-1} + 0.4314\ \text{Ln } GFCF_{t-1} \\ &\text{-} 0.0055\ (NR_t\text{-}INFLM_{t-1}) \end{aligned} \qquad (IV.17)$$

where *GFCF*, *Q*, *NR* and *INFLM* are as defined previously. Details of estimation results are given in Appendix 3.

IV.1.2b Labour Days of Employment Demand for labour in organized manufacturing is a function of real wage rates and expectations relating to demand conditions. Although adjustments in labour force in response to market conditions are subject to various regulations, especially in the organized manufacturing sector, labour force in this context is more flexible than the adjustment in capital stock. The supply of labour is assumed to be perfectly elastic at the going wage rate. The explanatory variables included in the labour demand equation in this study are the nominal wage rate (*NW*), rate of inflation and expected rate of growth in output. The general specification is,

$$LAB_t = L(NW_t, INFLC_t, (Q_{t-1}/Q_{t-2})) \tag{IV.18}$$

where *LAB* is the number of man days of employment in the ASI sector; *NW*, the nominal wage rate is the index of wage rates derived from wage payments and *LAB*; *INFLC* is the inflation rate measured in terms of the consumer price index and Q is the gross output of the manufacturing (ASI) sector. As nominal wage rate increases, labour costs of the firms would rise and demand for labour can be expected to decrease. The adjustment, however, would be effected with a lag and may not be immediate. The adjustment may also be on the basis of linkage between nominal wage rates and general price rise. As general price level increases (*INFLC*), nominal wage rates can be expected to increase, with a lag, and hence labour force adjustments may take place in response to general price changes directly. The demand for labour is, thus, expected to respond to changes in both the general price inflation and nominal wage rate. The expectations of growth in output would influence demand for labour as firms increase production level in anticipation of increased demand. The estimated equation for labour days of employment in the organized manufacturing is,

$$\begin{aligned}
\text{Ln } LAB_t = {} & 13.4582 + 0.1351\, t + 0.2535 \text{ Ln } (Q_{t-1}/Q_{t-2}) \\
& -0.0449 \text{ Ln } NW_t - 0.8740 \text{ Ln } NW_{t-1} - 0.2539 \text{ Ln } NW_{t-2} - 0.2717\, INFLC_t \\
& + 0.2697 \text{ Ln } INFLC_{t-1} + 0.1911\, INFLC_{t-2} + 0.3394\, INFLC_{t-3}
\end{aligned} \tag{IV.19}$$

where NW is the index of nominal wage rate, INFLC is the annual rate of change in the consumer price index and all the other expressions are as explained previously. Details of estimation results are in Appendix 3.

The estimated equation (IV.18) for labour days of employment captures a significant impact of nominal wage rate and the inflation rate in terms of consumer price index. The impact of consumer price inflation has to be interpreted in terms of its linkage to nominal wage rate. For instance, the negative impact of consumer price inflation on employment in the current year is combined with a smaller negative coefficient on *NW*. The subsequent lags have an opposite sign. Higher inflation induces labour demand and higher nominal wage rates depress it. In other words, general inflation rate affects expectations regarding nominal wage rate and hence influence labour demand by the firms. The impact of current period's consumer inflation rate on labour demand can also be interpreted in terms of an 'unexpected' inflation rate. The inflation rate with a lag of a year or more would be incorporated into the output prices and hence firms would attempt to restore demand for labour to the earlier levels. Thus, an increase in inflation rate first depresses demand for labour, but with a lag produces an increase in labour demand. If nominal wage rates respond to inflation rate through wage agreements, the impact of inflation rate on labour demand would be net of the indirect effect through wage rate.

IV.1.3 Wage Rates, Prices and Related Variables

IV.1.3a Nominal Wage Rate   In the organized manufacturing sector, collective bargaining is an important aspect of wage determination. Nominal wage rates are determined with attempts to protect and improve real wage rates. In other words, nominal wage rates are expected to be related to inflation rate of consumer prices and previous increases in output. The estimated equation incorporating these considerations is,

$$\text{Ln } NW_t = -2.0163 + 0.2653 \text{ Ln } Q\,t\text{-}1 + 0.7986 \text{ Ln } NWt\text{-}1$$
$$+ 0.7654 \text{ } INFLCt \qquad\qquad\qquad\qquad\text{(IV.20)}$$

where all the variables are as explained previously. Details of estimated equation are in Appendix 3.

In equation (IV.20) nominal wage rate is positively related to current inflation rate, lagged NW and lagged gross output. Relationship to current inflation rate is plausible because of the adjustment in nominal wage rates on the basis of consumer price index with just a few months' lag. In other words, pressures to maintain real wage rates are strong and reflected in the linkage of current NW with lagged NW and current inflation rate. Positive relationship between NW and lagged gross output is linked to expansion in production capacities on the basis of expected increase in demand for output.

IV.1.3b Change in Stock or Inventories   Accumulation of stock or its reduction is a function of mis-match between current levels of production and demand. Some level of stocks are held to meet the anticipated increase in demand during the periods when production can not be increased to meet the additional demand. Unanticipated inventory holdings occur when demand conditions change while production remains unaltered. Indications of unanticipated inventory holdings or demand conditions are sharp changes in the price situation: if there is a sudden increase in prices, it may lead to reduction in demand and accumulation of stocks with the producers. Faster increase in production may also lead to higher stocks in anticipation of increased sales or demand in the future. Taking these possible reasons for stock holding, following equation for stocks in the organized manufacturing is estimated,

$$(STQ/Q)_t = 0.0088 -0.0014\ t + 0.2239\ INFLM_t + 0.1726 \text{ Ln } (Q)_t/Q)_{t\text{-}1}) \qquad \text{(IV.21)}$$

where STQ is the level of stocks of output with the firms at the beginning of the year, Q is the level of real gross output and INFLM is the rate of inflation in terms of price index of manufactured products. Details of estimation results are given in Appendix 3.

IV.1.3c Gross Value of Manufacturing Output in the Organized Sector We estimate a statistical linking equation to predict the gross value of output from the gross value added from manufacturing the organized sector. The estimated equation is noted below and further details on the estimated equation are in Appendix 3.

$$\text{Ln } Q_t = 0.7790 + 1.0209 \text{ Ln } Q_{t-1} - 0.6887 \text{ Ln } Q_{t-2}$$
$$+ 0.4355 \text{ Ln } Q_{t-3} + 0.1976 \text{ Ln } GVAD_t \tag{IV.22}$$

IV.1.3d Value Added from Unorganized Manufacturing The output (value added) from unorganized manufacturing sub-sector is estimated from an equation linking it to the value added from organized sub-sector as,

$$\text{Ln } GVAD\_UR_t = 0.7496 + 0.5260 \text{ Ln } GVAD\_UR_{t-1} + 0.6569 \text{ Ln } GVAD_t$$
$$+0.5753 \text{ Ln } GVAD_{t-1} + 0.2991 \text{ Ln } GVAD_{t-2} \tag{IV.23}$$

where GVAD_UR is the real value added from the unorganized manufacturing sub-sector and GVAD is the real value added from the organized manufacturing. The details of estimated equation are given in Appendix 3.

IV.1.3e Price Index of Manufactured Products Manufactured product prices are sensitive to both the cost and demand pressures. As demand function is not directly estimated, the price of manufactured products is estimated as a reduced form equation. Taking the wholesale price index of manufactured products as the dependent variable, the following equation is estimated,

$$\text{Ln } PM_t = 3.3441 + 0.4188 \text{ Ln } PFPL_t + 0.0002 \ [(TAR*eR)_{t-1} + INDT_{t-1}]$$
$$+ 0.3461 \text{ Ln } PM_{t-1} - 0.4622 \text{ Ln } PM_{t-2}$$
$$+ 0.3102 \text{ Ln } (M3/GDPR)_t \tag{IV.24}$$

where PM is the wholesale price index of manufactured products, PFPL is the wholesale price index of fuel, power, light and lubricants group of commodities, TAR is the average collection rate of customs taxes (tax collections under customs divided by the value of imports of manufactured products), eR is the exchange rate (rupees per US dollar), INDT is the rate of domestic indirect taxes of the Central government per unit of value of gross output of manufacturing sector, M3 is measure of broad money at the end of year t and GDPR is the real GDP. Details of estimation are presented in Appendix 3.

IV.1.4 International Trade in Manufactured Products

IV.1.4a Exports of Manufactured Products Manufactured exports constitute about 70% of India's total merchandise exports. Textile products dominate the manufactured exports but the share of engineering goods has increased significantly beginning from mid-1980s. The trends in manufacturing exports relative to total merchandise exports are shown in Figure IV.5). A number of studies have estimated the demand function for Indian exports of manufactured products and they have shown sensitivity of exports to changes in exchange rate as well as international price relative to domestic (Indian price). The equation estimated in the present study is,

$$\text{Ln } XMFGt = 5.0739 + 1.9155 \text{ Ln } WGDP_{t-1} + 0.4833 \text{ Ln } XMFG_{t-1}$$
$$+ 0.3544 \text{ Ln } (UVIXM * XSUB / PM)_t$$
$$+ 0.3241 \text{ Ln } (UVIXM * XSUB / PM)_{t-1} \qquad \text{(IV.25)}$$

where XMFG is the quantum index of manufactured exports, WGDP is the real world GDP (trade weighted index of India's 10 major trade partners), UVIXM is the unit value index of manufactured exports (rupee terms), XSUB is the export subsidies per unit of manufactured exports and PM is as defined earlier. Exchange rate enters as an explanatory variable as UVIXM is a combination of international prices and exchange rate. Details of the estimated equation are in Appendix 3.

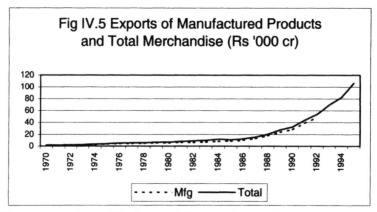

Fig IV.5 Exports of Manufactured Products and Total Merchandise (Rs '000 cr)

Note: These are manufactured Products excluding petroleum products.

IV.1.4b Imports of Manufactured Products Besides the petroleum products, the major items of manufacturing imports into India are the machinery or capital goods. The trends in imports of non-petroleum sector manufactured imports relative to total imports are shown in Figures IV.6). We distinguish between imports of petroleum products (POL) and other manufactured products mainly because of the fact that POL products are almost import dependent. Trade policy changes of the early 1990s have had significant impact on tariffs relating to manufactured products. Non-tariff measures relating to manufactured products have also been liberalized over the years. The consumer goods products which continued to enjoy non-tariff protection are now gradually brought under tariff protection. The estimated equation for manufactured imports is,

$$MMFG_t = -16.8342 + 2.1083 \text{ Ln } GDPR_t + 0.2419 \text{ Ln } MMFG_{t-1}$$
$$+ 0.5705 \text{ Ln } (UVIMM^* (1+ TAR) / PM)_t \qquad\qquad \text{(IV.26)}$$

where MMFG is the quantum index of imports of manufactured products other than petroleum products, GDPR is real GDP, UVIMM is the unit value index of manufactured products (in rupee terms), and TAR and PM are as defined previously. Details of the estimated equation are in Appendix 3.

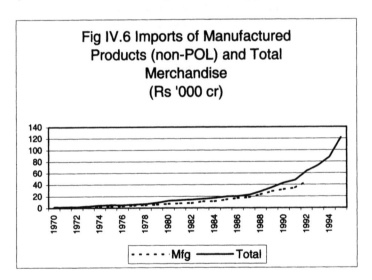

The estimated equation reflects sensitivity of manufactured imports to tariff rate changes, exchange rate changes and changes in both the international price conditions and domestic price conditions.

IV.2 Output of Other Non-Agricultural Sectors

The main sectors contributing to GDP besides agriculture and manufacturing are: (1) mining and quarrying (*MNG*), (2) construction, (3) electricity, gas and water supply (*EGW*), (4) transportation, storage and communications (*TSC*), (5) trade, hotels and restaurants (*THR*), (6) banking, insurance and financial services (*BIFS*),

(7) public administration and defense (*PAD*) and (8) other services. Among these categories, *MNG, EGW, TSC* and *PAD* are dominated by the government sector. It is only in recent years that private sector has been allowed to participate in some of the sub sectors. Hence, real *GDP* from all these four sub sectors is assumed be exogenous in the present model. In the other cases, we have estimated a set of equations linking *GDP* originating from these sectors to the *GDP* originating from agriculture and manufacturing or the total real *GDP*.

IV.2.1 Construction

Since construction is an investment activity that is undertaken by both the households and the business sector, expectations of household income and overall output of the economy play an important role in the determination of output of this sector. Output of construction is expected to be linked to lagged and current levels of real *GDP*. While the current levels of *GDP* reflect the availability of funds for investment, particularly for the household sector, lagged *GDP* levels along with the current level of *GDP* are indicators of expected growth of real *GDP*. In the estimation process, lagged levels of real *GDP* were not significant and the selected equation includes only the lagged construction output and current levels of real *GDP*. The estimated equation is noted below and the statistics relating to the estimated equation are given in Appendix 3.

$$\text{Ln } CONY_t = -0.8281 + 0.5007 \text{ Ln } CONY_{t-1} + 0.4442 \text{ Ln } GDPR \qquad \text{(IV.27)}$$

where *CONY* is the real *GDP* from construction and *GDPR* is the real *GDP*.

IV.2.2 Trade, Hotels and Restaurants (THR)

Activities relating to trade, hotels and restaurants are essentially demand determined and extension of activities relating to production in the other sectors. As production in sectors such as agriculture and manufacturing increases, demand for services of trade, hotels and restaurants would also rise. The equation selected from alternative estimates is noted below. Details of the estimated equation are reported in Appendix 3.

$$\text{Ln } THRY_t = -1.1045 + 0.7992 \text{ Ln } THRY_{t-1} + 0.5552 \text{ Ln } GDP1_t$$
$$- 0.2857 \text{ Ln } GDP1_{t-1} \qquad \text{(IV.28)}$$

where *THRY* is the real *GDP* from trade, hotels and restaurants and *GDP1* is defined as the sum of real *GDP* from agriculture and allied activities, manufacturing, public administration and defense and the mining sectors.

IV.2.3 Other Services

The sub groups included in the 'other services' category here are (1) banking, insurance and financial services, (2) real estate and ownership of dwellings and (3) personal services. Output from these services are strongly influenced by the overall economic activity. An equation capturing this linkage was estimated and reported below. Details of the estimated equation are presented in Appendix 3.

$$\text{Ln } OTHS\_GDP_t = -2.8059 + 0.6806 \text{ Ln } OTHS\_GDP_{t-1} + 0.2721 \text{ Ln } GDPR_t$$
$$+ 0.2413 \text{ Ln } GDP_{t-1} \qquad\qquad\qquad\qquad \text{(IV.29)}$$

IV.3 Overall Output Measures and Deflators

Various components of overall *GDP* and sectoral prices have been defined in the previous discussions. Formally, we define the overall measures of output, prices and inflation. The overall real *GDP* is the sum of real *GDP* originating from the various sectors. This measure is in terms of value added in factor cost.

$$GDPRt \equiv GDP1t + EGWYt + TSCYt + CONYt + THRYt + OTHSY_t \qquad \text{(IV.30)}$$

The other measure of real output often used in discussions is the real *GDP* measured in market prices. We have estimated a link equation to relate real *GDP* at market prices to real *GDP* at factor cost. While a direct proportionate relationship does not capture the divergence caused by the role of taxes and subsidies, we have retained a simple proportionate relationship given the overall purpose of the present study. The estimated equation is presented below and the estimation details are in Appendix 3.

$$\text{Ln } GDPMP_t = 0.0066 + 1.0091 \text{ Ln } GDPR_t \qquad\qquad\qquad \text{(IV.31)}$$

where GDPMP is the real GDP at market prices and *GDPR* is the real *GDP* at factor cost.

In order to derive the overall output measures in nominal terms, we have estimated deflators for the two series of *GDPMP* and *GDPR* in relation to the consumer price index. The estimated equations are noted below and the details of estimation are in Appendix 3.

$$\text{Ln } DEF\_FC_t = 0.1383 + 1.0045 \text{ Ln } CPI_t \qquad\qquad\qquad \text{(IV.32)}$$

$$\text{Ln } DEF\_MP_t = 0.1078 + 1.0090 \text{ Ln } CPI_t \qquad\qquad\qquad \text{(IV.33)}$$

where *DEF_FC* is the *GDP* deflator for *GDP* at factor cost and *DEF_MP* is the deflator for *GDP* at market prices, both dependent on consumer price index (CPI). The nominal *GDP* is derived from the real *GDP* and the corresponding deflators.

Chapter V

Integration of the Sectoral Details
in the Macroeconomic Framework

In the previous two chapters, details of specification and estimation of production, price and trade relating to agriculture and manufacturing sectors were discussed. Coverage of the other sectors of the economy was provided through link equations between the output of the respective sectors and agriculture, manufacturing or the overall GDP. Output of some of the sectors such as transportation, public administration and electricity generation was assumed to be exogenously determined. A complete description of the macro economy would also need to include the inter-relationships across the sectors achieved through the markets or other mechanisms. The three mechanisms that influence all the production sectors directly are the fiscal, monetary and foreign exchange rate related policies and their impact on other variables. These policies affect prices, input decisions and consumption decisions in different sectors. In this chapter, we first describe the quantification of inter-relationships between fiscal, monetary and foreign exchange variables and how they affect the sectoral level performance of the economy. We note at the outset that the macro economic framework adopted in this study is to provide the basic links between macro policies and the agricultural sector. These links are through the effect of macro level variables such as monetary variables, inflation rate, exchange rate and tax/subsidy policies that directly affect production sectors. Development of the macro economic model in this study has a focus on the analysis on these linkages. The selected equations for incorporation into the model are presented in this chapter below. Details of estimation are summarized in Appendix 3.

V.1 Fiscal Variables

Fiscal variables affect the production sectors through both general mechanisms and direct interventions in the form of taxes, subsidies and expenditures in specific sectors. The general mechanisms are such as the effect of a fiscal imbalance on overall inflation rate, interest rate and exchange rate, which in turn affect the sectoral prices and input prices.

Fiscal imbalances reached a critical level in the late 1980s and the macro economic crisis that erupted in 1991 focussed policy attention on these growing imbalances. Deficits in the fiscal account have implications to prices, interest rates and exchange rate, extent of the impact depending upon the type of monetary and exchange rate policy regimes in place. If fiscal imbalance leads to its monetization, then the impact on prices would be most significant. If fiscal imbalance leads to crowding out of private expenditure by public expenditure, then the reallocation is likely to be through the credit or interest rate changes. The reallocation of expenditures has consequences to growth and sustainability of the fiscal position. If fixed exchange rate policy is pursued, the pressures from fiscal imbalance on interest rate and prices would be greater. However, in the longer run, exchange rate adjustments would become necessary as capital inflows would depend on the ability of the economy to sustain a satisfactory growth which in turn will depend on stability in prices and interest rates. Thus, expenditure and revenue policies of the government with implications to fiscal balance also affect growth and distribution of income.

Agricultural subsidies and government investment in agriculture are two agriculture related government expenditures that have received attention with respect to their impact on growth and fiscal balance. In the central government account, agricultural subsidies comprise of food and fertilizer subsidies. The trends in food and fertilizer subsidies and government investment in agriculture, both in current prices, are shown in Figure V.1. Agricultural subsidies began to rise sharply in the 1980s. Both food and fertilizer subsidies accelerated during this period.

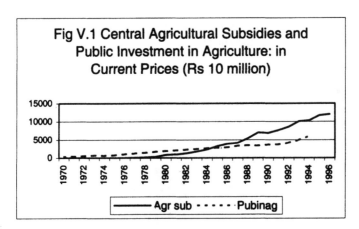

Fig V.1 Central Agricultural Subsidies and Public Investment in Agriculture: in Current Prices (Rs 10 million)

Government investment in agriculture, however, increased at a slower pace during the period of 1980s. The trends in agricultural subsidies and government investment expenditures in constant prices show that real government agricultural investment declined during the period of 1985-86 to the early 1990s (Figure V.2).

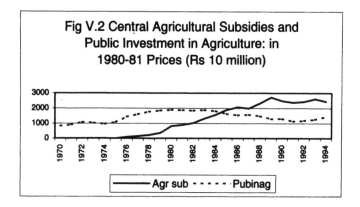

The trends in agricultural subsidies and public investment show a trade-off between the two types of expenditure, caused by the growing fiscal imbalance. Beginning in 1990s, however, the growth in subsidies in nominal terms has slowed down in comparison to the trends in 1980s. Real public investment in agriculture is showing signs of increasing trend. Beginning in the early 1990s, fiscal imbalance, measured by the ratio of gross fiscal deficit of the government (central, state and union territories) to nominal *GDP* at market prices, which rose during 1980s, began to reduce (Figure V.3) in the 1990s. Reduction in fiscal deficit was a result of slowing down of expenditures as well as rise in revenue growth. Slowing down of expenditure in part was a result of slower growth in subsidies and reduction in the growth of investment expenditures.

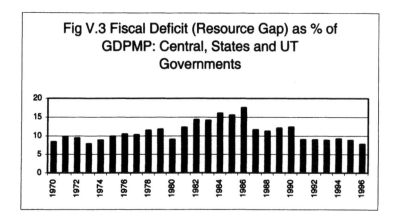

In order to estimate the fiscal imbalance, we first estimate the government revenue and expenditure equations that incorporate the policies affecting the agricultural sector. Within the government sector, we consider only the Central government expenditures, as the impact of the fiscal imbalances on the overall economy are primarily through the imbalances in the central government account.

The Central government has the option of monetizing its deficit whereas the state governments face a harder financing constraint in the sense that there are limits up to which the Central bank could lend. In the case of Central government, there are now limits mutually agreed upon between the Reserve Bank of India and the central government on the extent of financing the former would provide in the form of 'monetization'. However, there are still no statutory limits on this mode of financing.

V.1.1 Central Government Revenues

The impact of changes in fiscal imbalance on prices is through the impact on money supply. The impact on money supply is caused by the fiscal imbalance in the Central government account. To estimate the changes in Central government's fiscal imbalance, we model the tax revenues of tax revenues of the Central government. The tax revenues comprise of both the direct and indirect taxes. The direct taxes, consisting mainly of personal and corporate income taxes are levied on non-agricultural incomes. Contribution of agriculture to the direct taxes of the Centre is negligible. While within the non-agricultural sectors, contributions to Centre's direct tax originate from the various components we consider manufacturing sector's output as a proxy for the income or output of the non-agricultural sectors. The indirect taxes consist of the domestic indirect taxes and the customs duties levied primarily on imports. Bulk of the imports is inputs to the manufacturing process and collection of import duties is related to manufacturing output. As indirect taxes are mainly on ad-valorem basis, collections are a function of both the levels of production and price. Taking these factors into consideration, alternative estimates of the tax collection were made. The equation selected for further analysis is presented below.

$$\text{Ln } GTAX_t = -1.1354 - .0247 \, T_t + .3855 \text{ Ln } GTAX_{t-1} + .7903 \text{ Ln } IIPM_t$$
$$+ .0042 \text{ Ln } PM_t + .3011 \text{ Ln } PM_{t-1} + .8007 \text{ Ln } INDTR_t$$
$$- .3063 \text{ Ln } INDTR_{t-1} \qquad\qquad (V.1)$$

where *GTAX* is the level of tax revenues of the Central government, *T* is a time trend variable, *IIPM* is the index of industrial production representing the output of the manufacturing sector, *PM* is the wholesale price index of manufactured products and *INDTR* is the ratio of collection of indirect taxes to the value of gross output of the manufacturing sector. The output and price of the manufacturing sector are both positively related to the tax revenues of the Centre. The variations in output have a greater impact on tax collections than the variations in price. This may be related to the significance of customs revenues in the indirect taxes. Customs revenues are a function of imports that are in turn related to manufacturing output. The changes in tax rates also affect tax revenues positively. The estimated equation with estimation details is presented in Appendix 3.

The non-tax revenues are primarily profits from public sector enterprises and proceeds from the sale of public sector assets. We consider non-tax revenues as an exogenous variable in the present study. The total revenues of the Central government are estimated as the sum of tax and non-tax revenues,

$$GREV_t = GTAX_t + GNTAX_t \qquad (V.2)$$

V.1.2 Central Government Expenditures

Among the expenditure items we consider investment expenditures, expenditures on salaries and current consumption expenditures, interest in public debt and subsidies. The expenditures on investment are assumed to be exogenous.

V.1.2a Salaries and Consumption Expenditures   Expenditures on salaries and consumption are mainly the expenditures on salaries and operation of the government administration including defense. The growth in government employment and consumption of materials in real terms is a policy variable and reflects the overall fiscal stance of the government. In nominal terms the expenditures on this account are a function of the price conditions in the economy. The overall fiscal stance may also be influenced by the price conditions, but adjustments in expenditures are expected only over a longer period rather than on year-to-year basis. Hence, we assume that real expenditures on salaries and consumption are exogenous and related to real *GDP* from public administration and defense (also exogenous) and the nominal expenditures are determined by the price conditions. The estimated equation (with details of estimation) is presented in Appendix 3 and reproduced below,

$$\text{Ln } (GEXP1/WPI)_t = 2.4020 + 0.9985 \text{ Ln } PADY_t \qquad (V.3)$$

The estimated equation (V.3) clearly shows that the real government expenditures are closely related to the real *GDP* from public administration and defense and the nominal expenditures can be determined based on the wholesale price index.

V.1.2b Interest Payments   Interest on Central government's debt accounts for about 30 per cent of its total expenditures. It is related to the level and composition of debt in terms of the interest rate at which the borrowings are made. A simple relationship between interest payments and the level of debt has been estimated as,

$$\text{Ln } GINT_t = -1.9814 + .6427 \text{ Ln } GINT_{t-1} + .4608 \text{ Ln } DEBT_t \qquad (V.4)$$

where *GINT* is the level of interest payments during the year t and *DEBT* is the level of debt of the Central government at the beginning of the year 't'. The stock of debt is updated based on the previous debt and the net borrowings of the Central government. Details of the estimated equation are presented in Appendix 3.

V.1.2c Subsidies   Total subsidies consist of fertilizer, food and other subsidies. The shares of fertilizer, food and other subsidies in total Central government subsidies are shown in Figure V.4.

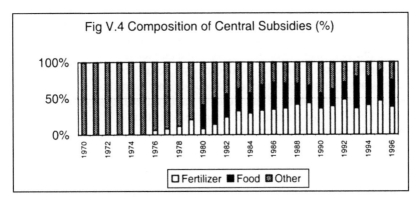

Fertilizer subsidy

Budgetary fertilizer subsidies are due to the difference between the prices paid by the farmers and the price the producers and importers of fertilizers receive. The price paid to the fertilizer suppliers (domestic producers and imports) is based on cost of production or import price. The government determines the price paid by the farmers. Cost of production of fertilizers is linked mainly to the cost of feedstock, energy and capital. Although cost of fertilizer production would increase as any component of the cost increases, increases in the energy or feed cost lead to changes in variable cost that may not be covered by the short term changes in prices paid by the farmers giving rise to the subsidy. The subsidy per unit of fertilizer consumption in nominal terms is, therefore, a function of the rise in the cost of production of fertilizers (or supply) relative to the price paid by the farmers. The equation representing this relationship is estimated as,

$$(FTSB/F)_t = -4.0519 + .1056\ T_t + 1.9798\ \text{Ln}\ (PFPL/PF)_t \tag{V.5}$$

where *FTSB* is the level of subsidy on fertilizers in nominal terms, *T* is the trend variable, *PFPL* is the price index of energy (power, fuel, light) and *PF* is the wholesale price index of nitrogenous fertilizers. Details of the estimated equation are in Appendix 3.

The price index *PFPL* is used as a proxy for the cost of production (or supply) of fertilizers and *PF* is the proxy for price index of all the fertilizers. The subsidy per fertilizer consumption is shown to have increased over time by the positive coefficient of the trend variable in equation (V.5) above. The rise in per unit subsidy is partly related to the rise in cost of production not directly related to the variable inputs, such as the capital expenditures of fertilizer plants. The relatively large coefficient of the price ratio (*PFPL/PF*) in equation (V.5) implies that the rise in input costs of the fertilizer plants (suppliers) is proportionately larger than the rise in *PFPL* whenever there is an increase in the latter relative to fertilizer price. One explanation for the relatively large coefficient on (*PFPL/PF*) is the composition of the index *PFPL*, which comprises of coal, electricity and petroleum products. As fertilizer inputs (feedstock for instance) do not include all these items in the same proportion, the rise in *PFPL* may imply disproportionate changes in fertilizer input costs and hence the disproportionate increase in subsidy. Secondly, while the input costs of fertilizer producers may go up proportionate to the input prices, the subsidy may rise faster as subsidy is only a fraction of the total cost. While a more accurate index of input cost to the fertilizer industry is desirable, for the present study, we have retained the estimated equation.

Total fertilizer subsidy is estimated as,

$$FTSB_t = (FTSB/F)_t * F_t \tag{V.6}$$

where *FTSB* is the total fertilizer subsidy and *F* is consumption of fertilizer.

Food Subsidy

Food subsidy arises due to the difference between the cost of procurement, storage and distribution of food grain by the government and the receipts from the sale of grain from distribution. Procurement of food grain is at a price (*PP*) fixed based on the cost of production of food grain and a reasonable return to the farmer, whereas the price at which they are distributed (*IP*) is a policy decision. Cost of storage and distribution (marketing) depend on the operation and maintenance of storage facilities and transportation. Change in these costs is a function of general price conditions of which consumer price index is one indicator. Food subsidy per unit of food grains distributed is, thus, as a function of (1) ratio of procurement price to the market price, and (2) ratio of issue price (proxy for sale price) to the consumer price index reflecting the general price conditions. As procurement and distribution of food grains is dominated by rice and wheat in terms of commodities, the price indices for PP, IP and market price relate to rice and wheat. The estimated equation with estimation details is reported in Appendix 3 and it is given below for reference:

$$\text{Ln}\,(FDSB/DIST)_t = 2.6603 + .1197\,T_t - 3.3569\,\text{Ln}(IP_t\,/\,CPI_{t-1})$$
$$- 3.8919\,\text{Ln}\,(PP/PRW)_t \tag{V.7}$$

where *FDSB* is the level of food subsidy, DIST is the level of food grains distributed through the public distribution system (PDS) and *IP, PP, CPI* and *T* are as defined previously.

The weighted average of wholesale price indices of rice and wheat, *PRW*, is used as a proxy for the market price of rice and wheat which influences level of procurement of grains by the government agencies. We have used *CPI* lagged by one period rather than the current period value to reflect the impact of accumulated cost increases that may not be covered by the changes in *IP* in the current period. A time trend variable is included to reflect the increase in the coverage of PDS over time in areas where additional expenses may be incurred for transportation and storage.

Total food subsidy is estimated as,

$$FDSB_t = (FDSB/DIST)_t * DIST_t \qquad (V.8)$$

Other Subsidies

The subsidies other than fertilizer and food in the Central government budget include subsidies to handicrafts, subsidies on exports and a number of government assistance programs. Generally, these subsidies are related to the cost in nominal terms while attempting to maintain a real level of support. The costs are related to the overall price conditions reflected by the general price level, *CPI*. The estimated equation is,

$$\text{Ln } OTHSB_t = 1.6674 + 0.0388 \ T_t + 0.7021 \ \text{Ln } OTHSB_{t-1}$$
$$- 0.6071 \ \text{Ln } (PFPL/CPI)_t \qquad (V.9)$$

where *OTHSB* is the level of other subsidies and all other variables are as defined previously. The estimated equation is presented in greater detail in Appendix 3.

V.1.2d Total expenditure Total government expenditure is estimated as,

$$GEXP_t = GINV'_t + GEXP1_t + GINT_t + FTSB_t + FDSB_t + OTHSB$$
$$+ OTHEXP'_t \qquad (V.10)$$

where *GINV* is the investment expenditure of the government and *OTHEXP* are the expenditures not covered by the components specified in the previous discussions. The symbol ' ' ' denotes the exogenous variable.

V.1.3 Fiscal Balances

From the estimates of government receipts and expenditures, we estimate the gross fiscal deficit of the Central government as,

$$GFISC_t = GEXP_t - GREV_t \qquad (V.11)$$

where *GFISC* is the gross fiscal deficit of the Central government and *GREV* and *GEXP* are government revenue and expenditure as defined previously.

The budget deficit of the Central government, after taking into account net borrowings by the government from domestic and external sources is specified as,

$$GBUDG_t = GFISC_t - DBOR'_t - EBOR'_t \qquad\qquad (V.12)$$

where *GBUDG* is the budget deficit of the Central government, *DBOR* is the net borrowing of the government in the domestic economy and *EBOR* is the net borrowing from the foreign or external sources. Borrowings by the government are specified as exogenous variables. Historically, budget deficit of the Central government was met by monetization. Hence, rising budget deficits led to automatic increases in 'base money' or 'reserve money' leading to increased money supply. Since the Central budget of 1996-97, there has been a limit on automatic monetization: deficit above the agreed limit is financed by the sale of government securities by the Reserve Bank of India. In other words, borrowing from the market would finance budget deficit in excess of the agreed limit. In this regime, budget deficit becomes 'exogenous' and government borrowing becomes an 'endogenous' variable.

Government borrowing leads to reduction of credit available to the private sector. Until the liberalization of interest rates (lending and borrowing) charged by the commercial banks, credit to the private sector was subject to quantitative restrictions. With the liberalization of interest rates, as credit available to the private sector is reduced, lending rates of the banks can be expected to rise. Higher interest rates lead to lower investment and hence lower demand for credit from the private sector. In effect, increased government borrowing results in crowding out of private expenditure.

In the previous regime of financing the budget deficit of the Central government, monetization of deficit led to increase in money supply and higher rate of inflation. Higher inflation reduced real consumption expenditures of the private sector and the government expenditure 'crowds out' private expenditure. Higher inflation rate decreases real interest rate when the nominal interest rate is 'fixed' but the positive impact on investment is offset by the adverse effect of a decrease in consumption demand.

In both the cases, therefore, rise in government expenditure relative to revenue would lead to a change in the composition of aggregate demand between private and government sectors, unless there are unutilized real or financial resources in the economy. If there are unutilized resources, then higher government expenditures financed by either monetization or borrowing would not lead to higher inflation or higher interest rates. In the present model, we specify nominal interest rate as an exogenous variable and assume that government budget deficit is financed by monetization.

V.2 Monetary Variables, the Consumer Price Index and the Inflation Rate

Monetary aggregates provide the link between fiscal variables and prices and through prices to the other real variables such as input use, output and trade. In the price formation equations specified in the earlier chapters, monetary aggregates *M1* or *M3* influence prices. The impact on prices is not neutral across sectors, as agricultural price policies tend to influence these prices in a particular direction.

Money supply is sensitive to fiscal balance and the manner in which deficits are financed. Money supply is also sensitive to the manner in which the monetary authorities try to accommodate growth and moderate inflation rate.

V.2.1 The Monetary Aggregates

In this study, we have estimated the supply of broad money, *M3*, as a function of 'base money or reserve money' and inflation rate. Reserve money in turn is a function of budget deficit and change in foreign exchange reserves. As reserve money expands, money supply increases. However, monetary authorities also react to the levels of inflation rate in the sense that higher inflation rates are likely to attract measures aimed at reducing money supply. The instruments such as credit controls, interest rate and reserve ratios of the banking sector are used by the Reserve Bank of India to regulate the rate of growth of money supply. The narrow money, *M1*, comprising of currency and demand deposits, follows the trends in broad money given the impact of credit expansion on demand deposits.

The estimated equations for reserve money, *M3* and *M1* are presented in Appendix 3 along with the relevant statistics. The equations are also noted below.

$$HM_t \equiv HM_{t-1} + BUDGC_t + \Delta\, FOREX_t \tag{V.13}$$

$$\Delta\, RM_t = -1788.5 + 0.5328\, \Delta\, RM_t + 347.0300\, T_t \tag{V.14}$$

$$Ln\, M3_t = 0.9515 - 0.6543\, INFLC_t + 1.0324\, Ln\, RM_t \tag{V.15}$$

$$Ln\, M1_t = 1.2884 + .8096\, Ln\, M3_t \tag{V.16}$$

In the equations (V.13)–(V.16) above, *HM* is the stock of high powered money at the end of the year t, *BUDGC* is the Central government's budget deficit that is monetized, *FOREX* is the foreign currency reserves of the banking sector, RM is the reserve money, *M1* and *M3* are the stocks of narrow and broad money at the end of year t, respectively, and *T* is the time trend variable. *INFLC* is the inflation rate in terms of consumer price index. Clearly, the estimated relationships in equations (V.14)–(V.16) represent long-term responses in the sense that we have not accounted for any adjustment lags. The specification, however, provides the link between fiscal balance affected by subsidy and expenditure policies and the production sectors. It also provides a link between foreign exchange transactions and the production sectors through their effect on money supply.

V.2.2 The Consumer Price Index and Inflation Rate

Among the alternative indices of consumer prices in India, the consumer price index for industrial workers is the more appropriate indicator of consumer prices in the context of relating these prices to nominal wage rate in the manufacturing sector. In the previous chapter, an equation for whole sale price index (*WPI*) was built up based on agricultural (crop) price index and the price index of manufactured products. The two indices, namely *WPI* and *CPI*, though differentiated in terms of (1) their composition and weights of aggregation and (2) the margins and taxes between the point of production and sale, they are also closely related. In Figure V.5, the pattern of the two indices is illustrated.

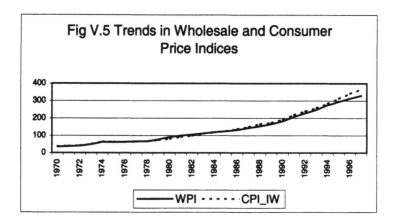

As noted above, besides the composition, it is the margin between the wholesale point and the retail point that differentiates the *CPI* from *WPI*. The margin is sensitive to changes in the parameters that affect the costs of distribution and storage. One of the parameters that can have an impact on such costs is the changes in money supply relative to the output. We have attempted to incorporate this effect into the CPI through the following equation,

$$\text{Ln } CPI_t = 2.9032 + 0.4779 \text{ Ln } (M1/GDPR)_t + 0.5264 \text{ Ln } WPI_t \qquad (V.17)$$

where *CPI* is the consumer price index (*CPI*, industrial workers), *WPI* is the wholesale price index, *M1* is the measure of narrow money supply, *GDPR* is the real *GDP*. Details of the estimated equations are presented in Appendix 3.

The measure of inflation is based on the estimated *CPI* and defined as,

$$INFLC_t = \text{Ln } CPI_t - \text{Ln } CPI_{t-1} \qquad (V.18)$$

V.3 The Balance of Payments Accounting

The exports of agricultural commodities and manufactured products other than petroleum products (non-POL, for products other than petroleum, oil and lubricants) were discussed in the previous chapters on agriculture and manufacturing. Imports of agriculture and non-POL manufactured products were also discussed previously. Imports of petroleum products account for 40% of

India's total imports. Imports of petroleum products are a function of the level of domestic economic activity as indigenous production of crude meets only 20% of requirements of crude equivalent of petroleum products. Some of petroleum crude produced in India is exported. The net imports of petroleum crude and products in value (real) terms can be considered as a function of output of the manufacturing sector. As there are lags in supply and demand of the products, lagged value of manufacturing output is used in the net imports function rather than the current level of manufacturing output. Domestic production of crude affects net imports both in terms of an export item and also as a substitute for imported crude. The estimated equation is presented in Appendix 3 and reported below,

$$\text{Ln } NMPOL_t = -3.0142 + .6547 \text{ Ln } NMPOL_{t-1} + 1.8839 \text{ Ln } IIPM_{t-1}$$
$$- 1.4262 \text{ Ln } QPOL_t \qquad\qquad (V.19)$$

where NMPOL is the neat imports of petroleum crude and products (real value), IIPM is the index of industrial production (manufacturing) and QPOL is the production of petroleum crude (physical units).

The trade deficit in rupee value can now be specified as,

$$TDEF_t \equiv MMFG_t * UVIMMFG + MWHT_t * UVIMWHT_t$$
$$+ NMPUL_t * UVIMPUL_t$$
$$+ NMPOL_t * UVIPOL_t - XRICE_t * UVIXR_t - XNFG_t * UVIXNFG$$
$$- XMFG_t * UVIXMFG - XOTHR'_t \qquad\qquad (V.20)$$

where *TDEF* is the trade deficit, *MMFG* is the imports of manufactured products (real terms), *MWHT* is the imports of food grains, *XRICE* is the exports of rice, *XNFG* is the exports of other agricultural commodities, *XMFG* is the exports of manufactured products other than *POL*, *NMOL* is the net imports of petroleum crude and products (real value) and *XOTHR* is the net exports of other merchandise, a balancing item specified exogenously. Price or unit value index of each of the export or import categories are used to obtain the value of exports or imports. These prices are indicated by the letters '*UVI*' in the equation (V.20) above. In the case of *NMPOL* and *XOTHR*, the values are in real rupee terms. Only when exchange rate or international price indices vary in comparison to some base year value, their impact can be simulated.

Balance of trade in invisibles is taken as an exogenous factor. With this assumption, current account deficit in a year is specified as,

$$CAD_t \equiv TDEF_t + INVDEF_t \qquad\qquad (V.21)$$

where *CAD* is the current account deficit and *INVDEF* is the deficit (debits minus credits) on trade in invisibles.

The change in foreign exchange reserves of the banking sector is expressed as,

$$\Delta\ FOREX_t = CAD_t + KINFL_t \tag{V.22}$$

where KINFL is the net inflow of foreign capital specified as an exogenous variable.

V.4 Integration of the Model Components

The various components of the model are described in the previous sections of this chapter and in Chapters III and IV in terms of production, prices and trade variables linked by fiscal and monetary variables. There is a regional dimension of agricultural production that is unique to the present model. An overview of the model is provided in Figure V.6. Agricultural production, in terms of both quantum and composition is modeled through input use and production efficiency. Prices, determined at national level, influence input use, inter-sectoral allocation of resources and composition of output within agriculture. Prices are influenced by government policies relating to agriculture directly and relating to other sectors as well. Policies affecting the procurement prices for food grains, tariff rates for manufactured imports, fiscal balance and external trade influence agricultural prices and production. Agricultural production explicitly incorporates a role for differences in technical efficiency among the producers. In the case of manufacturing, technical efficiency reflects the influence of variations in capacity utilization with variations in technical progress also being linked to technical efficiency.

Agricultural production is modelled in terms of crop output and output of allied sectors at the state level. Agricultural production is modelled in the framework of a production frontier with fertilizer, irrigation, tractors and labour as the inputs. Crop output composition is characterized by the share of rice and wheat in food grain output and by the ratio of food grain to non-food grain output. Technical efficiency in production is linked to rural literacy and infrastructure represented by the transportation facilities.

In the case of the manufacturing sector, output is modelled based on the output of organized manufacturing sub-sector. In the latter sub-sector, output is again modelled in the 'production frontier' framework. However, technical efficiency is explained by factors affecting capacity utilization, namely, the level of stocks or inventories relative to production. Higher the stocks, lower is the efficiency. The rate of technological progress is also found to be positively related to technical efficiency. In other words, in the years when technical efficiency is low, technological progress would also be low. Manufacturing output is thus, a function of capital stock, labour, technical efficiency and rate of technical progress. Capital stock is accumulated through investment. Employment of labour and investment in capital stock are influenced by rate of inflation.

Fig V.6 Overview of the Model Structure

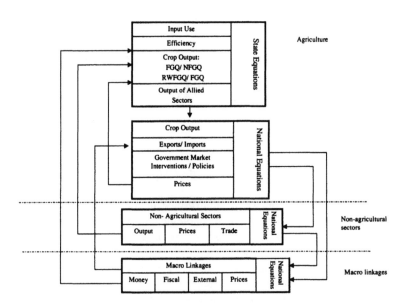

Rate of inflation is influenced mainly by variations in money supply relative to output. The impact of variations in money supply affects individual prices at different rates. The variation can be attributed partly to differences in adjustment lags in prices to money supply variations and partly to specific price interventions. The relationship between inflation rate and money supply is not unidirectional. Money supply responds to changes in the budget deficit of the Central government, changes in foreign exchange reserves and the response of monetary authorities to inflation rate. The level of foreign exchange reserves is influenced by current account deficit as net capital inflows are assumed to be exogenously determined. Current account deficit incorporates the effect of changes in domestic prices, international prices, exchange rate and tariff rates on imports. Exchange rate and net capital inflows are exogenously specified and hence changes in current account wdeficit have a negative relationship with money supply. Higher *CAD* leads to lower money supply and prices. Lower domestic prices raise exports and tend to reduce the initial rise in *CAD*.

The model outlined in Chapters III to V captures a number of inter-linkages between different sectors of the economy and different economic policies. The applications of the model are presented in the next chapter.

Chapter VI

Impact of Alternative Policy Choices on Agriculture: Applications of the Model

VI.1 Policies for Sustaining and Accelerating Agricultural Growth

Growth of agricultural output is of significance in the Indian economy from a number of perspectives. Input growth, technological progress and diversification of crop output have been pursued with a number of policy initiatives to raise and sustain agricultural output. There are, however, concerns relating to the sustainability of the past policies, particularly in relation to the policies that supported agricultural production through input subsidies and consumption through subsidies combined with restrictions on international trade. The prospect of increasing liberalization of trade in agricultural commodities around the world has also required an examination of appropriate policies for agricultural growth in the coming years.

The policy choices that have been frequently proposed and debated include: (a) liberalization of agricultural trade regime, (b) reduction and more efficient utilization of input subsidies, (c) targeting of consumer subsidies to the poor, (d) improved input supply systems for agriculture, (e) encouragement for agro-processing/food processing industry to improve demand for agricultural commodities, (f) encouragement for agricultural-technology industries to improve productivity in agriculture (g) investments in facilities for specialized storage and transportation requirements of diversified agricultural output and (h) strengthening of research and extension system. These are measures that have a direct impact on agricultural production. The measures that are likely to influence agricultural output indirectly, by operating on variables in other sectors of the economy or at the macro economic level, are those that affect 'terms of trade' or incentives that promote allocation of resources to agriculture. For instance, increased competition in the manufacturing sector would result in lower input prices of agriculture and hence induce more intensive use of such inputs raising agricultural production. Improved management of the macro economy resulting in lower inflation rate can also have a positive influence on agricultural production as it results in improvement in consumption demand.

Alternative policy measures influence agricultural output not merely in the aggregate but in terms of its composition as well. The composition of output in terms of food crops and non-food crops is of policy importance given the implications for food security. In a broader context, policies affect different sectors in an asymmetric manner: some sectors respond to policies more rapidly than the other sectors resulting in an asymmetric impact. An assessment of the impact of policy changes on different sectors of the economy is of importance because of the potentially divergent effects across sectors or enterprises within a sector.

VI.1.1 How the Policies Affect Agriculture

In a broad sense, all the policies discussed above affect agricultural production by influencing input use, investment or demand for agricultural products. For instance, liberalization of international trade has a direct effect on agricultural prices. Reduction in input subsidies implies higher price for agricultural inputs. Incentives for agro-based industries are expected to increase demand for agricultural commodities; improved input supply system or better research and extension system for agriculture would reduce the cost of agricultural production; improved terms of trade for agriculture would increase investment in agriculture leading to increased production capacity. In this sense, the policy choices influence either the supply of agricultural output or its demand. Effectiveness of the policies can be measured by the response of agricultural output to various policy changes.

Two important areas that have an influence on the performance of agriculture and consequences for policy that have received relatively less attention in the past studies relate to efficiency in the utilization of inputs in agriculture and the inter-state or inter-regional variations in agricultural production. While the implications of improvements in technical efficiency in agricultural production are the same as those of improvements in technology, inter-regional variations in performance draw attention to the need for region-specific policies. Efficiency in production also provides a linkage between human capital dimensions of agricultural production management and productivity. Regional variations in input use efficiency provide one link between policies at the national level and their regional impact.

VI.1.2 Focus of the Present Stud

A number of studies have examined the impact of alternative policy choices relating to the reforms of economic policies, on agricultural production and inputs. However, in empirical evaluations of the impact of alternative policies, often, the economy-wide setting is not utilized and the regional differences in the impact within the national setting are also not considered. The studies relating to the role of input use efficiency and regional dimensions of the impact are few. In the present study, we focus on the role of input use efficiency in influencing agricultural output both at the national and state level in response to changes in policies at the national level.

In the model developed in the present study, an attempt is made to capture these two dimensions of analytical framework. The regional variations in agricultural output performance are captured primarily through the 'efficiency' of the states in transforming the inputs into crop output. The regional or state-level differences are captured in the frontier production function model for crop production. The model developed in the previous chapters has been used to assess the impact of number of alternative scenarios that are expected to be important in the design of policies to sustain and accelerate the growth of agricultural output.

The scenarios examined below can be grouped into two broad categories: (a) policy measures that seek to raise agricultural output directly and (b) policy measures seek to raise agricultural output by providing a more favourable overall macro economic environment. The specific simulations carried out within the broad categories are,

a.   Measures that increase agricultural output directly
       1. Improvement in the rural literacy rate
       2. Improvement in physical infrastructure for agriculture
       3. Improvement in rural literacy and physical infrastructure
       4. Improvement in irrigation
       5. Increase in agricultural prices as a result of liberalization of agricultural trade
       6. Measures to reduce input (fertilizer) subsidies

b.   Measures that affect agricultural output indirectly
       1. Depreciation of the exchange rate of the rupee
       2. Reduction in trade protection to manufacturing sector and
       3. Measures to improve overall fiscal balance achieved by reducing government expenditures

The various measures affect agricultural output in a variety of ways. First, they may affect the efficiency of input use. Second, they may affect input use by influencing the price of input relative to price of output. Third, they may affect 'terms of trade' and influence investment in irrigation leading to output effects. In an economy-wide setting there are also the effects due to the interaction of supply and demand for agricultural output. The increase in agricultural output would imply lower agricultural prices unless there is also a corresponding increase in demand for agricultural output. The overall impact of the selected policy measures on agricultural output would also be influenced by their impact on the composition of crop output in terms of food grain and non food grain output and in terms of state level variations in crop output response. The model developed in the present study is applied to capture several of these diverse impacts on agricultural production.

VI.1.3 Measurement of the Impact of Policies

The impact of alternative policies can be measured by comparing the results of the model *with the policy change* relative to the model results *without the policy change*. The latter results are also termed conventionally, the 'base run' or 'reference run' results of the model. The model can be solved for the simulation analysis either for the future periods or 'within sample' or past time period. The within sample analysis provides an estimate of the impact if policies were implemented in the specified time period. If the impact is expected to vary in different time periods, both the analyses would be useful. In the present study, we have restricted the analysis to the 'within sample' simulations. The base run scenario is the period 1975-76 to 1990-91. We have preferred the 'within sample' simulations as the values of exogenous variables for the in-sample simulations are readily available, whereas for the future projections, the exogenous variables would have to be separately projected. Secondly, a comparison of the impact for selected variables over a period of time does not indicate significant variation in the results for different time periods.

A second aspect of the measurement of the impact of policy changes is the dynamics of the impact. For instance, a specific policy change has an initial impact on a number of variables but these variables in turn may impact on each other or other variables to produce subsequent rounds of impact over time. Thus, there are the 'short-run' and the 'long-run' impacts. In the present study the model is solved with the policy change in each of the years in the reference period 1975-76 to 1990-91. The 'average' impact for the entire period, thus, includes both the short-run and the long-run impacts.

VI.1.4 The Initial Condition

The simulations of the model provide an assessment of the impact of alternative scenarios of policy on the endogenous variables of the model. Due to the interaction between variables or non-linear relationships among the variables, the impact is a function of the levels of variables also. The main variables whose initial levels are of importance in assessing the impact of alternative simulations are (1) those affecting general efficiency in agricultural production and (2) the proportion of irrigated area out of gross crop area. For example, general efficiency in agricultural production is a function of rural literacy, transportation infrastructure and a measure of diversification of crop output. The impact of rural literacy on efficiency, however, depends on infrastructure and the impact of infrastructure on efficiency depends on level of rural literacy. Further, the impact of each of these variables in turn depends on the initial level of efficiency itself: lower the initial level of efficiency, greater is the impact. Hence, the initial conditions of these variables are important in assessing the level of impact of alternative scenarios. With this in view, we discuss the initial conditions of selected variables that are useful in examining the model simulation results.

State level variations in the levels of rural literacy are shown in Table VI.1 for the Census years of 1971, 1981 and 1991. In 1971, the rural literacy rate was the lowest in Rajasthan (16.44%) and the highest in Kerala (68.54%). In 1991, the lowest rate of rural literacy was still in Rajasthan and the highest in Kerala (88.92%) although, Rajasthan's rural literacy rate increased by about 85% over the 20 year period. The bottom three states in terms of rural literacy rate were

Rajasthan, MP and Bihar in 1971. The top three states (in ascending order) were Maharashtra, Tamilnadu and Kerala in 1971. The same pattern has continued in 1991 as well. The literacy rates have improved over the years but the difference across the states has widened. The trends and patterns in rural literacy are also presented in Figure VI.1.

Variations in transportation infrastructure (per capita TSC) across the states are indicated in Table VI.2 and Figure VI.2. As in the case of literacy, the extent of variation in transportation infrastructure on a per capita basis is significantly large across the states. The states of Orissa, Bihar and West Bengal had the lowest per capita TSC in 1971. In 1981 as well as in 1991, the same three states were at the bottom of the list of 15 states. Tamilnadu, Maharashtra and UP were the top three states in 1971 and 1981. But in 1991, Maharashtra, Gujarat and Tamilnadu are the three top states in terms of per capita TSC.

Table VI.1   Rates of Rural Literacy (%) across States

State	Year: 1971	State	Year: 1981	State	Year: 1991
Rajasthan	16.44	Rajasthan	21.01	Rajasthan	30.37
MP	20.08	MP	24.62	Bihar	33.83
Bihar	20.13	Bihar	26.03	AP	35.74
UP	21.29	AP	26.49	MP	35.87
AP	22.30	UP	26.70	UP	36.66
Haryana	25.92	Haryana	35.09	Orissa	45.46
Orissa	28.09	Karnataka	35.57	Karnataka	47.69
Karnataka	29.48	Orissa	35.70	Assam	49.32
WB	30.63	WB	37.90	Haryana	49.85
Assam	31.26	Assam	38.72	WB	50.50
Punjab	32.02	Punjab	39.94	Punjab	52.77
Gujarat	33.31	Gujarat	41.46	Gujarat	53.09
Maharashtra	36.09	Maharashtra	43.47	TN	54.59
TN	37.04	TN	43.54	Maharashtra	55.52
Kerala	68.54	Kerala	77.55	Kerala	88.92

Note: States are arranged in ascending order of rural literacy.

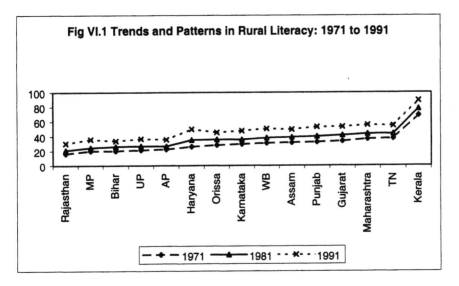

Fig VI.1 Trends and Patterns in Rural Literacy: 1971 to 1991

Table VI.2   Level of Real Net State Domestic Product from Transportation, Storage and Communication Per Capita across States (1980-81 Prices)

State	1971	State	1981	State	1991
Orissa	14.64	Orissa	19.10	Bihar	25.03
Bihar	19.38	Bihar	23.45	Orissa	33.30
WB	22.22	WB	25.97	WB	42.98
Punjab	23.24	Assam	33.27	MP	45.62
Assam	24.92	MP	37.47	Punjab	60.13
MP	26.82	Punjab	38.06	Assam	64.30
Kerala	38.48	Karnataka	54.81	AP	79.47
Karnataka	38.81	Kerala	55.53	Karnataka	85.01
Gujarat	41.77	AP	63.02	Rajasthan	90.98
AP	43.96	Rajasthan	63.04	UP	106.57
Haryana	44.84	Gujarat	70.81	Kerala	110.25
Rajasthan	52.12	Haryana	73.41	Haryana	147.96
UP	52.52	UP	75.57	Maharashtra	176.75
Maharashtra	89.41	Maharashtra	116.58	Gujarat	181.23
TN	123.92	TN	131.34	TN	189.34

Note: States are arranged in ascending order of NSDP from TSC per capita.

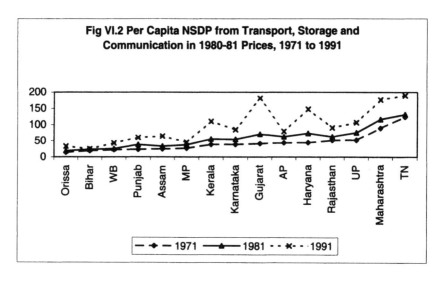

Fig VI.2 Per Capita NSDP from Transport, Storage and Communication in 1980-81 Prices, 1971 to 1991

The estimates of general efficiency in agricultural production for three periods at the state level are presented in Table VI.3 and Figure VI.3. Averages for 3 years, rather than a specific year are presented for comparison. For the period TE 1972 (TE= three year period ending in) Maharashtra has the lowest level of efficiency (63.58%) whereas Tamilnadu has the highest efficiency (97.54%). The three states at the bottom of the list of 15 states in terms of general efficiency are Maharashtra, Bihar and West Bengal in TE1972; Bihar, West Bengal and Madhya Pradesh (MP) in TE1982 and Bihar, MP and Maharashtra in TE1992. The three states with the highest levels of general efficiency were Assam, Kerala and Tamilnadu in TE1972; Tamilnadu, Kerala and Assam in TE1982 and Tamilnadu, Punjab and Kerala in TE1992. Thus, the impact of factors influencing efficiency is likely to be greater in the states of Maharashtra, Bihar, West Bengal and MP where the level of efficiency is relatively lower during the early years of the simulation period. However, it may be noted that general efficiency is lower in these states even in TE1992 suggesting the general pattern would hold even for the more recent period.

Table VI.4 and Figure VI.4 present the percentage of irrigated area out of gross cropped area in the 15 states for three selected periods of TE1975, TE1980 and TE1992. The initial level of the ratio of irrigated area to gross crop area affects the response of fertilizer consumption to changes in relative price of fertilizer: higher the irrigated area relative to total area, lower is the elasticity of fertilizer consumption with respect to price of fertilizer relative to output price. The proportion of irrigated area is the lowest in MP, Maharashtra and Karnataka in TE1975 and TE1980. The proportion is the lowest in Maharashtra, Kerala and MP in TE1992. The states of UP, Punjab and Haryana are among the top four states in terms of irrigated area as a proportion of gross crop area in TE 1975, TE1980 and TE1992. In other words, the impact of a change in fertilizer price on fertilizer consumption is likely to be greater in the states of Maharashtra, MP and Karnataka where the percentage of irrigated area out of gross cropped area is lower among the 15 states considered in this study. The impact is likely to be less in the states of Punjab, Haryana and UP.

VI.2 Policy Measures Affecting Agricultural Output Directly

Among the six simulations of the model grouped under this category, the first three relate to the policies that affect general efficiency of the states in crop production. Rural literacy and physical infrastructure (represented by transportation, storage and communication) can be influenced by government policies either by direct programs or by providing incentives for the development of appropriate facilities. The fourth simulation under this category of measures with direct impact on agricultural output is development of irrigation: or increase in irrigated area. Raising public investment in agriculture in the present model carries out this simulation. The fifth simulation under the present category is the impact of an increase in agricultural price by 5% for all the crop groups. The final simulation under this category is the increase in fertilizer price paid by the farmers to reduce fertilizer subsidy. Results of each of the simulations are discussed below.

Table VI.3   Estimated General (Intercept) Efficiency in Agricultural Production across States (% to Potential)

State	TE1972	TE1982	TE1992
Maharashtra	63.58	74.98	69.77
Bihar	73.78	61.12	58.10
West Bengal	74.49	66.27	72.83
Orissa	77.07	74.77	71.00
Gujarat	77.71	79.22	72.54
MP	78.22	67.73	61.34
UP	80.59	69.81	72.74
AP	80.83	75.88	73.68
Karnataka	81.41	79.47	78.45
Rajasthan	81.91	70.57	74.85
Punjab	83.70	80.55	86.26
Haryana	87.50	76.96	81.09
Assam	89.75	93.94	84.90
Kerala	95.42	91.42	93.67
TN	97.54	86.61	92.19

Note: States are arranged in ascending order as of TE1972.

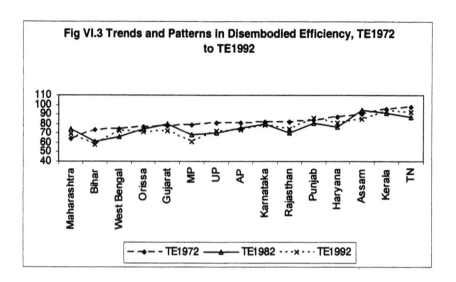

Table VI.4   **Gross Irrigated Area as a Percentage of Gross Crop Area across States**

State	TE1975	TE1980	TE1992
MP	8.73	11.92	22.09
Maharashtra	10.44	12.37	16.42
Karnataka	14.78	16.63	24.60
West Bengal	17.23	20.83	37.34
Gujarat	17.50	23.07	30.90
Assam	17.66	18.77	23.17
Rajasthan	18.37	24.16	29.28
Orissa	18.53	21.11	28.24
Kerala	23.21	16.57	18.73
Bihar	28.53	33.46	41.95
AP	34.00	36.60	41.39
UP	37.37	41.85	65.42
Tamilnadu	38.67	41.06	39.51
Haryana	50.84	59.84	80.39
Punjab	56.67	56.09	62.31

Note: States are arranged in ascending order as of TE1975.

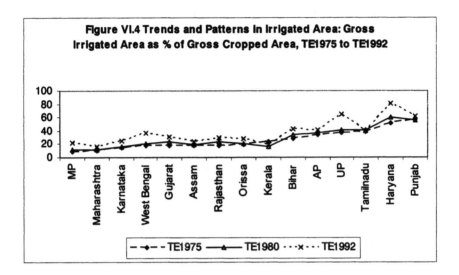

Figure VI.4 Trends and Patterns in Irrigated Area: Gross Irrigated Area as % of Gross Cropped Area, TE1975 to TE1992

VI.2.1 *Impact of Rural Literacy and Physical Infrastructure on Agricultural Production*

General efficiency of crop production has been modelled as a function of rural literacy, transportation infrastructure, farm size, crop diversification and a time trend in Chapter II. Among these five explanatory variables, farm size and time trend are not policy variables. The rural literacy and transportation infrastructure (represented by per capita real NSDP from transport, storage and communication) can be influenced by policy. The extent of crop diversification can be influenced by policy only indirectly, as it is determined as a function of price of non-food grain crops relative to food grains. Therefore, we examine the impact of rural literacy and infrastructure on agriculture and a number of other variables under three simulations: two simulations are carried out to assess the impact of improvements in rural literacy and TSC, separately; in the third simulation, both rural literacy and per capita TSC are increased by 10% over the base run levels.

In the first simulation, SIMLIT, the rate of rural literacy is increased exogenously by 10% for all the states relative to the base-run values. In the second simulation, the level of real NSDP from TSC per capita is increased by 10% in all the states. In Table VI.5, the results for simulation on rural literacy are summarized under SIMLIT and the results for improved infrastructure are under SIMTR.

The impact of changes in rural literacy and TSC on agricultural production is through their effect on efficiency of the states in crop production. The response of efficiency of the states is sensitive to the initial levels of efficiency, initial levels of literacy and per capita TSC. For example, the elasticity of efficiency with respect to rural literacy increases with the initial level of literacy as well as with the initial level of per capita TSC. The same pattern holds for elasticity with respect to per capita TSC. In other words, physical infrastructure and literacy are complementary in raising production efficiency. The impact of each of the two variables is, however, affected by the initial level of efficiency: the impact is greater when the initial level of efficiency is lower. This feature reflects limits to the increases in efficiency, as the potential for increase in efficiency declines as the initial level of efficiency is higher.

The impact of increasing rural literacy and transportation infrastructure on selected number of variables is summarized in Table VI.5 at the national level and in Tables VI.5a-VI.5b at the state level. The results are in terms of average percentage change per year for the selected variables relative to the base run scenario.

VI.2.1a National Level Results   It was noted in the previous section that levels of rural literacy vary significantly across states. The latest decennial census for 1991 puts the rural literacy rate for nine of the 15 states at below 50%. While there would be improvements in rural literacy since the last census, the gap between the states with more literate rural population and those with lower literacy rates is likely to be substantial. The simulation presented in this section points to the potential benefits from increase in rural literacy.

Table VI.5   The Impact of Improvements in Rural Literacy and Physical Infrastructure

Variables	SIMLIT	SIMTR	SIMLIT_TR
I. Agriculture Related			
A. Gross Output			
1. Rice and wheat	0.5122	0.2608	0.7945
2. Other food grain	0.5552	0.2473	0.8203
3. Total food grain	0.5061	0.2450	0.7704
4. Non-food grain	0.8099	0.3946	1.2361
5. Total crop	0.6323	0.3072	0.9639
B. Crop GDP	0.5523	0.2674	0.8409
C. Prices			
1. Rice and wheat	-0.5057	-0.2392	-0.7614
2. Other food grain	-0.7278	-0.3082	-1.0542
3. Food grain	-0.5613	-0.2564	-0.8346
4. Non-food grain	-0.1943	-0.0942	-0.2948
5. All crops	-0.3089	-0.1447	-0.4633
D. Inputs			
1. Fertilizer	-0.2839	-0.1365	-0.4294
2. Tractor purchases	0.5623	0.1911	0.7741
3. Irrigated area	0.0516	0.0238	0.0773
4. Gross crop area	0.0067	0.0028	0.0097
E. Productivity			
1. Crop yield per ha	0.6044	0.2892	0.9167
2. General efficiency	0.5900	0.2506	0.8591

Table VI.5   **The Impact of Improvements in Rural Literacy and Physical Infrastructure (Continued)**

Variables	SIMLIT	SIMTR	SIMLIT_TR
F. Trade			
1. Crop exports	1.2467	0.5686	1.9029
2. Crop imports	-0.7263	-0.3070	-1.0481
3. Total CAD index	0.5897	0.2677	0.8794
G. Government operations			
1. Procurement	0.3445	0.1955	0.5565
2. Distribution (PDS)	-0.2175	-0.1044	-0.3291
3. Stocks	1.2614	0.5577	1.8648
4. Procurement price	-0.3043	-0.1246	-0.4371
H. Manufacturing			
1. ASI value added			
(real)	0.0600	0.0323	0.0948
2. ASI GFCF (real)	0.0044	0.0021	0.0066
3. ASI employment	0.0961	0.0502	0.1502
4. General efficiency	0.0184	0.0102	0.0294
I. Macro variables			
1. Overall GDP (real)	0.2631	0.1269	0.4001
2. M3	-0.5359	-0.2425	-0.7955
3. WPI	-0.2272	-0.1050	-0.3398
4. CPI	-0.4097	-0.1882	-0.6114
5. Inflation rate (CPI)	-0.0503	-0.0267	-0.0788
J. Other variables			
1. Food subsidy	-2.0102	-0.8245	-2.8766
2. Fertilizer subsidy	-0.2310	-0.1059	-0.3441
3. Budget deficit index	-1.9567	-0.9261	-2.9424
4. Fiscal deficit	-0.3285	-0.1605	-0.4988
5. Price of manufactured			
products (WPI)	-0.2317	-0.1067	-0.3464
6. Terms of trade (PA/PM)	-0.0772	-0.0380	-0.1168

Note: SIMLIT= increase in literacy rate by 10% over the base; SIMTR= increase in per capita real NSDP from Transportation, storage and communication by 10%; SIMLIT_TR= SIMLIT and SIMTR combined.

Table VI.5a   State Level Impact of Efficiency Improvement in Agriculture through Increase in Rural Literacy (by 10%): Percentage Change in Selected Variables over the Base

State	Fertilizer	Tractor (purchase)	Tractor stock	General efficiency	Crop yield	Crop output
AP	-0.2594	0.6358	0.2823	0.7519	0.7409	0.7659
Assam	-0.3556	-0.1680	-0.0467	0.1118	0.0576	0.0669
Bihar	-0.2882	-0.0742	-0.0197	0.1694	0.1301	0.1382
Gujarat	-0.3118	0.7432	0.2141	0.8527	0.8271	0.8663
Haryana	-0.1912	0.8676	0.3422	0.8916	0.8982	0.9566
Karnataka	-0.3302	0.4935	0.1615	0.6873	0.6500	0.6715
Kerala	-0.3861	0.0890	0.0110	0.3711	0.3142	0.3212
MP	-0.4166	0.7611	0.3625	0.8955	0.8632	0.8997
Maharashtra	-0.3876	1.2924	0.4683	1.3720	1.3469	1.3868
Orissa	-0.3174	0.3647	0.1292	0.5589	0.5230	0.5378
Punjab	-0.1966	0.6647	0.2117	0.7262	0.7220	0.7742
Rajasthan	-0.3131	0.3831	0.1198	0.5482	0.5159	0.5443
Tamilnadu	-0.2263	0.0785	0.0328	0.2833	0.2584	0.2735
UP	-0.2616	0.3060	0.0904	0.4856	0.4616	0.4872
West Bengal	-0.3418	-0.0725	-0.0192	0.1944	0.1459	0.1576
All	-0.2839	0.5623	0.1928	0.5900	0.6044	0.6323

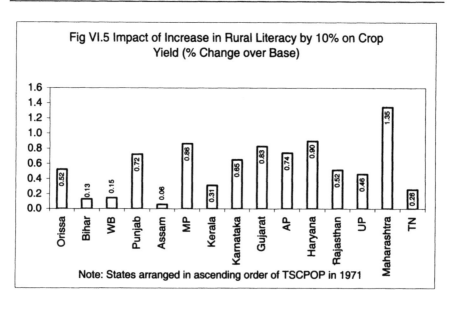

Fig VI.5 Impact of Increase in Rural Literacy by 10% on Crop Yield (% Change over Base)

Note: States arranged in ascending order of TSCPOP in 1971

Table VI.5b	**State Level Impact of Efficiency Improvement in Agriculture through Increase in Transportation Infrastructure (by 10%): Percentage Change in Selected Variables over the Base**

State	Fertilizer	Tractor (purchase)	Tractor stock	General efficiency	Crop yield	Crop output
AP	-0.1249	0.2270	0.0850	0.3132	0.3042	0.3190
Assam	-0.1702	-0.0957	-0.0237	0.0512	0.0255	0.0303
Bihar	-0.1378	0.0512	0.0180	0.1655	0.1488	0.1543
Gujarat	-0.1499	0.2094	0.0436	0.3069	0.2905	0.3189
Haryana	-0.0917	0.2342	0.0730	0.3038	0.3000	0.3319
Karnataka	-0.1565	0.0801	0.0230	0.2071	0.1857	0.1968
Kerala	-0.1840	0.2191	0.0613	0.3552	0.3326	0.3355
MP	-0.2010	0.0353	0.0158	0.1702	0.1439	0.1558
Maharashtra	-0.1842	0.5444	0.1731	0.6219	0.6067	0.6369
Orissa	-0.1509	0.0221	0.0021	0.1573	0.1360	0.1434
Punjab	-0.0958	0.0327	0.0051	0.1334	0.1238	0.1381
Rajasthan	-0.1511	0.0086	0.0006	0.1342	0.1147	0.1245
Tamilnadu	-0.1092	0.1673	0.0635	0.2627	0.2538	0.2678
UP	-0.1268	0.4152	0.1324	0.4766	0.4715	0.4956
West Bengal	-0.1639	0.1106	0.0200	0.2333	0.2125	0.2231
All	-0.1365	0.1911	0.0583	0.2506	0.2892	0.3072

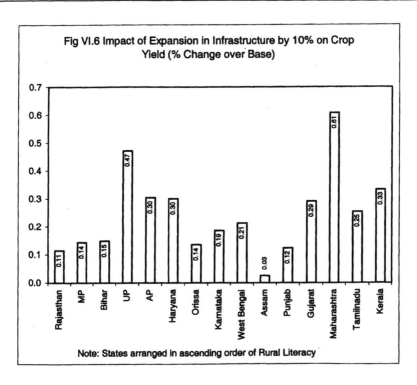

Fig VI.6 Impact of Expansion in Infrastructure by 10% on Crop Yield (% Change over Base)

Note: States arranged in ascending order of Rural Literacy

In the case of an increase in rural literacy rate, across the states, by 10%, crop output increases by 0.63% per year. The increase in crop output results from the increase in general efficiency in crop production (by 0.59%). General efficiency raises crop yield per hectare that in turn leads to an increase in crop output. Increase in crop output, however, implies a reduction in agricultural prices (-0.31%). If there is no corresponding increase in the demand for crop output, higher level of production implies a drop in output price in order to raise consumption levels to absorb the higher output. As a second order effect, lower crop output price, relative to input prices leads to a reduction in the demand for inputs in crop production, if the input prices are not affected by the lower overall inflation rate. For instance, Table VI.3, indicates a reduction in fertilizer use (-0.28%) when there is an improvement in general efficiency due to the rise in rural literacy. Thus, although general efficiency improves, the level of input use is lower in the case of some inputs.

The lower agricultural prices, have a positive impact on manufacturing output as lower inflation rate, resulting from lower agricultural price, induces marginally higher fixed investment demand (less than 0.01%) and demand for labour (+0.1%) in the manufacturing sector. The labour employment in manufacturing improves as lower inflation rate reduces nominal wage rate. The general efficiency in manufacturing production, a measure that reflects the level of capacity utilization, increases marginally (+0.02%) as a result of the drop in stock levels which in turn is caused by lower inflation rate. Thus, improvement in general efficiency in agriculture also leads to higher output in the manufacturing sector. The overall real GDP increases by 0.26% in the case of a rise in rural literacy by 10%.

The impact of an improvement in infrastructure (increase in real *NSDP* from transport, storage and communication, *TSC* per capita by 10%) for all the states, raises crop output in real terms by 0.31% per year. The linkages by which the changes in efficiency, crop yield and output followed by the second order effects on crop prices and manufacturing output are effected are the same as described above in the case of increase in rural literacy.

A key factor influencing crop output is irrigated area. A change in irrigated area relative to total or gross crop area affects crop output in a number of ways. It influences crop yield directly, affects the use of other inputs such as fertilizers and purchase of tractors, influences total crop area under crops and it also has an impact on the cropping pattern. In the present model, cropping pattern is affected by irrigated area through its effect on the ratio of output of rice and wheat to total food grains and the ratio of non-food grain output to food grain output. The ratio of output of rice and wheat to total food grain output increases with a rise in irrigated relative to gross crop area. The ratio of food grain to non-food grain output increases with the rise in irrigated area relative to gross crop area, following the impact of irrigated area on rice and wheat output. Thus, it is the food grain output other than rice and wheat that declines when irrigated area increases relative to total crop area. There may be an increase in both rice and wheat output and the output of non-food grains.

Irrigated area is affected by changes in crop output price relative to manufacturing price as well as by changes in crop yield relative to manufacturing price. In SIMLIT and SIMTR, irrigated area increases by .05% and .02% whereas gross cropped area increases by less than .01%. In other words, irrigated area as a proportion of gross cropped area increases under both the simulations although only marginally. Although crop prices decline when crop output increases, increase in the crop yield offsets the negative impact of lower crop price on irrigation. Similar impact is obtained on the purchase of tractors. Although crop output prices are lower, due to the higher irrigated area, tractor purchases are higher than in the base run. Increase in irrigation to some extent offsets the negative impact of lower crop prices on fertilizer consumption. In other words, while crop prices decline to induce demand for higher output, thus, thereby reducing the initial impact of enhanced efficiency on output, a number of interactions increase the input use and hence reduce the adverse impact of lower crop prices on input demand.

Lower prices are obtained, relative to the base run, in all the three crop groupings considered. However, the decline is the smallest in the case of non-food grain crops, followed by larger decline in the price of 'rice and wheat' group and largest decline coming in the price of 'other food grains'. Changes in crop output also follow a corresponding pattern: output of non-food grain increases the greatest, followed by output of rice and wheat, and by 'other food grains'. The variations in price response to output changes in different crop groups reflect differences in implicit price elasticity of demand. In the case of non-food grain crops, price elasticity is larger leading to smaller price response although output changes are greater. Increase in the output of non-food grain crops is caused by the sharper fall in the price of food grains relative to non food grains that implies a shift towards non-food grain production. Thus, the rise in efficiency initiated by the improvements in literacy and infrastructure is supplemented by crop diversification effect.

There is a decline in the amount of fertilizer consumption relative to the base run. This decline is due to the drop in crop price relative to the input price. In the case of fertilizer, as fertilizer price is held at levels determined by policy, drop in crop prices would adversely affect fertilizer consumption. In the case of tractors, although tractor prices also decline as they are linked to manufacturing price, the drop in crop price is greater. In the case of fertilizer, the adverse effect of lower crop prices is partially offset by increased irrigated area. In the case of tractor demand, increase in irrigated area compensates for the drop in the relative price of crops. We note that the drop in fertilizer (and the rise tractor demand) may be slightly overstated (understated) in the model as the direct impact of higher efficiency on fertilizer and tractor demand is not captured in the input demand equations.

Although agricultural exports increase and imports decline as a result of lower agricultural prices, the current account deficit increases as petroleum imports increase. Government revenues improve as manufacturing output increases and government expenditures decline. Both fertilizer and food subsidies decrease. Fertilizer subsidy decreases as fertilizer consumption declines and food subsidy decreases, as quantum of food distributed under the public distribution system is lower following the drop in market prices of rice and wheat. Food grain stock with the government increases as the level of food procurement rises and distribution is reduced. Although rice exports increase, the impact of higher procurement and lower distribution on food grain stock is greater.

The impact of a combined increase in rural literacy and improved infrastructure are approximately additive. At the national level, crop output increases by 0.96% as compared to the increase of 0.63% under SIMLIT and 0.31% under SIMTR (Table VI.5). Similar nearly additive results are obtained in the case of all other variables of interest.

The results point to the need for enhancing demand for agricultural products when policies shift the supply function upwards. If agricultural prices do not decline, the impact on input demand would not be adverse and the rise in crop output would be greater. However, the lower crop prices induce lower overall price leading to a rise in consumption demand for non-agricultural products.

VI.2.1b State Level Results   The model provides estimates of the impact on fertilizer consumption, purchase of tractors, efficiency and crop yield at the state level under alternative policy scenarios. Table VI.5a provides the estimates for the simulation in which rural literacy in all the states has increased by 10%. The impact of improved infrastructure at the state level is summarized in Table VI.5b. The effect of combined increase in rural literacy and infrastructure improvement at the state level is summarized in Table VI.5c. The state level variations are largely influenced by the changes in efficiency at the state level. Efficiency changes vary across the states as the response of efficiency to changes in literacy and transportation infrastructure depends on the initial level of efficiency itself and the levels of rural literacy and transportation infrastructure in each state. The response or elasticity is greater when initial level of efficiency is lower and the impact of literacy is greater when the infrastructure is superior. The impact is greater also when the initial level of literacy is higher.

Considering the impact of higher literacy on general efficiency first, the state in which the impact is the greatest is Maharashtra. It is followed by MP, Haryana and Gujarat. The impact is the lowest in Assam, Bihar and West Bengal. As noted in Table VI.2, level of per capita NSDP from transport, storage and communication (*TSC*) is the highest in the case of Tamilnadu followed by Maharashtra in TE1971 and TE1981. Therefore, the large response of efficiency to the increase in rural literacy in Maharashtra is partly explained by the relatively better infrastructure in the state. Gujarat and Haryana rank among the top five states in TE1981 and 1991. Bihar and West Bengal are among the bottom three states in terms of per capita *NSDP* from *TSC* in 1981 and 1991. The complementary effect of better infrastructure is, thus, greater in Maharashtra, Gujarat and Haryana and lower in Bihar and West Bengal (Figures VI.5 and VI.6). In the case of Assam, the initial level of general efficiency is among the highest (Table VI.3) out of all the 15 states considered. In contrast, MP has the third lowest level of general efficiency among the 15 states in TE1982. Maharashtra, Gujarat and Haryana have relatively lower levels of efficiency in the initial years of the simulation period. Thus, a combination of state level features determine the net impact of improvement in rural literacy rate on general efficiency in each state. The availability of adequate physical infrastructure, which in the present model is represented by *TSC*, is an important determinant of the impact of changes in rural literacy.

The state level results for the impact of improvements in infrastructure (per capita *TSC*) are presented in Table VI.5b. The impact on general efficiency is the highest in the case of Maharashtra, followed by UP and AP. It is the smallest in the case of Assam, Punjab and Rajasthan. As in the case of literacy, the impact is greater when initial level of literacy is higher, per capita *TSC* is greater and general efficiency level is lower. In the case of Maharashtra and UP, initial levels of *TSC* are relatively high and the initial levels of general efficiency are relatively low. In the case of AP the general efficiency has dropped over time significantly increasing its response to changes that affect efficiency. In the case of Rajasthan, although per capita *TSC* is relatively high levels of literacy are low in all the periods. Again, the determinants of net impact of improvement in infrastructure are initial levels of per capita *TSC*, rural literacy and general efficiency itself.

The combined improvements in rural literacy and infrastructure result in the largest gains in crop output in the states of Maharashtra, Haryana and Gujarat (Table VI.5c). The impact is the least in the states of Assam, Bihar and West Bengal where the initial levels of parameters (literacy and infrastructure) are poor or efficiency is high.

The results point to the positive impact of improvements in rural literacy and physical infrastructure on general efficiency in crop production which in turn result in higher crop output for the same level of inputs. The results across the states indicate that the states where initial levels of efficiency are relatively low are likely to respond more to policies influencing efficiency. The results also point to the interaction or complementarity between physical infrastructure development and human capital improvement. At the state level, therefore, policies aiming at improving literacy in rural areas and improving infrastructure for transportation are likely to result in significant growth of agricultural output.

The variation across the states in the impact on fertilizer consumption and purchase of (demand for) tractors is indicated in Tables VI.5a and VI.5b for the two simulations, SIMLIT and SIMTR, respectively. In the case of fertilizer consumption, there is a decline in all the states when there is an improvement in efficiency. The drop in crop prices relative to the exogenously 'fixed' fertilizer price results in lower fertilizer consumption. The drop in fertilizer consumption is the steepest in MP, Maharashtra and Kerala. It is the least in the case of Haryana, Punjab and Tamilnadu. The estimated equations for fertilizer consumption suggest lower price elasticity in the states with higher irrigated to total crop area. The relatively larger irrigated area in Haryana, Punjab and Tamilnadu, thus, implies smaller impact of increase in the relative price of fertilizer. In the case of MP, Maharashtra and Kerala, irrigated area as a proportion of gross cropped area is among the lowest of all the 15 states.

The purchase of tractors decreases in Assam, Bihar and West Bengal when rural literacy is increased by 10% whereas in all the other states, tractor purchases improve. Under SIMTR, tractor purchases decrease only in Assam. The drop in tractor demand is related to the fact that in the estimated tractor demand equation, tractor demand is positively related to the lagged value of crop output. Given the result that efficiency improvements are the least in the case of Assam, Bihar and West Bengal, crop output increase is also the lowest in these three states. Under SIMTR, the improvement in crop output is greater as the drop in crop price is less steep which implies smaller decrease in the use fertilizer per hectare. Thus, tractor demand is linked not only to the price of tractors relative to crop output price but also to variations in the level of crop output. The purchase of tractors increases by the highest percentage under SIMLIT in Maharashtra, Haryana and MP. As efficiency improvements result in relatively large gains in output in the states of Maharashtra, Haryana and MP, purchase of tractors in these states is affected more than in the other states.

The state level variations in the response to efficiency enhancing measures suggest that state-specific policies may be important to ensure maximum impact from such policies. The states where efficiency levels are presently low are likely to provide greater gains than the states where efficiency levels are relatively high. The states where both rural literacy and infrastructure are poor, the potential gains in efficiency are substantial.

VI.2.2 Agricultural Prices and Supply Response (Trade Liberalization)

A number of previous studies in the context of liberalization of agricultural trade policies have pointed to the 'dis-protection' provided to Indian agriculture. The dis-protection is, however, not uniform across the crops, and in some important cases, the studies have estimated positive rates of protection. In terms of broad implications of a more liberal trade regime for agriculture, this would imply higher domestic prices where there is dis-protection and lower prices where there is protection. The price changes in turn will induce changes in crop output and could increase aggregate crop output if agriculture is initially 'dis-protected'. The model developed in the present study could be used to examine the extent of supply response if agricultural prices increase as a result of trade liberalization in agriculture. As trade liberalization at the crop level can not be examined in the present model, we have considered only the impact of changes in overall crop prices. In SIMPA, crop prices of all the three crop groups are increased by 5% over the base run. In this sense, we are not considering any specific sequence of liberalization but merely assessing the extent of supply response if agricultural prices were to increase as a result of trade liberalization in agriculture.

The simulation SIMPA uses a restricted version of the model developed in the previous chapter. First, we recognize that the agricultural export supply functions incorporated in the model do not capture the trade environment resulting from trade liberalization. In the case where the crops are 'dis-protected', liberalization would raise domestic prices. But, in the export market, the non-price restrictions would be liberalized so that exports can increase at the prevailing export prices. As the implicit 'tax' on agricultural exports has not been incorporated in the estimation of the export functions, it is not possible to use the estimated export equations to simulate the effect of removal of an implicit 'export tax' on exports. Instead, we assume that the export market would absorb the 'excess supply' of crop output at the higher prices. The crop prices are specified as exogenous variables (in effect determined in the world market). Since, we have not explicitly modeled exports; the impact on current account deficit has also not been modeled in the restricted version of the model. Secondly, the increased domestic crop prices would also mean higher prices for the grains procured by the government. Higher market prices also increase the demand for PDS sales increasing subsidies on PDS. The PDS is likely to require strengthening and improved targeting of population segments when agricultural prices, particularly food grain prices, increase. In general, food subsidies are expected to be higher with the extent of the increase depending on the targeting or coverage under the PDS. In the present analysis, we restrict the model such that the changes in subsidy levels do not affect the budgetary imbalance and hence in turn influence overall prices.

The main changes in the restricted version of the model, thus, are: (1) crop prices are exogenously specified, (2) agricultural exports are determined not from the originally estimated export equations but as residuals or the excess supply at the prevailing domestic prices, and (3) changes in current account deficit or subsidies do not affect money supply. The restrictions imply that the model simulates only the supply response of agriculture to changes in crop output prices.

The national level impact of the increase in agricultural prices by 5% for all the crop groups is summarized in Table VI.6. The state level impact is summarized in Table VI.6a.

VI.2.2a National Level Results   The increased agricultural price leads to a rise in the price of crop output relative to the inputs such as fertilizer and tractors, leading to increased application of fertilizers and tractors. Crop yields improve as fertilizer consumption and tractors per hectare of crop area increase. Higher crop prices and higher crop yields imply improved barter terms of trade in favour of agriculture and investments resulting in increased irrigated area. The rise in irrigated area leads to the second round effects on fertilizer consumption and purchase of tractors enhancing the previous increase in crop yields. The rise in irrigated area also leads to changes in the crop output mix by raising the ratio of rice and wheat within food grains. The ratio of non food grain output to food grain output turns in favour of food grain as their price ratio remains unchanged relative to the base run. Thus, although all crop prices rise by the same proportion, crop output composition changes because of the variation in the response of crop output to changes in agricultural investments (irrigation).

Crop yield increases by 1.66% over the base run but general efficiency declines marginally (-0.01%) due to the adverse crop diversification effect. The decline in the ratio of non food grain output to food grain output implies a reduction in value of output per hectare in constant prices.

The model does not estimate the impact of increased output on crop exports and imports but provides an estimate of the increase in demand for PDS issues of 1.53% over the base run. As the PDS demand increases, with the selling prices for PDS constant, the subsidies on food are estimated to increase by 3.77%. Fertilizer subsidy increases by 4.68% as fertilizer consumption increases. The central government's budget and fiscal deficit increase.

Table VI.6　　The Impact of Increase in Irrigated Area and Increase in Crop Prices

Variables	SIMPA_RM	SIMIA_FM	SIMIA_RM
I. Agriculture Related			
A.　Gross Output			
1. Rice and wheat	2.1728	0.3912	0.6251
2. Other food grain	1.5858	-0.2392	-0.1605
3. Total food grain	1.8704	0.1480	0.3163
4. Non-food grain	1.7960	0.4373	0.2426
5. Total crop	1.8395	0.2682	0.2857
B.　Crop GDP	1.6024	0.2308	0.2441
C.　Prices			
1. Rice and wheat	5.0000	-0.6737	0.0000
2. Other food grain	5.0000	-0.1323	0.0000
3. Food grain	5.0000	-0.5383	0.0000
4. Non-food grain	5.0000	-0.1100	0.0000
5. All crops	5.0000	-0.2457	0.0000
D.　Inputs			
1. Fertilizer	4.8617	0.0619	0.3169
2. Tractor purchases	28.2731	0.3847	0.9872
3. Irrigated area	0.6772	0.6640	0.6787
4. Gross crop area	0.1006	0.1089	0.1111
E.　Productivity			
1. Crop yield per ha	1.6615	0.1520	0.1688
2. General efficiency	-0.0089	0.0389	-0.0093

Note: SIMIA_FM= Increase in irrigated area due to 10% increase in real public investment in agriculture (full model); SIMIA_RM= same as SIMIA_FM but with restricted model without the output impact on prices; SIMPA_RM= increase in all crop prices by 10% with restricted model without the output impact on prices.

Table VI.6   The Impact of Increase in Irrigated Area and Increase in Crop Prices
(Continued)

Variables		SIMPA_RM	SIMIA_FM	SIMIA_RM
F.	Trade			
	1. Crop exports	--	1.6702	0.0000
	2. Crop imports	--	-0.9163	0.9185
	3. Total CAD index	--	0.0630	0.5058
G.	Government operations			
	1. Procurement	--	0.3620	0.3620
	2. Distribution (PDS)	1.5329	-0.2458	-0.0243
	3. Stocks	0.0000	1.7702	0.0000
	4. Procurement price	0.0000	-0.4622	0.0000
H.	Manufacturing			
	1. ASI value added			
	(real)	-0.0081	0.0302	0.0000
	2. ASI GFCF (real)	-0.0029	0.0044	0.0000
	3. ASI employment	-0.0122	0.0492	0.0000
	4. General efficiency	-0.0023	0.0089	0.0000
I.	Macro variables			
	1. Overall GDP (real)	0.7072	0.1121	0.1096
	2. M3	0.0000	-0.2997	0.0000
	3. WPI	1.0910	-0.1401	0.0000
	4. CPI	0.6434	-0.2238	0.0000
	5. Inflation rate (CPI)	0.0374	-0.0223	0.0000
J.	Other variables			
	1. Food subsidy	3.7700	-2.4735	-0.0286
	2. Fertilizer subsidy	4.6830	0.0937	0.3055
	3. Budget deficit index	13.4845	-1.4180	0.1512
	4. Fiscal deficit	1.9001	-0.2355	0.0298
	5. Price of mfd products (WPI)	0.0000	-0.1191	0.0000
	6. Terms of trade (PA/PM)	5.0000	-0.1266	0.0000

Note: SIMIA_FM= Increase in irrigated area due to 10% increase in real public investment in agriculture (full model); SIMIA_RM= same as SIMIA_FM but with restricted model without the output impact on prices; SIMPA_RM= increase in all crop prices by 10% with restricted model without the output impact on prices.

Table VI.6a   State Level Impact of Increase in Crop Output Prices by 5%:
Percentage Change in Selected Variables over the Base

State	Fertilizer	Tractor (purchase)	Tractor stock	General Efficiency	Crop yield	Crop output
AP	4.4758	27.9049	9.5869	-0.0140	1.6567	1.8217
Assam	5.8235	27.9594	5.7552	-0.0026	1.6977	1.8859
Bihar	5.0306	26.1759	7.9748	-0.0186	1.6637	1.7972
Gujarat	5.1660	27.8926	6.5406	-0.0057	1.6059	1.8029
Haryana	3.9900	29.3284	9.7607	-0.0081	1.5646	1.7927
Karnataka	5.5893	25.4227	6.1595	-0.0075	1.6824	1.8463
Kerala	6.3076	24.8467	6.6851	-0.0060	1.8587	1.9528
MP	6.4586	28.0620	9.6175	-0.0127	2.0600	2.2855
Maharashtra	6.3524	26.6199	7.2424	-0.0089	1.9058	2.0802
Orissa	5.4405	27.0979	7.7103	-0.0140	1.7429	1.8837
Punjab	3.7022	29.5225	8.4897	-0.0061	1.4360	1.6629
Rajasthan	5.0244	29.0353	7.8547	-0.0066	1.6622	1.8662
Tamilnadu	3.9256	25.3562	7.3044	-0.0035	1.4164	1.5961
UP	4.5466	27.8327	8.5004	-0.0172	1.5930	1.7583
WB	5.6543	26.9048	4.4805	-0.0159	1.5588	1.7085
ALL	4.8617	28.2731	8.2637	-0.0087	1.6615	1.8395

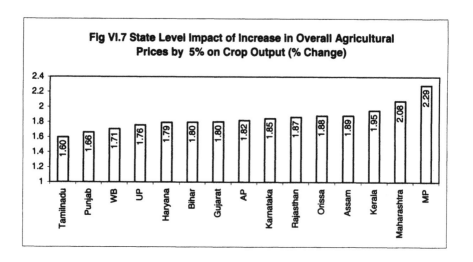

Table VI.6b	State Level Impact of Increase in Irrigated Area due to a Rise in Public Investment in Agriculture by 10% (Full model): Percentage Change in Selected Variables over the Base

State	Fertilizer	Tractor (purchase)	Tractor stock	General efficiency	Crop yield	Crop output
AP	0.0853	0.3076	0.2456	0.0640	0.1813	0.2972
Assam	-0.0744	0.0006	0.0462	0.0119	0.0813	0.1937
Bihar	0.0635	0.3190	0.2077	0.0840	0.1935	0.3125
069						
Gujarat	-0.0011	0.1227	0.0922	0.0253	0.1137	0.2288
Haryana	0.3189	0.7659	0.4616	0.0372	0.2187	0.3400
Karnataka	-0.0779	-0.0063	0.0497	0.0336	0.1003	0.2139
Kerala	-0.1238	-0.0302	0.0461	0.0272	0.0852	0.1939
MP	-0.1680	-0.0840	0.0392	0.0573	0.1091	0.2273
Maharashtra	-0.1605	-0.1142	0.0141	0.0399	0.0875	0.2013
Orissa	-0.0227	0.1331	0.1131	0.0638	0.1475	0.2608
Punjab	0.2537	0.6406	0.3544	0.0278	0.1920	0.3106
Rajasthan	-0.0299	0.0486	0.0824	0.0297	0.1117	0.2270
Tamilnadu	0.1094	0.2871	0.2155	0.0156	0.1358	0.2492
UP	0.1347	0.4665	0.2783	0.0783	0.2106	0.3285
West Bengal	-0.0441	0.1203	0.0541	0.0720	0.1489	0.2645
All	0.0619	0.3847	0.2336	0.0389	0.1520	0.2682

Table VI.6c	State Level Impact of Increase in Irrigated Area due to a Rise in Public Investment in Agriculture by 10% (Restricted model): Percentage Change in Selected Variables over the Base

State	Fertilizer	Tractor (purchase)	Tractor stock	General efficiency	Crop yield	Crop output
AP	0.3215	0.8793	0.4525	-0.0149	0.1769	0.2925
Assam	0.2286	0.6508	0.1814	-0.0028	0.1499	0.2682
Bihar	0.3230	0.8322	0.3736	-0.0198	0.1664	0.2797
Gujarat	0.2718	0.7486	0.2417	-0.0062	0.1595	0.2785
Haryana	0.5225	1.3988	0.6798	-0.0087	0.2414	0.3640
Karnataka	0.2029	0.5576	0.1895	-0.0080	0.1402	0.2564
Kerala	0.2021	0.5329	0.2008	-0.0063	0.1413	0.2519
MP	0.1777	0.5064	0.2495	-0.0137	0.1319	0.2504
Maharashtra	0.1620	0.4705	0.1773	-0.0095	0.1287	0.2448
Orissa	0.2527	0.6937	0.2798	-0.0150	0.1503	0.2642
Punjab	0.4517	1.2928	0.5469	-0.0066	0.2241	0.3455
Rajasthan	0.2404	0.6927	0.2607	-0.0071	0.1534	0.2720
Tamilnadu	0.3177	0.8663	0.3854	-0.0037	0.1849	0.3026
UP	0.3780	1.0175	0.4566	-0.0184	0.1866	0.3025
West Bengal	0.2501	0.6656	0.1489	-0.0170	0.1374	0.2523
All	0.3169	0.9872	0.4161	-0.0093	0.1688	0.2857

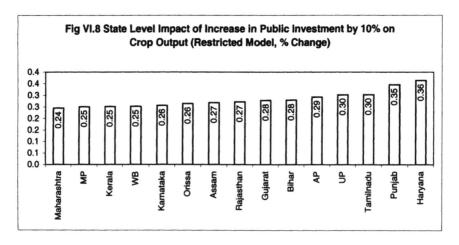

Fig VI.8 State Level Impact of Increase in Public Investment by 10% on Crop Output (Restricted Model, % Change)

The model simulation shows that for an increase in agricultural prices by 5% crop output increases by 1.84%. Nearly all the increase in crop output is from increased application of inputs, with a small proportion coming from increased crop area. The crop diversification effect is negative as the ratio of food grain output to non-food grain output increases. Impact on the other sectors in the economy is only partially covered in the present model. As crop prices increase, there is an increase in overall price level which depresses consumption demand and hence lower utilization of capacity in the manufacturing sector. Impact of the rise in agricultural income on the demand for non-agricultural output is not captured in the present simulation. The overall real GDP increases by 0.71% but real GDP from manufacturing is seen to decline by 0.01% as a result of higher rate of inflation.

As demand for non-agricultural sectors may rise due to higher agricultural income the overall effect on GDP is under-estimated in the present simulation. The simulation also does not allow for changes in the relative prices of different crops. If for instance, crop prices change in favour of price of rice and wheat, the share of food grains in crop output would increase more than indicated in the present simulation.

VI.2.2b State Level Results   The state level variations in fertilizer consumption, purchase of tractors, general efficiency, crop yield and crop output, summarized in Table VI.6a, show that the state where the increase in crop output is the highest is MP followed by Maharashtra and Kerala. The impact is the lowest in Tamilnadu followed by Punjab and West Bengal (Figure VI.7). This pattern is a reflection of the response of fertilizer consumption to changes in the price of fertilizer relative to crop prices. In other words, as crop prices increase relative to the fertilizer price, fertilizer consumption increases the most in the states with relatively lower irrigation coverage. Thus, fertilizer consumption increases in the states of MP,

Maharashtra and Assam relatively more than in the states of Tamilnadu, Punjab and West Bengal.

The demand for the purchase of tractors increases sharply by 28.27% over the base run at the national level. The rise in the purchase of tractors is the combined effect of the increase in the price of crop output relative to the price of tractors, increase in irrigated area and the increase in crop output due to the increase in fertilizer consumption. The sharp increase in tractor purchases is the result of highly price elastic demand estimated in Chapter II. While the short- term price elasticity is 1.69, the long-term elasticity is about 6.0. The relatively large price elasticity is partly the result of sharp increase in the purchase of tractors from a low base. Increase in the percentage increase in the purchase of tractors under SIMPA is the largest in Bihar, Punjab and Haryana and the least in Kerala, Tamilnadu and Karnataka. The larger increase in the case of Bihar, Punjab and Haryana is related to the higher proportion of irrigated area out of the gross cropped area. Over time, the shares of Punjab, Haryana and Bihar in the total irrigated area in the country as a whole are estimated to decrease, with the decline in the case of Bihar being slower than in the other two states. Hence the impact of relatively higher irrigated area in Bihar results in larger increase in demand for tractors.

The crop output increase is the largest in MP, Maharashtra and Kerala largely following the pattern of fertilizer consumption increase. The impact on crop output is the least in Tamilnadu, Punjab and West Bengal following the pattern of increase in crop yield per hectare. The impact of increase in crop prices at the state level is, therefore, is affected by the variations in the production conditions at the state level. Variation in the response of input application to changes in relative prices of inputs is a key factor in explaining the difference in the impact among the states. The present model does not imply differences in production response to input application but it does indicate differences in input use as a result of differences in production conditions. The increase in agricultural prices generally is seen to affect consumption of current inputs such as fertilizer more in the states with lower extent of irrigation but the demand for durable inputs such as tractors is affected more when the extent of irrigation is greater.

VI.2.3 Expansion in Irrigated Area

Irrigation provides the major difference in production conditions in agriculture by raising the potential for crop yields from a unit of crop area. While the potential for irrigation varies across the states, the extent of exploitation of this potential has also varied. Measures aiming to increase irrigation potential or to improve its efficiency remain important policy initiatives in agriculture. The expansion of irrigation facilities through direct investment by government has reduced in recent years as compared to the increase from private investment in tube wells and the use of electric or diesel powered pumps. Provision of credit for such private investment through the banking system is encouraged by government policies. As noted previously, increase in irrigation affects agricultural output in a number of ways, through its effect on input application, cropping pattern and raising the potential for higher output per unit of crop area. In the simulation SIMIA, public investment in agriculture is increased by 10% that results in an increase in irrigated area.

As irrigated area expands, crop output increases leading to a decline in output prices, unless the higher output can be absorbed by other sources of demand without affecting crop prices. The model is restricted in an alternative simulation where crop output prices are fixed at their base run level to assess the impact of increase in irrigation without the 'price effect'. The restricted model as outlined in the previous simulation is used to carry out the simulation with no price effects. The simulation with price effects is termed 'SIMIA_FM' (full model) and the simulation without the price effects is termed 'SIMIA_RM' (restricted model). The national level results are in Table VI.6 and the state level results are summarized in Tables VI.6a and VI.6b.

VI.2.3a National Level Results   The irrigated area increases by 0.66% under SIMIA_FM when public investment in irrigation increases by 10%. The overall crop prices decrease by 0.25% as a result of increase in the crop output by 0.27%. The increase is slightly higher (0.68%) under SIMIA_RM when the crop prices are held fixed at the base run level. The non-food grain output increases relative to food grains and within food grain the output of rice and wheat increases relative to other crops. Thus, increase in irrigation has a significant impact on cropping pattern. There is switch from coarse grains to rice and wheat and from food grain to non- food grains. Prices of non-food grains decline by 0.11% under SIMIA_FM as compared to a decrease in rice and wheat price by 0.67% and that of coarse grains by 0.13%. The larger fall in the price of rice and wheat is related to the higher increase in output as well as relatively lower price elasticity of demand for this group of crops.

Total crop output increases by 0.27% under SIMIA_FM and by 0.29% under SIMIA_RM. The output of rice and wheat increases by 0.39% under SIMIA_FM and by a significantly higher proportion of 0.63% under SIMIA_RM. In other words, the price effects are more significant in determining the cropping pattern rather than the aggregate output. The share of rice and wheat and food grains in total crop output is higher when crop prices do not decline as a result of higher crop output resulting from increased irrigation. When crop prices do not decline as a result of higher crop output, the level of input application is greater. When prices do adjust resulting in changes in cropping pattern, there is an increase in general efficiency in production due to the 'diversification effect'. Efficiency declines slightly under SIMIA_RM as diversification is less than in the full model simulation.

The higher crop output and lower prices under SIMIA_FM also result in positive impact on the output of manufacturing. Crop exports are estimated to increase by 1.67% and imports to decline. Overall current account deficit is estimated to increase as output related imports rise. The overall real GDP is estimated to increase by 0.11%. Food subsidy is estimated to decrease (-2.47%) but fertilizer subsidy to rise (+0.09%). The overall macroeconomic results comprise of increase in real output and lower inflation. However, the net effect on terms of trade for agriculture are not favourable: agricultural prices decrease by more than the price of manufactured products. It may be noted here that when agricultural prices were increased under SIMPA_RM, irrigated area increased by roughly the same proportion as under SIMIA_FM but the impact on crop output was greater as price of crop output relative to input prices increased. Under SIMIA_FM the relative price of crop output has decreased. Under SIMIA_RM the relative prices have remained constant. Thus, if irrigation expansion is stimulated by changes in relative prices rather than direct investment, the output effect is likely to be greater for the same level of increase in irrigation.

VI.2.3b State Level Results   When crop prices respond to higher output induced by increased irrigation, fertilizer consumption decreases in Assam, Gujarat, Karnataka, Kerala, MP, Maharashtra, Orissa, Rajasthan and West Bengal. In the other states of AP, Bihar, Haryana, Punjab, Tamilnadu and UP, fertilizer consumption increases under SIMIA_FM (Table VI.6b). The increase in fertilizer consumption reflects the positive effect of higher irrigated area in the latter group of states relative to the first set of states. In other words, at higher levels of irrigated area, the impact of relatively higher fertilizer price is smaller, hence the positive effect of irrigation. The demand for tractors decreases under SIMIA_FM in the states of Karnataka, Kerala, MP and Maharashtra: the states where irrigation is relatively lower. Efficiency improves in all the states as crop diversification effect is realized. The impact on crop output is the largest in the states of Haryana, Punjab and UP. It is the lowest in Assam, Kerala and Maharashtra.

The state level results under the restricted model simulation on irrigation (Table VI.6c, Figure VI.8) are similar to the results under the full model in terms of the pattern across the states. However, fertilizer consumption increases in all the states whereas efficiency decreases in all the states due to the decrease in crop diversification.

The states with relatively higher proportion of irrigated area relative to gross crop area benefit more than other states when irrigated area increases at the same rate in all the states. State specific programs, therefore, would have to be developed to target improvement in crop output in specific states.

VI.2.4 Reduction in Fertilizer Subsidy by Raising Fertilizer Price by 10%

Among the input subsidies in agriculture, fertilizer subsidies are prominent in the Central government's budget. There have been changes in the manner in which fertilizer subsidies are subsidized and the extent of coverage under the subsidy program since the early 1990s. Urea which is the largest and most common of the fertilizer materials used in Indian agriculture is still governed by the same pattern of subsidy which has been in existence since the late 1970s. In the case phosphatic and potassic fertilizers, there is a 'flat rate' subsidy and in the case of urea, there is the subsidy based on cost of production or the 'retention price'. Periodically, fertilizer prices are increased to reflect the higher cost of supplying fertilizers. Increased fertilizer price is clearly a disincentive to fertilizer use and hence attracts opposition from the farming community. However, fertilizer subsidy is only one of the many interventions by the government in agricultural markets. Hence, it is useful to consider the measures to reform government intervention as a package rather than raising input price as a separate measure.

In the previous simulations, we have examined the type of reforms that can benefit agriculture directly. In the case of reduction in fertilizer subsidy by raising fertilizer price paid by the farmers, there are adverse effects on agriculture. In order to balance these adverse effects with the positive effects, it is important to assess the dimensions of the adverse effects. In simulation SIMFT, the impact of a 10% increase in fertilizer price paid by the farmers is examined.

VI.2.4a National Level Results   Table VI.7 presents the national level estimates of the impact of SIMFT on selected variables. Increase in fertilizer price has its first impact on fertilizer consumption. Fertilizer consumption is projected to decrease by 8.27% over the base run. Crop yield decreases by 2.37% and irrigated area by 0.16%. However, demand for tractors increases by 0.84% on account of higher crop prices. Crop prices increase in the aggregate by 1.53% as compared to an increase of 0.61% in the price of manufactured products. Crop prices increase as a result of reduction in crop output which in turn follows the decrease in fertilizer consumption and irrigated area. Output of non-food grains decreases (-3.6%) more steeply than food grains (-1.6%). The asymmetric impact follows from the relatively sharper increase in food grain prices (3.03%) as compared to non-food grain prices (0.83%). The relatively higher increase in food grain prices is a result of upward adjustment in procurement price following the rise in input prices. Procurement price of rice and wheat is projected to increase by 2.67% following the hike in fertilizer price. Thus, the rise in fertilizer price is offset at least partially by the higher procurement price.

The decrease in the output of non-food grains relative to food grain output implies a drop in general efficiency in crop production (crop diversification effect). The higher crop prices imply reduction in exports and increased level of imports of agricultural commodities. Although procurement price is higher, level of procurement of rice and wheat is lower by 0.32% over the base run as the rise in market is price is greater than the increase in procurement price. The distribution of food grains through PDS is projected to increase and the food grain stocks with the government decrease by 4.46%. Attempts to reduce fertilizer subsidy may increase subsidy relating to government operations in food grains. Food subsidy is projected to rise by 12.44% whereas fertilizer subsidy is projected to decrease by 24.16%.

Rise in the overall price index both at the consumer and producer level following the increase in crop prices leads to a rise in the price of manufactured products as well. The manufacturing sector's output (real GDP) decreases slightly (-0.03%) as both investment and employment decline in the organized sector. Thus, increase in fertilizer price has generally a contractionary effect on output in both agriculture and manufacturing leading to a decrease in overall real GDP by 0.98% over the base run. The measure, therefore, has a number of adverse consequences, which need to be taken into account for its successful implementation as a part of the reform process.

VI.2.4b State Level Results At the state level, results are influenced by the sensitivity of fertilizer consumption to changes in fertilizer price. Table VI.7a provides state level impact of the increase in fertilizer price by 10%. Figure VI.9 summarises the impact on crop output at the state level. MP, Maharashtra and West Bengal are projected to record the largest percentage decrease in fertilizer consumption. The decline is the least in the case of Punjab, Haryana and Tamilnadu. As noted in the previous simulations, relatively lower ratio of irrigated area to gross cropped area in MP, Maharashtra and West Bengal have meant higher sensitivity to changes in fertilizer price. In the case of Punjab, Haryana and Tamilnadu, the reverse is the case. The purchase of tractors are projected to decrease in MP, Maharashtra and West Bengal due to (1) the relatively sharp decrease in crop yield following the decrease in fertilizer consumption and (2) lower extent of irrigated area in these states. In the other states, the decrease in fertilizer consumption and the consequent impact on crop output is offset by the larger increase in crop prices relative to the increase in the price of tractors. There is a decline in general efficiency as a result of the increase in food grain output relative to non-food grain output.

Table VI.7   The Impact of an Increase in Fertilizer Price

Variables	SIMPF
I. Agriculture Related	
A. Gross Output	
1. Rice and wheat	-1.7209
2. Other food grain	-1.4791
3. Total food grain	-1.5616
4. Non-food grain	-3.6051
5. Total crop	-2.4107
B. Crop GDP	-2.1466
C. Prices	
1. Rice and wheat	2.8606
2. Other food grain	3.5340
3. Food grain	3.0290
4. Non-food grain	0.8324
5. All crops	1.5305
D. Inputs	
1. Fertilizer	-8.2656
2. Tractor purchases	0.8383
3. Irrigated area	-0.1603
4. Gross crop area	-0.0242
E. Productivity	
1. Crop yield per ha	-2.3679
2. General efficiency	-0.2833

**Table VI.7   The Impact of an Increase in Fertilizer Price
(Continued)**

Variables	SIMPF
F. Trade	
1 .Crop exports	-4.3175
2. Crop imports	3.0856
3. Total CAD index	-2.6530
G. Government operations	
1. Procurement	-0.3169
2. Distribution (PDS)	1.0970
3. Stocks	-4.4551
4. Procurement price	2.6679
H. Manufacturing	
1. ASI value added (real)	-0.0318
2. ASI GFCF (real)	-0.0418
3. ASI employment	-0.1073
4. General efficiency	0.0038
I. Macro variables	
1. Overall GDP (real)	-0.9849
2. M3	1.2050
3. WPI	0.7827
4. CPI	1.2570
5. Inflation rate (CPI)	0.0150
J. Other variables	
1. Food subsidy	12.4400
2. Fertilizer subsidy	-24.1574
3. Budget deficit index	-4.4610
4. Fiscal deficit	-1.2743
5. Price of mfd products (WPI)	0.6134
6. Terms of trade (PA/PM)	0.9172

Note: SIMPF= increase in fertilizer price by 10% over the base run.

The state level results point to the greater impact of higher fertilizer prices in the states where spread of irrigation is lower. While fertilizer usage is more intensive in the states where irrigation is more widely spread, the sensitivity of fertilizer demand is estimated to be lower in such states as the potential for changing the crop mix and access to other agricultural infrastructure can be

Table VI.7a   State Level Impact of Increase in Fertilizer Price by 10%: Percentage Change in Selected Variables over the Base

State	Fertilizer	Tractor (purchase)	Tractor stock	General efficiency	Crop yield	Crop output
AP	-7.1539	0.8851	-0.1195	-0.4570	-2.1263	-2.1713
Assam	-10.0693	0.5600	-0.1721	-0.0856	-2.4477	-2.4705
Bihar	-8.5190	0.2167	-0.3521	-0.6031	-2.6015	-2.6397
Gujarat	-9.2725	0.6390	-0.1641	-0.1865	-2.3593	-2.3909
Haryana	-6.4011	1.3148	0.0690	-0.2660	-1.7500	-1.7949
Karnataka	-10.0044	0.2315	-0.2986	-0.2442	-2.5889	-2.6234
Kerala	-9.6993	0.2826	-0.3261	-0.1949	-2.4782	-2.5026
MP	-11.8323	-0.4212	-0.8526	-0.4151	-3.2475	-3.3023
Maharashtra	-11.0228	-0.0656	-0.4732	-0.2903	-2.8923	-2.9294
Orissa	-9.7988	0.0993	-0.3785	-0.4570	-2.7565	-2.7944
Punjab	-6.0421	1.5861	0.1862	-0.2003	-1.5932	-1.6312
Rajasthan	-8.4405	0.9431	-0.0858	-0.2161	-2.1891	-2.2233
Tamilnadu	-6.5553	1.2812	0.0455	-0.1132	-1.6318	-1.6579
UP	-7.6226	0.5838	-0.1738	-0.5605	-2.3428	-2.3961
West Bengal	-10.1443	-0.0423	-0.2108	-0.5185	-2.8927	-2.9396
All	-8.2656	0.8383	-0.1152	-0.2833	-2.3679	-2.4107

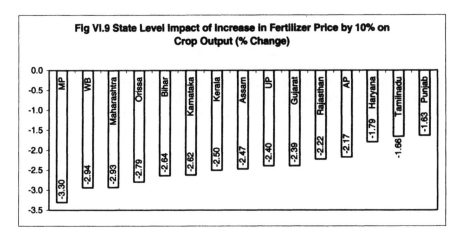

Fig VI.9 State Level Impact of Increase in Fertilizer Price by 10% on Crop Output (% Change)

expected to be greater there. In other words, fertilizer use can be expected to be affected in all the regions and the effect is not necessarily greater in the states where fertilizer use is more intensive.

VI.3 Policy Measures Affecting Agriculture Indirectly

Input use and the choice of output mix in agriculture are affected by a number of policy measures that may not be directly related to agriculture. Policies that affect terms of trade between agriculture and the other sectors can influence inter-sectoral flow of resources and hence affect production. Some of the policies may have differential impact on different crops depending upon the variations in price-support mechanisms or trade policy variations across the crop groups. For example, considerations of food security may have led to more restrictive trade regime for food grains than in the case of non-food grains/crops. Similar considerations have also led to government operations in food grain procurement and distribution at prices that are fixed by policy, unlike the case of non food grain crops. Thus, in a broad sense, the impact of policies at the macro level or outside of agriculture may affect agriculture differently from the other sectors and they may also affect food and non food grain crops differentially. In simulation SIMER, we examine the impact of a depreciation of the rupee; in simulation SIMTAR, the impact of a reduction in tariff rate on the imports of manufactured products is examined; and in SIMFISC1 and SIMFISC2, the impact of a reduction in government expenditure is analysed.

VI.3.1 Devaluation of the Rupee

The exchange rate variations affect agricultural sector through their impact on output prices and on the input prices. The transmission of the effect is, however, influenced by the restrictions on international trade and by rigidities in price adjustments. For example, fixed fertilizer prices at the subsidized levels are not affected by exchange rate variations unless the fertilizer prices are varied through policy measures. The trade restrictions in the case of food grains imply that price response to exchange rate variations in the case of non-food grains is likely to be greater than in the food grains. The estimated price equation for non-food grains includes exchange rate as an explanatory variable whereas in the equations for rice and wheat, and 'other food grains' exchange rate is not included as an explanatory variable. Nominal exchange rate also influences price of the manufactured products such that a depreciation of the rupee increases the price of manufactured products (PM). Thus, a depreciation (or appreciation) of the nominal exchange rate produces asymmetric impact across sectors depending upon the trade regime faced by each sector. In the present model, price of non-food grain crops and price of manufactured products increase relative to the price of food grain as a result of a depreciation of the rupee. The resulting changes in crop output reflect the altered pattern of price incentives to the producers.

VI.3.1a National Level Results   The aggregate or national level results of the simulation SIMER, where exchange rate of the rupee is depreciated by Rs 0.5 per US dollar relative to the base run are summarized for the national level in Table VI.8. First consider the price scenario resulting from the exchange rate depreciation. Price of non-food grains increases by 0.95% whereas the price of food grains increases by only 0.22%. The price of manufactured products increases by 0.50%. The changes in relative prices produce a corresponding output effect. Output of food grains decreases by 0.03% on account of the decline in the output of 'other food grains' by 0.13%. The non-food grain output increases by 1.02%. The output of rice and wheat increases marginally (+.02%) primarily due to the increase in irrigated area that raises the share of rice and wheat in food grain output. Although the rise in irrigated area relative to gross cropped area implies a reduction in the ratio of non food grain to food grain output, the positive impact of the rise in non food grain prices dominates the negative effect of irrigation expansion on non food grain production.

Irrigated area increases by 0.07% as compared to a smaller increase of 0.01% in gross cropped area. Increase in irrigated area is a result of improved terms of trade as price of manufactured products increases by 0.50% as compared to the increase in crop prices by 0.70%. The relatively higher increase in crop prices also induces higher demand for tractors (+1.86%) and fertilizer consumption (+0.60%). Aggregate crop yield increases by 0.38% and general efficiency increases by 0.14%. The rise in efficiency is the 'crop diversification effect' as the ratio of non-food grain to food grain output increases.

Crop exports increase along with imports of agricultural commodities. Exports rise as price of exports in rupee terms increases relative to the domestic price. As domestic prices also increase, imports rise. Procurement of food grains by the government is projected to decrease, as the increase in procurement price (0.11%) is lower relative to the increase in the market price of rice and wheat (0.23%). Distribution through PDS increases by 0.09% and the food grain stocks with the government decrease by 0.81%. Thus, depreciation of the rupee is projected to result in higher agricultural prices and increased crop output. However, crop output mix is projected to change with larger proportion of non-food grain output than in the base run. With lower procurement and larger distribution through PDS, supplies of food grain with the government are likely to be smaller. Thus, in the longer run better targeting of PDS is important.

The manufacturing sector shows a marginal change in output as a result of depreciation of the rupee. Although fixed investment increases modestly, there is a drop in employment as nominal wage rate increases. Real *GDP* from manufacturing of the organized sector increases marginally by less than 0.01%. The overall real *GDP* increases by 0.17%.

The impact of rupee depreciation is projected to be favourable to the current account deficit, which is projected to decrease by about 7%. Thus, although domestic prices increase, the rise in export prices is relatively larger leading to increase in export earnings. The overall results suggest that agricultural production is likely to benefit from exchange rate depreciation more than the manufacturing sector especially when some of the input prices remain insulated from the effect of exchange rate changes.

VI.3.3b State Level Results   The state level results in Table VI.8a show that the crop diversification effect is the largest in Bihar (efficiency improves by 0.30%), followed by UP (0.28%) and West Bengal (0.26%). It is the least in the states of Assam (0.04%), Tamilnadu (0.06%), Gujarat (0.09%) and Kerala (0.09%). Figure VI.10 shows the pattern of the impact of exchange rate depreciation on crop output at the state level. The pattern across the states is a result of the initially low levels of efficiency in Bihar, UP and West Bengal and the relatively high levels of general efficiency in Assam, Tamilnadu, Gujarat and Kerala. Thus, changes in cropping pattern are likely to result in greater impact on the crop output in those states where crop yield is relatively low for the same levels of input use. As level of efficiency is already at a high level in the states of Assam, Kerala, Tamilnadu and Gujarat, the change in cropping pattern does not increase efficiency as much as in the states with lower initial levels of general efficiency.

The pattern of changes in fertilizer consumption and demand for tractors follows broadly the pattern noticed when all agricultural prices were increased under SIMPA. The per cent increase in fertilizer consumption is the highest in Maharashtra, MP and Kerala where irrigated area as a proportion to gross cropped area is the least; the increase is the smallest in Punjab, Haryana and Tamilnadu where the coverage of crop area under irrigation is greater. The rise in purchase of tractors is the highest in UP, MP and AP and the least in Tamilnadu, Kerala and Assam. A combination of patterns of initial levels of irrigation (which influence demand for tractors positively) and the changes in general efficiency produced by exchange rate depreciation influences state level variation in demand for tractors. The efficiency gains are among the largest in UP and AP. And they are among the least in the case of Tamilnadu, Kerala and Assam. In the case of MP and AP, the ratio of irrigated to total crop area is relatively higher than the states with similar increases in efficiency. Bihar, MP and UP are projected to record the largest percentage gains in crop output as a result of rupee depreciation. The impact is the smallest in percentage terms for Tamilnadu, Assam and Punjab.

VI.3.2 Reduction in Tariff Rate Manufacturing Imports

The package of economic reforms of the early 1990s saw sustained and significant decrease in the tariff rates on the manufactured products. The period also saw sharp devaluation of Indian rupee. The reduction in import tariffs reduced protection afforded by trade policy to the manufacturing sector. This has meant a cap on manufactured product prices and hence improved terms of trade for agriculture. How strong could be this effect? The model developed in the present study was used to estimate the effect of lower import tariffs of manufacturing sector on agricultural sector's output and related variables. It should be noted at the outset that the actual reduction in tariff rates has followed fairly complex selection, reclassification and sequencing of items and rates over a period of time. The simulation carried out here is at the aggregate level.

VI.3.2a National Level Results   Table VI.8 also provides the impact of SIMTAR on the national level aggregates.   As noted earlier, reduction in import tariffs lowers the cap on the manufactured product prices. In terms of estimated equation for price of manufacture products, lower import tariff rate actually implies a reduction in the price of manufactured products. The manufactured product prices are estimated to decrease by 2.5% when import tariff rate is reduced by 10%. The lower manufacturing product prices lead to an improvement in terms of trade for agriculture which in turn causes rise in irrigated area. Demand for tractors is projected to rise by 12.69%, as there is an increase in irrigated area as well as a rise the relative price of crops vis-à-vis price of tractors. In the model, price of tractors is linked to the price of manufactured products and hence when price of manufactured products decreases, price of tractors also decline.

Crop prices, at the aggregate level, decrease by 0.30% as crop output increases by 0.21%. Crop output increases following the increased irrigated area and increased stock of tractors. Fertilizer consumption, however, decreases by 0.20% over the base run as fertilizer price is held fixed while crop prices decrease. Increase in food grain output (0.27%) is greater in percentage terms than in the non-food grain output (0.12%). The differential impact on output is a result of the difference in the impact of higher irrigated area on the output of rice and wheat relative to other food grains and on food grain output relative to non food grain output. Because of the decline in manufactured product price, the procurement price of rice and wheat is also projected to decline by 0.09% over the base run scenario.

As the ratio of food grain output to non-food grain output increases, level of general efficiency decreases by 0.02%. Crop yield increases by 0.16% as irrigated area and tractor purchases increase. As a consequence of higher crop output, particularly of food grains, procurement of food grains by the government increases by 0.23% and distribution through PDS decreases by 0.10% leading to a rise in food grain stock with the government by 0.39%. Agricultural exports increase by 0.47% and imports decrease by 0.19%.

The manufacturing sector output increases as a result of higher employment resulting from lower nominal wage rates. Investment demand is projected to be lower as the manufactured product prices decrease but output increases in the organized sector by 0.46% over the base run. Overall real GDP is projected to increase by 0.21%. Both food and fertilizer subsidies are projected to decrease. Thus, the reduction in trade protection given to the manufacturing sector can be beneficial to agriculture when it results in improved terms of trade for agriculture. The impact could be greater if the additional crop output could be absorbed without the adverse price effect which in turn limits the impact on input demand.

Table VI.8   **The Impact of a Depreciation of the Rupee and Reduction in Tariffs on Manufacturing Imports**

Variables	SIMER	SIMTAR
I. Agriculture Related		
A. Gross Output		
1. Rice and wheat	0.0243	0.3750
2. Other food grain	-0.1305	0.1330
3. Total food grain	-0.0324	0.2722
4. Non-food grain	1.0174	0.1213
5. Total crop	0.4038	0.2095
B. Crop GDP	‛0.3592	0.1762
C. Prices		
1. Rice and wheat	0.2294	-0.2215
2. Other food grain	0.1988	-0.1458
3. Food grain	0.2218	-0.2026
4. Non-food grain	0.9528	-0.3450
5. All crops	0.7071	-0.2997
D. Inputs		
1. Fertilizer	0.5958	-0.1976
2. Tractor purchases	1.8639	12.6861
3. Irrigated area	0.0675	0.2263
4. Gross crop area	0.0103	0.0260
E. Productivity		
1. Crop yield per ha	0.3843	0.1598
2. General efficiency	0.1417	-0.0190
F. Trade		
1. Crop exports	8.4777	0.4682
2. Crop imports	4.8155	-0.1886
3. Total CAD index	-6.9994	15.9209
G. Government operations		
1. Procurement	-0.2057	0.2299
2. Distribution (PDS)	0.0863	-0.1026
3. Stocks	-0.8118	0.3930
4. Procurement price	0.1079	-0.0871
H. Manufacturing		
1. ASI value added (real)	0.0094	0.4627
2. ASI GFCF (real)	0.0659	-0.0755
3. ASI employment	-0.0039	0.7864
4. General efficiency	0.0002	0.1500
I. Macro variables		
1 Overall GDP (real)	0.1668	0.2109
2. M3	0.4040	-5.1346
3. WPI	0.4712	-1.7128
4. CPI	0.3459	-2.7855
5. Inflation rate (CPI)	0.0485	-0.3542

Table VI.8 **The Impact of a Depreciation of the Rupee and Reduction in Tariffs on Manufacturing Imports (Continued)**

Variables	SIMER	SIMTAR
J. Other variables		
1. Food subsidy	-0.9836	-9.3398
2. Fertilizer subsidy	0.6623	-0.1376
3. Budget deficit index	1.8949	-9.5798
4. Fiscal deficit	0.1966	-1.5279
5. Price of mfd products (WPI)	0.4957	-2.5039
6. Terms of trade (PA/PM)	0.2114	2.2043

Note: SIMER= Depreciation of the rupee by Rs 0.5 per USD over the base run; SIMTAR= reduction of tariff rate on imports by 10% over the base run.

Table VI.8a **State Level Impact of Depreciation of the Rupee by Rs 0.5 per USD: Percentage Change in Selected Variables over the Base**

State	Fertilizer	Tractor (purchase)	Tractor stock	General efficiency	Crop yield	Crop output
AP	0.5460	1.9221	0.8513	0.2226	0.4273	0.4481
Assam	0.7336	1.6727	0.4544	0.0418	0.2598	0.2727
Bihar	0.6267	1.9170	0.7459	0.2985	0.5133	0.5294
Gujarat	0.6353	1.7342	0.5345	0.0941	0.2967	0.3127
Haryana	0.4718	1.8700	0.8073	0.1290	0.3132	0.3390
Karnataka	0.7305	1.6670	0.5238	0.1207	0.3393	0.3537
Kerala	0.7966	1.6398	0.5725	0.0941	0.3349	0.3420
MP	0.7968	1.9323	0.8700	0.2062	0.4742	0.4993
Maharashtra	0.8236	1.7819	0.6317	0.1444	0.3938	0.4089
Orissa	0.7001	1.9003	0.6895	0.2242	0.4493	0.4656
Punjab	0.4228	1.8238	0.6800	0.0980	0.2620	0.2845
Rajasthan	0.6109	1.8094	0.6435	0.1072	0.3130	0.3303
Tamilnadu	0.4724	1.5590	0.5874	0.0554	0.2216	0.2363
UP	0.5382	1.9921	0.7707	0.2756	0.4749	0.4982
West Bengal	0.7115	1.9080	0.3999	0.2565	0.4667	0.4867
All	0.5958	1.8639	0.7041	0.1417	0.3843	0.4038

Table VI.8b   State Level Impact of Reduction in Tariffs on Manufacturing Imports by 10%: Percentage Change in Selected Variables over the Base

State	Fertilizer	Tractor (purchase)	Tractor stock	General Efficiency	Crop yield	Crop output
AP	-0.1700	12.4334	3.0840	-0.0315	0.1965	0.2419
Assam	-0.3011	12.6314	1.9316	-0.0058	0.1188	0.1690
Bihar	-0.1958	11.5439	2.5570	-0.0412	0.1451	0.1799
Gujarat	-0.2420	12.6072	2.1801	-0.0123	0.1413	0.1990
Haryana	-0.0166	13.2975	3.2167	-0.0183	0.2433	0.3153
Karnataka	-0.2775	11.1527	1.9894	-0.0165	0.1128	0.1568
Kerala	-0.3355	10.5950	2.0773	-0.0134	0.1145	0.1421
MP	-0.3883	12.3309	3.0351	-0.0281	0.1631	0.2230
Maharashtra	-0.3507	11.5851	2.3013	-0.0195	0.1198	0.1665
Orissa	-0.2499	11.8721	2.4785	-0.0313	0.1383	0.1746
Punjab	-0.0683	13.4793	2.8550	-0.0137	0.2160	0.2884
Rajasthan	-0.2580	13.2091	2.6260	-0.0145	0.1680	0.2288
Tamilnadu	-0.1463	11.3176	2.3908	-0.0077	0.1749	0.2287
UP	-0.1549	12.3471	2.7555	-0.0384	0.1709	0.2161
West Bengal	-0.2798	11.9695	1.4978	-0.0354	0.0637	0.0984
All	-0.1976	12.6861	2.7149	-0.0190	0.1598	0.2095

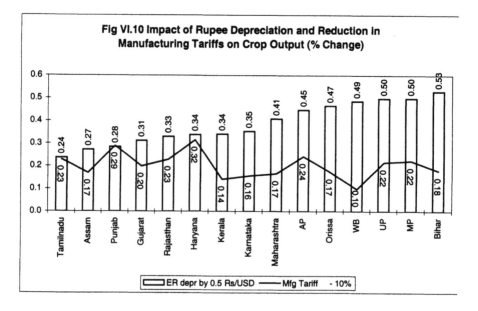

Fig VI.10 Impact of Rupee Depreciation and Reduction in Manufacturing Tariffs on Crop Output (% Change)

VI.3.2b The State Level Results   The state level results are summarized in Table VI.8b. The impact on crop output at the state level is presented in Figure VI.10. The variation in the impact at the state level is related to the differences in the impact on demand for tractors, demand for fertilizers and on general efficiency. Fertilizer demand is projected to decrease the most in percentage terms in MP, Maharashtra and Kerala as these are the states with relatively lower coverage of crop area under irrigation. The states where the decrease in fertilizer consumption is the least are Haryana, Punjab and Tamilnadu where the coverage of crop area under irrigation is relatively high. In the case of fertilizer consumption, irrigated area is negatively related to the elasticity with respect to fertilizer price: higher the irrigation coverage, lower is the price elasticity. Although fertilizer consumption is positively related to irrigation, there is a negative relationship between price response and irrigated area. But in the case of demand for tractors, irrigated area is positively related to demand for tractors and does not influence price elasticity of tractor demand directly. Increase in the purchase of tractors is the steepest in percentage terms in Punjab, Haryana and Rajasthan.

The decline in general efficiency as a result of reduction in crop diversification is greater in the states with already lower levels of efficiency: Bihar, UP and West Bengal. The decline is the least in the case of Assam, Tamilnadu and Gujarat. Crop output increases the most in percentage terms in the states of Haryana, Punjab and AP and the least in the states of West Bengal, Kerala and Karnataka.

VI.3.3 Improved Fiscal Balance

In the previous simulations, the asymmetric impact of exchange rate changes and reduction in the tariff rate for manufacturing sector imports, on the agricultural sector were noted. The asymmetry is noticed within agricultural sector as well. The implications of such a differential impact are important from a policy perspective. Providing adequate safeguards against unintended adverse consequences in terms of food security and inflation would require consideration of the impact of macro level policies at the sectoral level. Besides the exchange rate variations and trade policy changes, the policies at the macro level that are often implemented relate to expenditure policies. In the context of reducing fiscal deficit to provide greater macro economic stability, reduction in government expenditure (or its growth) is a major option. Reduction in subsidies, interest payments on public debt, expenditure on public administration are alternative options in reducing expenditures. Reduction in government expenditure may have a demand effect in the sense that it reduces aggregate demand. There may also be such government expenditures whose reduction would not entail reduction in aggregate demand as such functions can be transferred to the private sector.

Reduction in government expenditure that reduces fiscal and budgetary deficit has the effect of reducing inflationary pressures in the economy. The impact of such a deflationary pressure, however, may not be uniform across the sectors, particularly when there are significant sector specific subsidy and price policies. In the estimated price equations for crop groups of rice and wheat, other food grains and non food grains, the differences in the response of price to the macro level factors such as exchange rate variations and money supply were captured. The exchange rate variations affected the price of non-food grains directly and affected other crop prices only indirectly. Money supply relative to overall real GDP appears as an explanatory variable only in the case of non-food grain crops among the three crop groups considered. The indirect effects on crop prices can be reflected through the input prices, which respond to deflationary pressures as manufactured products.

Two simulations were carried out using the model developed in the present study to assess the impact of improvement in fiscal balance achieved by reducing government expenditures. In SIMFISC1, government expenditure is reduced by 10% without affecting aggregate demand. In SIMFISC2, the real expenditure on public administration and defense is reduced by 10%. The second of the two simulations has a direct effect on aggregate demand as it reduces real *GDP* by curtailing expenditure on public administration. Table VI.9 provides the estimates of the impact at the national level and the state level impact is summarized in Tables VI.9a and VI.9b.

VI.3.3a National Level Results   Reduction in expenditure without affecting aggregate demand results in a reduction in the price level of all the crop groups, with the non-food grain crops registering the steepest decline. Price of 'other food grains' decreases by a smaller percentage than the price decline in rice and wheat. Price of manufactured products decreases by 6.06% as compared to the decline in the crop prices by 1.03%. Thus, the fiscal contraction results in improved terms of trade for agriculture. This general result holds in the case of SIMFISC2 as well. Crop prices decline by a smaller percentage than the manufactured product price.

There are some important differences in the results of two simulations. First, under SIMFISC2, output of food grains decreases unlike the case of the first simulation. The non-food grain output increases under SIMFISC2, thus resulting in a higher ratio of non-food grain to food grain output. The results vary so sharply with respect to output mix because of the differences in the price response to changes in overall demand. If real *GDP* declines, then the demand for rice and wheat would also decline resulting in lower prices. Although price of non food grain crops also decreases due to the drop in overall demand, the price response is smaller than in the case of rice and wheat. As the price of rice and wheat decreases, distribution through PDS would also be lower. Although export of rice is higher, procurement of rice and wheat is also greater and hence there is an increase in the food grain stock with the government. The procurement price is projected to decrease as a result of lower manufactured product price and higher level of food grain stock with the government. The lower procurement price also reduces the price of 'other food grains'.

The net impact on the prices of different crop group depends on whether the expenditure reduction results in a decline in aggregate real demand or not. The decline in the price of food grain crops relative to non food grain crops, leads to an increase in the ratio of output of non food grains to food grain output. The general result is that the price of food grains is more sensitive to overall demand conditions than in the case of non-food grain crops. The implicit higher sensitivity of price with respect to income for food grains reflects the access to PDS when purchasing power of the consumer declines: consumers shift to PDS from the market resulting in greater downward pressure on price.

Table VI.9   The Impact of Reduction in Government Expenditures

Variables		SIMGEXP1	SIMGEXP2
I.	Agriculture Related		
A.	Gross Output		
	1. Rice and wheat	1.0173	-0.2945
	2. Other food grain	0.4570	-0.1462
	3. Total food grain	0.7731	-0.2288
	4. Non-food grain	0.0081	0.4306
	5. Total crop	0.4552	0.0452
B.	Crop GDP	0.3769	0.0364
C.	Prices		
	1. Rice and wheat	-0.5677	-2.2680
	2. Other food grain	-0.4230	-0.9694
	3. Food grain	-0.5315	-1.9434
	4. Non-food grain	-1.2594	-1.0439
	5. All crops	-1.0272	-1.3276
D.	Inputs		
	1. Fertilizer	-0.7910	-1.2465
	2. Tractor purchases	36.3384	8.8549
	3. Irrigated area	0.5415	0.1442
	4. Gross crop area	0.0607	0.0164
E.	Productivity		
	1. Crop yield per ha	0.3373	0.0076
	2. General efficiency	-0.0989	0.0883
F.	Trade		
	1. Crop exports	1.3611	6.3223
	2. Crop imports	-0.4062	-2.8397
	3. Total CAD index	-8.8012	-11.4226
G.	Government operations		
	1. Procurement	0.6917	1.4723
	2. Distribution (PDS)	-0.2704	-0.7792
	3. Stocks	0.9731	5.7612
	4. Procurement price	-0.1668	-1.4234
H.	Manufacturing		
	1. ASI value added (real)	1.3499	0.4265
	2. ASI GFCF (real)	-0.0456	-0.0162
	3. ASI employment	2.1762	0.7526
	4. General efficiency	0.4431	0.1153
I.	Macro variables		
	1. Overall GDP (real)	0.5546	-1.3677
	2. M3	-18.3879	-10.2943
	3. WPI	-4.2103	-2.1273
	4. CPI	-9.0333	-4.1949
	5. Inflation rate (CPI)	-1.0280	-0.3755

Table VI.9   The Impact of Reduction in Government Expenditures
(Continued)

Variables	SIMGEXP1	SIMGEXP2
J. Other variables		
1. Food subsidy	-28.0373	-17.4730
2. Fertilizer subsidy	-0.5904	-1.0485
3. Budget deficit index	-142.3404	-88.4146
4. Fiscal deficit	-15.7729	-9.9527
5. Price of mfd products (WPI)	-6.0554	-2.7472
6. Terms of trade (PA/PM)	5.0282	1.4196

Note: SIMGEXP1= reduction in central government expenditures by 10% without affecting the aggregate demand; SIMGEXP2= reduction in central government expenditure by 10% with a corresponding effect on aggregate demand.

Table VI.9a   State Level Impact of Reduction in Government Expenditure by 10%
without Affecting Aggregate Demand: Percentage Change in Selected
Variables over the Base

State	Fertilizer	Tractor (purchase)	Tractor stock	General efficiency	Crop yield	Crop output
AP	-0.7004	35.6237	9.2328	-0.1614	0.4268	0.5340
Assam	-1.1042	36.0668	5.7466	-0.0301	0.2615	0.3832
Bihar	-0.7931	32.9942	7.6285	-0.2123	0.2552	0.3356
Gujarat	-0.9214	36.0324	6.4976	-0.0646	0.3131	0.4528
Haryana	-0.2858	38.1965	9.6183	-0.0939	0.5876	0.7638
Karnataka	-1.0198	31.9229	5.9443	-0.0854	0.2234	0.3276
Kerala	-1.2168	30.4088	6.2334	-0.0687	0.2316	0.2959
MP	-1.3687	35.2186	9.0756	-0.1455	0.3260	0.4667
Maharashtra	-1.2498	33.1327	6.8796	-0.1014	0.2292	0.3394
Orissa	-0.9451	33.9672	7.4024	-0.1610	0.2588	0.3435
Punjab	-0.4034	38.6807	8.5214	-0.0705	0.5256	0.7039
Rajasthan	-0.9574	37.7483	7.8304	-0.0754	0.3825	0.5297
Tamilnadu	-0.6073	32.5203	7.1588	-0.0397	0.4295	0.5622
UP	-0.6721	35.3426	8.2250	-0.1975	0.3368	0.4419
West Bengal	-1.0411	34.0899	4.4404	-0.1823	0.0385	0.1163
All	-0.7910	36.3384	8.1061	-0.0989	0.3373	0.4552

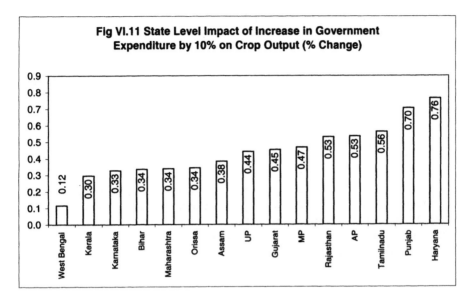

Fig VI.11 State Level Impact of Increase in Government Expenditure by 10% on Crop Output (% Change)

Table VI.9b **State Level Impact of Reduction in Government Expenditure by 10% with Corresponding Reduction in Aggregate Demand: Percentage Change in Selected Variables over the Base**

State	Fertilizer	Tractor (purchase)	Tractor stock	General efficiency	Crop yield	Crop output
AP	-1.1427	8.7720	2.5129	0.1460	0.1047	0.1421
Assam	-1.5447	8.5575	1.5001	0.0270	-0.1679	-0.1441
Bihar	-1.2700	8.1762	2.0776	0.1913	0.0914	0.1196
Gujarat	-1.3604	8.6510	1.7219	0.0574	-0.0802	-0.0454
Haryana	-0.8752	9.2739	2.5904	0.0847	0.1007	0.1560
Karnataka	-1.4424	7.7322	1.5812	0.0765	-0.1038	-0.0757
Kerala	-1.6763	7.3471	1.6520	0.0620	-0.1512	-0.1324
MP	-1.7898	8.5384	2.4241	0.1304	-0.0324	0.0133
Maharashtra	-1.6806	8.0061	1.8258	0.0907	-0.1159	-0.0852
Orissa	-1.3910	8.3463	1.9973	0.1452	0.0089	0.0363
Punjab	-0.8837	9.3702	2.2861	0.0632	0.0553	0.1067
Rajasthan	-1.3593	9.0771	2.0807	0.0674	-0.0429	-0.0035
Tamilnadu	-1.0010	7.8853	1.9174	0.0356	-0.0279	0.0051
UP	-1.1533	8.7657	2.2472	0.1784	0.1216	0.1625
West Bengal	-1.4878	8.3735	1.1906	0.1640	-0.0378	-0.0097
All	-1.2465	8.8549	2.1808	0.0883	0.0076	0.0452

The improved terms of trade for agriculture results in higher investments in developing irrigation facilities: irrigated area increases by 0.54% in SIMFISC1 and by 0.14% in SIMFISC2. Higher irrigated area results in the changes in input use and output mix as discussed in the previous simulations: increase in the demand for tractors and change in crop mix so that the proportion of rice and wheat in food grain and the ratio of food grain to non food grain output increases. The increase in the purchase of (demand for) tractors is substantial (36.33%) under SIMFISC1 given the sharp decline in manufactured product prices and the rise in irrigated area. Fertilizer consumption declines in both the simulations, as fertilizer price remains unchanged while crop prices decrease.

VI.3.3b State Level Results   The state level results vary between the two simulations with respect to the impact on general efficiency, crop yield and crop output. Under SIMFISC1 (Table VI.9a), general efficiency decreases for all the states as the ratio of food grain to non-food grain output increases. Crop yield and crop output increase for all the states as purchase of tractors increases significantly, driven by the fall in the relative price of tractors and the increase in irrigated area. The variation in impact across states is shown in Figure VI.11.

Under SIMFISC2 (Table VI.9b) the general efficiency increases in all the cases since the ratio of non-food grain to food grain output increases. However, the net impact on crop yield and crop output, of lower fertilizer consumption and higher efficiency is mixed across the states. Crop yield and output decline relative to the base run in Assam, Gujarat, Karnataka, Kerala, Maharashtra, Rajasthan and West Bengal. In MP and Tamilnadu, crop yield decreases relative to the base run but crop output increases due to the increase in crop area. The decline in crop yield is on account of lower fertilizer consumption as well as lower proportion of rice and wheat in the food grain output. In the remaining states of AP, Bihar, Haryana, Orissa and UP, crop yield as well as crop output increase due to the rise in efficiency partly from the 'crop diversification effect'.

The state wise results vary significantly between the two simulations due to the differential response of input use to price changes depending on production conditions such as irrigation and initial level of efficiency. Thus, even when output response to input use may not vary across the states, input use may vary due to the production conditions. The macro level policies influence not only crop output composition in terms of crops but also composition of output in terms of states.

VI.4 Lessons from Model Simulations

The alternative simulations of the model reflecting elements of diverse set of policies provide some important insights into the implications for policies towards agriculture. Policies were grouped into two main categories of (1) those affecting agriculture directly and (2) those affecting agriculture indirectly. The results point to the potential for raising agricultural output through alternative policy measures and the likely impact on a number of other variables relating to agriculture and other sectors in the economy. The results also point to the variation in the responses of different states to policy changes at the macro level or at the sector level. We summarize below the main results in terms of their implications for policies to accelerate and sustain agricultural growth.

VI.4.1 Inputs and Agricultural Growth

Growth in the use of yield enhancing inputs such as irrigation, fertilizers and machinery has been the major source of growth of agricultural output in India. Technical progress in the form of development and adoption of high yielding varieties of crops, has enabled intensive cultivation of land and led to the relaxation of the land constraint on crop production. Growth in the use of inputs has been facilitated from interventions of the government in terms of input subsidies, expansion of input supply outlets, expenditures on the development and promotion of agricultural technologies. The fiscal constraints on sustaining some of these expenditures have been reflected in the slowing down of government investment in agriculture in real terms and attempts to reduce input subsidies. Both the reduced government investment in agriculture and reduction in input subsidies would have an adverse impact on agricultural output unless the adverse effects are offset through some other measures.

The impact of public investment in agriculture is brought out by one of the simulations where public investment in irrigation is increased by 10%. A 10% increase in public investment results in an increased crop output of 0.23% when crop prices adjust downward due to the higher output. The impact of lower crop prices is, however, not significant as indicated by an alternative scenario where crop prices do not adjust when output increases. Conversely, when public investment in agriculture decreases, crop output would decrease by 0.24% if crop prices do not increase and by a marginally lower 0.23% if crop prices do increase. Gross irrigated are decreases by about 0.67% (in the simulation increases), indicating that the private investment in irrigation does not offset the decline in public investment due to the impact of higher crop prices alone.

The increase in fertilizer price paid by the farmers by 10% is estimated to result in a reduction of fertilizer consumption by 8.27% and crop output by 2.41%. Although crop prices increase by 1.53%, effecting an increase in the purchase of tractors irrigated area decreases. Thus, again, the rise in fertilizer price reduces fertilizer subsidy but also leads to a decline in fertilizer use and crop output. Although crop output prices increase by 2.67%, the rise is not enough to maintain fertilizer consumption or increase irrigated area.

The attempts to reduce fiscal pressures by reducing public investment in agriculture and increasing fertilizer prices paid by the farmers, therefore, need to be balanced by other policies in order to sustain growth of agriculture.

VI.4.2 Efficiency in Agricultural Production

Variations in crop output across the producing units, either the individual farms or geographical units are not fully explained by the variations in the level of inputs used and agro-climatic factors. The aggregate crop yield function estimated in this study does not indicate significant variations in production response across states to applications of fertilizer, irrigation or mechanization (implied by the use of tractors) but indicates significant variation in crop yield after allowing for differences in the levels of inputs used. In other words, crop yield or output may differ across the states for the same level of inputs due to the difference in the efficiency of the producers in utilizing inputs for production. If efficiency could be influenced by policies, then not merely subsidizing inputs or direct investments by the government but improving production efficiencies can also influence crop output.

Crop production efficiency is estimated as a function of rural literacy rate, physical infrastructure and an indicator of crop mix at the state level. Literacy rate signifies the level of farmers as managers to absorb new information relating to crop production as well as their ability to participate in other production opportunities in the off-farm sectors in rural area. A developed physical infrastructure in the region is more likely to give the producers more efficient access to inputs and markets, than a poorly developed infrastructure. In the present study, per capita real output (value added) from transportation, communication and storage is taken as an indicator of the level of development of infrastructure. Both literacy and infrastructure, therefore, have a positive impact on crop output. Although improvements in both require investments either by the government or the private sectors, these are not programs with an impact on agriculture alone. There are likely to be significant spill over effects.

Increase in rural literacy is estimated to result in an increase in crop output by 0.64% and increase in per capita real NSDP from transportation, storage and communication is estimated to increase crop output by 0.31%. Increasing agricultural growth, therefore, is possible not merely by raising the level of input use but considerable potential exists to raise agricultural output by improving production efficiency.

VI.4.3 Supply Response of Agriculture

The role of crop output prices in increasing agricultural output has been debated in the development literature extensively. More recent studies point to the impact of higher agricultural prices on investment in agriculture and the subsequent effects on agricultural growth. While higher agricultural prices induce higher output, they also have an adverse effect on consumption. In the simulations on improvements in rural literacy and infrastructure, higher crop output was accompanied by a reduction in crop prices. The impact of initial increase in crop output prices on crop output may be reduced by lower consumption demand subsequently unless there are other sources of demand for the increased output.

Subsidized Public Distribution System props up consumption in the face of higher crop prices for selected crops. This is particularly so when higher crop prices result from increased support prices for agricultural products. However, the restrictions on agricultural trade which result in an implicit tax on agricultural output point to another source of improved price for agricultural output without the accompanying decline in consumption demand when trade restrictions are lowered. While domestic consumption demand may decrease as crop prices rise, export demand for agricultural output would absorb the increased output. In the simulation where crop prices increase by 5%, real gross crop output increases by 1.84%. The crop yield increases by 1.66% as consumption of fertilizers, demand for tractors, gross irrigated area and gross crop area increase relative to their levels in the base run scenario. The estimated increase in crop output (1.84%) implies relatively low supply response to the price rise of 5%. Therefore, the impact of lowering trade restrictions on agricultural output would depend on the extent of dis-protection afforded to agriculture in the present trade regime.

The estimated rise in agricultural output is based on the constant input prices-- input prices do not change although crop prices change. In the case of fertilizers this also implies a rise in subsidies as fertilizer consumption increases but per unit subsidy remains the same.

VI.4.4 Macro Level Policies, Inter-sectoral Linkages and Agriculture

Macroeconomic policies such as those relating to exchange rate and fiscal balance influence different sectors in the economy differently depending on the flexibility for adjustment at the sector level. The flexibility of the sector is reflected in the variation in its price response to the overall shock. The differential impact on prices across sectors leads to the 'terms of trade' effect that influences the use of inputs in agriculture supplied by the manufacturing sector. As price of agricultural output varies relative to the price of manufactured products, input use in agriculture is affected. Improvement in the terms of trade, thus, implies more intensive use of inputs and hence larger agricultural output. Inter-sectoral linkages therefore, influence the transmission of changes in macro economic parameters to the sectoral level.

Results of the present study show that depreciation of the rupee is likely to benefit agriculture relative to manufacturing as crop exports respond to the rise in export price and non-food grain prices respond relatively more than the food grain prices. As the price of one of the key inputs, namely Fertilizer, remains fixed, higher crop prices result in more intensive use of inputs. In the case of manufacturing sector, depreciation implies higher input prices along with higher exports. The higher prices of manufactured products affect consumption demand adversely. However, the rise in manufactured products stimulates fixed investment leading to a marginal increase in the output of the manufacturing sector. Thus, while both agricultural and manufacturing outputs increase, the rise in agricultural output is relatively greater than in the case of manufacturing.

Reduction in government expenditures also appears to have a differential impact at the sector level. Lower government expenditure which translates into lower budgetary deficit with or without affecting aggregate demand, leads to an increase in the output of both agricultural and manufacturing output. In the case of agriculture, lower budget deficit translates into higher output from the terms of trade effect: the fall in manufacturing prices is greater than the fall in crop output price. Although fertilizer prices do not decrease, tractor prices decrease since they are linked to manufactured product prices. Irrigated area increases as the price of manufactured products decline relative to crop prices. The impact on manufacturing output is greater as the decline in the price of manufactured product price leads to a rise in consumption demand. The rise in demand leads to an increase in employment. Fixed investment decreases as the rise in consumption demand is accompanied by lower price of manufactured products.

Reduction in the tariff rate for the imports of manufactured products results in a decrease in the domestic price of manufactured products. Reduction in the price of manufactured products implies lower price of inputs in agriculture that are produced in the manufacturing sector. As agricultural prices are unaffected, improved terms of trade lead to an increase in the use of inputs in agriculture and hence an increase in output.

VI.4.5 Crop Output Composition

Crop output composition is of policy relevance due to the issue of food security. How would different policies affect the composition of output? In the present study an attempt has been made to differentiate crop output in terms of three groups: rice and wheat, other food grains and non- food grains. There are two basic mechanisms by which the crop output composition is influenced in the present model: (1) by the difference in the response of prices of different crop groups to various shocks and the subsequent response of output ratios to price changes; and (2) the response of crop output composition to changes in the production conditions reflected in access to irrigation.

The impact of policy changes on the output of various crop groups is summarized in Table VI.10.

The pattern resulting from alternative policy changes is a complex one given the role of regional variations in output response and the variation in the price response of crops to output changes which in turn influence crop- mix. The ratio of rice and wheat increases relative to other food grains in all the simulations except in the case when there is an improvement only in physical infrastructure, there is an increase in fertilizer price and there is a reduction in government expenditure with a corresponding reduction in aggregate demand. The ratio of food grain output to non food grain output decreases in a number of cases both when total crop output increases and when it decreases.

The relative changes in output growth are a function of a number of factors. At the regional or state level, change in the relative price of crop groups is a critical determinant of crop mix. However, changes in irrigated area can also have a direct influence on crop mix apart from the influence induced through price changes. At the aggregate or national level, the regional variations in output response to other factors assume a significant role.

Some broad conclusions that can be drawn are, if the policy change begins with an increase of aggregate output, then the resulting price decline is the sharpest in the case of 'other food grains', followed by rice and wheat and non- food grains. This indicates the pattern of implicit price elasticity of demand: elasticity being greater for non food grains, followed by rice and wheat, and other grains. This in turn increases the proportion of rice and wheat in food grains and the ratio of non-food grain to food grain, when there is an increase in output. If there is an initial decrease in output, then the subsequent price changes imply that the decrease in output would be the lowest in the case of other food grain, followed by rice and wheat and non-food grains. The ratio of rice and wheat output to other food grain would decline and the ratio of food grain output to non-food grains would also decline, assuming that rice and wheat output dominates the food grain output. The results are opposite of the results for an increased crop output. However, these results are modified by the state level variations in the initial output response to policy changes.

Table VI.10   Summary of the Impact of Policy Changes on the Output of Crops

Pattern of growth rates		g(RWQ) > g(OFGQ)		g(RWQ) < g(OFGQ)
g(FGQ) > g(NFGQ)	1.	Increase in agricultural	1.	Improvement in prices by 5% physical infrastructure by 10%
	2.	Increase in public investment in agriculture by 10% without price effects	2.	Increase in fertilizer price by 10%
	3.	Reduction in tariffs on manufacturing imports		
	4.	Reduction in government expenditure without affecting aggregate demand		
g(FGQ) < g(NFGQ)	5.	Increase in rural literacy by 10%	3.	Reduction in government expenditure combined with a corresponding reduction in aggregate demand.
	6.	Increase in rural literacy and physical infrastructure by 10%		
	7.	Depreciation of the rupee		
	8.	Increase in public investment in agriculture by 10% with price effects on output		

Note: g(RWQ) = growth rate of rice and wheat output; g(OFGQ) = growth rate of output of other food grains; g(FGQ)= growth rate of food grain output; and g(NFGQ)= growth rate of non-food grain output. All the growth rates are over the base run of the model.

When policy changes influence crop prices first, then the resulting pattern of output depends on how the prices are affected. That is, for instance, when there is exchange rate depreciation, the prices of non-food grain are affected more than others; when there is a contraction of government expenditures (without the cut in aggregate demand), non-food grain prices respond to money supply more than the other crop prices.

Any generalization of the impact of policy changes on the crop mix is difficult. For some specific policies, the model results indicate that (1) a depreciation of the exchange rate increases the ratio of non-food grains to food grain output while both the outputs increase, (2) an increase in fertilizer price increases the ratio of food grain to non-food grain output while both the outputs decreases, (3) for a cut in tariffs on manufacturing imports, the ratio of food grain output to non-food grains increases and (4) for a uniform rise in all the crop prices, the ratio of food grain to non-food grain output increases. In the other cases, the results are affected by the combination of related policies.

VI.4.6 Government Operations in Food Grains

The government operations in the food grain sector to provide support prices to the farmers and subsidized food grains to selected consumer groups are affected by specific policy choices relating to agriculture. For instance, policies that result in a reduction in the prices of rice and wheat may decrease the demand for food grains distributed through the PDS. But the policies that increase food grain prices, increase the demand for food grains sold through PDS. When the prices increase, it is not the support price mechanism that is relevant but the coverage of PDS. In the various simulations carried out in this study, the demand for PDS sales is projected to decrease when (1) there is improvement in production efficiency, (2) increased public investment in agriculture, (3) tariff on manufacturing imports are reduced and (4) fiscal deficit is reduced by decreasing government expenditure. In the first three cases, there is an increase in food grain output and a decrease in their price, but in the last case, food grain output as well as price decrease when aggregate demand is reduced. The demand for PDS sales is projected to increase when (1) fertilizer price is increased, (2) exchange rate is depreciated and (3) agricultural prices increase. In all these three cases, price of food grain increases. The decline in demand for PDS sales when there is a decrease in the food grain price suggests increased access to the supply in the market relative to PDS. However, the result that demand for PDS sales declines when output is lower (as in the case of reduced government expenditure and aggregate demand) should be viewed with caution. The drop in PDS demand results from the decline in the market price of food grains due to the decrease in aggregate demand. The implicit scenario is that there is a decline in the demand for food grains as a whole. The demand can not fall below the nutritional requirements, a condition not incorporated in the model. To this extent, the result for PDS demand when there is a general decline in demand does not hold, especially if the PDS caters to low income households. Judging the demand for PDS, therefore, should be based on the impact of policies not only on food grain price but also on food grain availability. There is a need to strengthen PDS in all the cases where there is a likely increase in food grain prices or a decline in the supply of food grains.

VI.4.7 The Regional Dimensions of Policy Impact

Regional variations in the response of agricultural output arise due to differences in production conditions. Two channels through which crop output is influenced is the level of input application and the efficiency with which inputs are utilized. While production response to input use has been found to differ little across states, there is significant variation in the efficiency in production among the states. Efficiency is estimated to vary across the states in response to changes in the levels of rural literacy, physical infrastructure, structure of production in the state and composition of crop output. Changes in these factors affect production efficiency in each state depending upon their existing levels and hence produce variation in the state's response to policy changes. Secondly, while production response to input use does not vary across states, demand for inputs is estimated to vary and result in variations in output response to policy changes. The net result of different factors provides an assessment of the impact of the policies on different states.

Improvement in efficiency resulting from improvements in rural literacy are estimated to be influenced by initial levels of literacy as well as physical infrastructure. The states with higher literacy and better infrastructure benefit relatively more from the same percentage change in rural literacy. However, the impact is greater in states with initially lower level of efficiency as the potential for improvement decreases as efficiency increases. In this sense, the states with developed infrastructure and higher levels of rural literacy will benefit relatively more from a uniform development policy all across the country. The impact in the states with initially poor infrastructure and other development indicators is likely to be more gradual. Thus, from among Bihar, MP and Rajasthan, the states with lowest rates of literacy only MP ranks among the three states where efficiency increases the most when rural literacy is increased by 10% in all the states. Relatively low initial level of efficiency makes it more sensitive to the change in the rate of rural literacy. States of Orissa, Bihar and West Bengal, with the least developed infrastructure, the impact of improvement in infrastructure by 10% is among the lowest.

The impact of increase in fertilizer price is estimated to affect fertilizer consumption relatively more in those states where the coverage of crop area under irrigation is less. Thus, the percentage decrease in fertilizer consumption is the greatest in MP, Maharashtra and West Bengal and it is the lowest in the states of Punjab, Haryana and Tamilnadu. The lower sensitivity of fertilizer use with respect to fertilizer price is related to higher levels of fertilizer use per hectare in states with relatively more crop area under irrigation.

When there is an increase in the proportion of non-food grain output relative to the output of food grains, there is an increase in efficiency in the sense that output per hectare is greater from the non food grain crops. Thus, the policies which influence the composition of output mix produce variable impact at the state level in terms of efficiency, crop yield and crop output. When exchange rate depreciates, efficiency increases the most in Bihar, UP and West Bengal. Although the ratio of food grain to non-food grain output changes at the same rate in all the states, the impact is greater in the states where initial level of efficiency is lower. The impact is less in the states of Assam, Tamilnadu, Kerala and Gujarat where the initial levels of efficiency are higher. A similar pattern emerges when the policy changes influence crop output mainly by inducing changes in crop-mix. A change in the relative price of crops, therefore, will result in a greater change in total output in the states with relatively lower levels of efficiency.

Chapter VII

Summary and Conclusions

The importance of agricultural sector in the Indian economy is evident from the fact that 25% of economy's output originates from this sector and about 65% of the labour force of the economy continues to be employed there. Agriculture's fortunes are also important due to the fact that bulk of India's poor are in the villages and improvement in agricultural growth can have a significant impact on rural poor. There is a further dimension to the issue: agriculture is the predominant source of income in regions that are at the bottom of per capita economic output. Economic reforms that are aimed at improving the efficiency of the economy as a whole, therefore, can not ignore the relevant policy changes necessary to improve the performance of agricultural sector in terms of output, productivity and income derived from agriculture.

Growth of agricultural sector has lagged behind the pace of growth of non-agricultural sectors throughout the past nearly five decades. While industrialization remained the focus of development effort, the investments needed to enable agricultural growth in the development of institutions and systems for the supply of credit, irrigation, marketing and new technology were also part of the overall plan strategy. Initial phases of agricultural policy also involved attempts at reforming system of land tenure by protecting the rights of the cultivator of the land. Economic policies towards agriculture have been fashioned by the need to obtain self sufficiency in the food sector with imports being used only as a last resort given the chronic deficit experienced by India on the external account.

As a result, Indian agriculture has grown steadily at rates above the rate of growth of population, leading to self-sufficiency in meeting the basic needs of food requirement. Expansion of crop area under cultivation provided the major source of output growth in the initial two decades of planned development. Irrigation and mechanization helped raise intensity of cultivation of cropland. Technological changes, particularly the green revolution of the late 1960s and early 1970s, opened up the potential for raising crop output per hectare through intensive use of land along with fertilizers. Recent studies have shown that the overall policy framework resulted in an incentive structure that reduced returns to agriculture, relative to the case if there were no government interventions in the markets. The industrial sector was provided protection through trade policy and exchange rate policy. This in turn has led to the need for government investments in agriculture and continued input subsidies to sustain the growth of input use essential for the output growth. These measures alone were not adequate to ensure food security necessitating price support operations. The higher agricultural output prices, in turn led to consumer subsidies, in the sense that the cost of food grain purchase and marketing by the government agencies were not met by the returns from their sale through the Public Distribution System.

In the 1980s, the price of crop output increased steadily relative to the price of inputs. The investment in fixed capital stock by the private sector accelerated during this period, while the public investment stagnated or declined. The slower rise in input prices was a reflection of growing input subsidies and the decline in real public sector investment in agriculture reflected the fiscal pressures generated by the rising current government expenditures which included subsidies. The agricultural sector, thus, has been subject to policies with conflicting objectives: the need to achieve higher output growth but without the higher output prices that may be required to induce the growth. The strategy may have reached a point where it is not sustainable.

Performance of agricultural sector is also influenced by macro economic policies. The rising fiscal deficit can bring about macroeconomic instability and in turn lead to cuts in expenditure affecting agriculture. The need to contain inflationary pressures resulting from expansionary fiscal policy may also affect agriculture through the impact on credit availability, input prices and demand for the output. Exchange rate variations influence agriculture through their impact on prices. The impact of macro economic policies may differ across sectors depending upon the relative flexibility of the respective prices and the type of government interventions in different sectors. For instance, price support mechanisms in agricultural commodities may limit the adjustments in agricultural prices when contractionary macro policies are undertaken. A uniform reduction in government investment expenditure would affect different sectors differently depending upon the share of government investment in different sectors. The differences in the rates of adjustment in prices and output in turn lead to changes that may accentuate or narrow the inter-sectoral differences in the impact. A key mechanism of the indirect effects is the 'terms of trade' variable or the ratio of inter-sectoral prices that influences resource allocation decisions of the producers. Thus, differences in the adjustment in the prices of agriculture and manufacturing, for instance, would alter the terms of trade and affect investment and hence output. The differential impact of exchange rate on agricultural and manufacturing prices, influence terms of trade and hence affect agricultural output.

Indian agriculture has an important regional dimension. Across the country, agro-climatic conditions as well as the level of development of the economy differentiate the states. Agricultural productivity, measured in terms of output per hectare varies with the extent of adoption of modern inputs of high yielding seed, fertilizer and machinery. Output also varies due to access to irrigation and markets. The pace of agricultural growth over time has also varied significantly over time, and there is some evidence that growth rates have a tendency to converge. This convergence, however, does not imply convergence of levels of land productivity. Access to irrigation increases the options for raising productivity per unit of land and hence, the variation across states in terms of land productivity is likely to be determined by the extent of development of irrigation in the states.

Besides the intensity of application of inputs per unit of land, agricultural productivity per hectare of crop area is also determined by the variation in the technical efficiency with which inputs are used. Alternatively, besides the broad agro- climatic factors, which influence productivity per hectare, farm level and farmer characteristics also have an impact on agricultural productivity. Input application is governed by the relative prices of inputs and output, choice of technology, and physical and marketing infrastructure and the efficiency of application is dependent on knowledge, experience and incentives of the producer. The range of factors that influence productivity provides the basis for policy interventions to promote performance of the agricultural sector. The roles of price and non-price factors have been distinguished in agricultural policies in the past. While the discussion on reforms has focussed on prices and incentives so far, the role of efficiency in growth needs to be examined.

The methodological innovation of this study is the formulation and application of the disequilibrium macroeconometric modelling for policy analysis. The disequilibrium approach through the frontier production function (FPF) modelling provides an analytical framework that provides the role for both price and non-price factors in the production process, including the effect of efficiency on output. When applied at the regional level, the framework provides for incorporation of regional variations in the production conditions. In this study, we have developed a varying coefficients frontier production function framework for modelling agricultural production using state level data. In the case of manufacturing sector, the FPF approach is used to model production using the national level data. The details of production in agriculture and manufacturing are embedded in a macro econometric model. The macro econometric model, thus, provides a framework for analyzing the impact of alternative macro economic policies on agriculture besides the analysis of sector specific policies.

The macro econometric model, incorporating the FPF approach to modeling agricultural and manufacturing production, has been used to simulate the impact of alternative policy scenarios on agriculture. The model also permits estimation of the effect of the policy changes on the aggregates of national income and overall prices, as the output and prices of all the sectors are also specified in the model. The key conclusions that emerge from the alternative simulations are summarized below.

1. Development of human capital resources and physical infrastructure has a significant impact on productivity in agriculture. The two factors are complementary to each other in the sense that they enhance the effect of each other: the impact of rural literacy is greater when physical infrastructure is more developed and the impact of infrastructure is greater when the rural population is more literate. The impact of increased rural literacy is greater when the initial level of literacy is higher. In other words, the gains from rural literacy accelerate as rural literacy begins to rise. The same result holds in the case of infrastructure also. Therefore, sustained improvements in human capital development and infrastructure development would continue to provide benefits in terms of higher efficiency.

2. A 10% increase in rural literacy results in 0.61% increase in crop output and 0.26% in overall real *GDP*. A 10% increase in per capita Net State Domestic Product (*NSDP*) from transportation, storage and communication (*TSC*) results in 0.31% in crop output and 0.13% increase in overall real *GDP*. It may be noted that in 1991, the average rate of rural literacy was just over 50% and in a number of states; the rate of rural literacy was well below 50% indicating considerable potential for gains from improvements in rural literacy. In the case of infrastructure, represented by per capita *NSDP* from *TSC*, the difference across the states is large: the ratio of the largest to lowest in 1991 was over a factor of 7. Hence improvement in physical infratsructure could become a major source of efficiency gains in agriculture.

3. Improvements in efficiency in agricultural production result in output gains in the other sectors of the economy as well, mainly due to lower rate of inflation. Improvements in rural literacy and infrastructure would require expenditures either by the government or the private sector. The impact of such additional expenditures is not captured in the simulations presented in this study. Incorporating the cost of providing additional resources to literacy programs and infrastructure development would reduce the projected decline in inflation rate.

4. The impact of policies affecting production efficiency is greater in regions with relatively lower levels of efficiency. As efficiency level increases, the potential for further improvement decreases and hence at lower levels of efficiency, the gains are higher. In the three-year period 1990-92, the general efficiency of production in agriculture was the least in Bihar, MP and Maharashtra. Orissa, UP and West Bengal formed the next three states in terms of efficiency level. Thus, some of the states with low productivity and income can benefit from efficiency improvement.

5. The impact of increasing rural literacy by 10% on general efficiency is the highest in Maharashtra, MP, Haryana and Gujarat. The impact is the least in the states of Assam, Bihar and West Bengal. The explanation for the pattern is a mixture of factors influencing the impact of rural literacy on efficiency: initial levels of literacy and infrastructure and initial level of efficiency itself. The results show that while there is a positive impact of improvement in literacy and infrastructure on efficiency and hence output the degree of impact varies from one state to another. Hence, greater efforts will have to be made in states where the current levels of literacy and infrastructure are low in order to get the same degree of benefit as the states with higher levels of literacy and infrastructure.

6. Agricultural output is estimated to increase by 1.6% for an increase in crop prices by 5%. The rise in output is contributed by increase in input use: irrigated area, fertilizers and tractors. The crop mix effect, captured as a part of general efficiency, is negative as the ratio of non-food grain to food grain output decreases. The rise in crop output price relative to other prices, leads to higher private investment in agriculture leading to increased irrigated area. Irrigation shifts cropping pattern in favour of rice and wheat from other crops, given the availability of high yielding varieties of rice and wheat that perform better than the other crops. Thus, even though all crop prices increase by the same proportion,

changes in crop mix may emerge due to the differences in crop output to investments in agriculture.

7. Higher agricultural output may not imply positive impact on the output of non-agricultural sectors, as it is accompanied by higher price level. The higher agricultural prices result in higher level of inflation rate with adverse effects on manufacturing output. The input supplying industries, however, benefit as demand for fertilizers and tractors increases with the increase in crop output prices. The model results do not capture the effect of higher agricultural income on the demand for non-agricultural output. But the results also do not account for the decline in the real income of the recipients of non-agricultural income with an increase in the general price level.

8. Irrigation has been a key element of various strategies to increase agricultural output. An increase in irrigated are by 0.68% is estimated to increase crop output by 0.29%, if agricultural prices do not decrease as a result of higher crop output. The higher crop output is a result of higher crop yield per hectare as application of fertilizer and machinery increases on per hectare basis. The rise in irrigated area increases the proportion of food grain output relative to non- food grain output. Thus, the crop- mix effect is negative.

9. When we take into account the possible decrease in crop output price when crop output rises, the increase in crop output is slightly lower at 0.27%. The crop-mix effect, however, is no longer negative. The higher food grain output resulting from expansion of irrigation also leads to larger fall in price, thus, moving the relative price ratio in favour of non-food grain crops. Thus, even though production pattern may shift in favour of food grain production as a result of supply effects (such as expansion of irrigation), the demand preferences may change relative prices in favour of non-food crops and hence move the production pattern in favour of non-food grains.

10. The state level impact of higher crop prices varies across the states influenced by the production conditions. Thus, although output response to input application does not vary across states, input application itself varies with the production conditions. In states with higher extent of irrigated area relative to gross cropped area, fertilizer consumption is less sensitive to changes in the price of fertilizer relative to crop output. Higher irrigated area (relative to crop area), however, increases demand for tractors. The production conditions are a major determinant of input demand.

11. Increase in fertilizer price alone reduces demand for fertilizers leading to a decline in output. Although fertilizer subsidy decreases, the overall adverse effect on crop output is not offset by the improvement in fiscal balance. Crop prices increase but at a lower rate than the rise in fertilizer price. Higher crop output prices lead to higher prices in the other sectors also resulting in lower consumption demand and hence a decline in overall real *GDP*.

12. A devaluation or depreciation of the exchange rate is estimated to increase agricultural output and increase the share of non-food grain output relative to food grain output. Crop prices increase with a depreciation of the currency the extent of the impact depending upon the degree of influence of international trade on crop

prices. As the non-food grain sector is relatively more open to trade, the impact of depreciation of the exchange rate can be expected to affect non-food grain prices more than the rest. The crop output increase is, thus, contributed by input use per hectare and an increase in crop-mix effect.

13. A reduction in tariff protection to the manufacturing sector results in improved terms of trade for agriculture and raises agricultural output. A 10% reduction in import tariff rate on manufacturing sector increases crop output by 0.21%. Manufacturing output also improves as the rise in crop output combined with lower manufactured prices, leads to lower inflation rate. A more competitive manufacturing sector, thus, can enhance the performance of agriculture.

14. Improvement in fiscal balance can be achieved by increasing government revenues or by reducing government expenditures. Reduction in government expenditures may lead to reduction in aggregate demand if the (corresponding) services provided by the government are withdrawn completely. Alternatively, if there is no withdrawal of aggregate demand, the impact of improved fiscal balance would be mainly through lower inflation rate. The impact of improved fiscal balance affects prices through its effect on money supply. The impact on prices is uneven across the two key sectors considered in this study. The price of manufactured products decreases more sharply relative to the agricultural prices. This in turn leads to higher terms of trade for agriculture and a rise in crop output. Manufacturing output also expands as consumption demand increases due to lower inflation rate. When there is a reduction in aggregate demand accompanying expenditure reduction, the crop output gain is marginal. Manufacturing output does increase but overall real *GDP* decreases. Thus, improved fiscal balance appears to have a positive impact on agriculture, mainly due to the uneven impact on prices. One of the explanations for the uneven sectoral price response to overall macro conditions is the sector specific price policies. Hence, to the extent that the price policies remain, the differential impact of the macro level policies will also persist.

15. The various simulations draw attention to the role of demand for agricultural output for sustained increases in output levels. Any supply side stimulus, either in the form of efficiency improvement or expansion of irrigation, leads to increased output but also downward pressure on prices unless the increased output is absorbed by demand at the prevailing prices. Absorption of the increased output by the market demand is possible only when there is an increase in income in a closed economy or when there is a large international market for the produce. In the past, market support was provided by the price policies resulting in growing subsidies. Therefore, for technology improvements to be sustained, an expanding market is essential.

16. The state level variations in efficiency indicate the potential for improving productivity at the regional level, without the increase in crop prices which generally accompanies output increase. Although there are variations in the ranking of states in terms of efficiency over time, the states that are backward in terms of other indicators of development are also inefficient. Although a state like Maharashtra is also low in ranking by efficiency despite its development in terms of per capita *NSDP*, infrastructure and rural literacy, the relatively low efficiency

may also suggest lack of complementarity between agriculture and other sectors. The findings suggest that focus on the development of human resources as well as infrastructure resources in rural areas would play an important role in reducing variations in productivity at the regional or state level.

17. Macroeconomic policies such as exchange rate policy, fiscal policy and monetary policy can have asymmetric impact on different sectors in the economy with respect to output effects. The study shows that exchange rate depreciation and improvement in fiscal balance has a positive impact on agricultural output. Reduction in tariff protection to manufacturing sector also has a positive effect on agricultural output. However, part of the explanation for the asymmetric effects may lie in the price support policies for agriculture. Therefore, agricultural price policies play an important role in sustaining agricultural growth during macroeconomic stabilization.

Appendix 1

Data Details

1.1 List of Crops Used to Calculate the Value of Crop Output at the State-level

I. Food Grains
1. Cereals
2. Pulses

II. Oilseeds
1. Groundnut
2. Rape and mustard
3. Sesamum
4. Linseed
5. Castor
6. Safflower
7. Nigerseed
8. Coconut
9. Soybean
10. Sunflower

III. Fruits and Vegetables
1. Banana
2. Tapioca
3. S Potato
4. Potato
5. Onion
6. Papaya

IV. Fibres
1. Cotton
2. Jute
3. Mesta
4. Sanhemp

V. Condiments and Spices
1. Chillies
2. Ginger
3. Turmeric
4. Pepper
5. Cardmom
6. Garlic

VI. Plantation Crops
1. Coffee
2. Rubber
3. Tea

VII. Other
1. Sugarcane
2. Tobacco
3. Guarseed
4. Arecanut

Appendix 1.2   **Data on Crop Output and Inputs by States and Over the Period 1970-71 to 1992-93**

State	St ID	Year	Value of Output	Gross Area	Gross Irrigated Area	Rainfall	Agri-cultural Labour	Fertilizer	Tractors
AP	1	1970	2267.1	13347.0	4223.0	4479.1	12349.1	283.1	1140
AP	1	1971	2295.0	12652.0	3787.0	2760.0	12624.0	297.0	1207
AP	1	1972	2023.0	12314.0	3573.0	2658.0	12905.0	275.2	2010
AP	1	1973	2690.7	13238.0	4154.0	3682.1	13192.3	280.8	3001
AP	1	1974	2776.4	12860.0	4423.0	4415.0	13485.9	306.6	3859
AP	1	1975	2562.9	12500.0	4528.0	4637.1	13786.1	412.1	5846
AP	1	1976	2028.4	11390.0	4156.0	4099.1	14093.0	401.5	7565
AP	1	1977	2609.4	12090.0	4378.0	4301.0	14406.7	521.8	8754
AP	1	1978	2901.1	12650.0	4698.0	5738.1	14727.4	604.0	10602
AP	1	1979	2702.4	11830.0	4237.0	3621.0	15055.3	534.8	12260
AP	1	1980	2745.3	11780.0	4342.0	3395.1	15390.4	575.6	14581
AP	1	1981	3328.4	12530.0	4678.0	4960.1	15733.0	655.5	17181
AP	1	1982	3220.2	12240.0	4518.0	3724.1	16075.7	731.9	19995
AP	1	1983	3473.0	12820.0	5058.0	7610.1	16425.8	908.6	23699
AP	1	1984	2975.1	11650.0	4470.0	3508.0	16783.6	980.3	29744
AP	1	1985	3123.3	11500.0	4337.0	3735.1	17149.2	888.1	34494
AP	1	1986	2837.3	11070.0	4360.0	3030.1	17522.7	901.5	37753
AP	1	1987	3114.6	11520.0	4298.0	4240.0	17904.4	966.7	40869
AP	1	1988	3942.0	12450.0	5440.0	7260.1	18294.4	1355.3	43988
AP	1	1989	4065.0	12510.0	5454.0	5350.1	18692.8	1532.4	48241
AP	1	1990	4133.2	12430.0	5059.0	3280.1	19100.0	1619.6	53749
AP	1	1991	4184.8	12440.0	5075.5	4760.1	19516.0	1582.3	59854
AP	1	1992	4145.6	11920.0	5085.0	3350.1	19941.1	1514.1	58135
Assam	2	1970	644.3	2773.0	469.0	14490.0	2754.8	8.7	2695
Assam	2	1971	666.4	2834.0	479.0	12942.0	2817.0	8.2	2853
Assam	2	1972	741.9	3035.0	488.0	12261.0	2880.6	10.3	2987
Assam	2	1973	737.7	3076.0	498.0	14707.0	2945.7	8.3	3105
Assam	2	1974	717.8	2710.0	508.0	17967.0	3012.2	6.7	3285
Assam	2	1975	766.0	2870.0	518.0	11890.0	3080.3	5.6	3544
Assam	2	1976	758.4	2950.0	528.0	16018.0	3149.8	3.8	3820
Assam	2	1977	801.0	2950.0	539.0	14149.0	3221.0	5.9	4061
Assam	2	1978	824.6	2980.0	550.0	14419.0	3293.7	7.9	4312
Assam	2	1979	765.9	2900.0	561.0	17106.0	3368.1	6.8	4613
Assam	2	1980	903.3	3090.0	572.0	11845.0	3444.2	9.4	4878
Assam	2	1981	873.2	3080.0	589.0	14108.0	3522.0	10.8	5160
Assam	2	1982	946.9	3190.0	607.0	15102.0	3601.6	13.0	5334
Assam	2	1983	957.1	3210.0	625.0	20206.0	3683.0	17.3	5642
Assam	2	1984	983.0	3350.0	644.0	14608.0	3766.2	13.8	6283
Assam	2	1985	1053.2	3420.0	663.0	15960.0	3851.3	16.7	7568
Assam	2	1986	975.2	3260.0	683.0	14530.0	3938.4	16.8	7603
Assam	2	1987	1051.5	3310.0	703.0	16290.0	4027.4	23.8	7799
Assam	2	1988	1018.2	3250.0	725.0	19350.0	4118.4	25.5	8074
Assam	2	1989	1070.8	3350.0	746.0	18390.0	4211.5	23.6	8446
Assam	2	1990	1134.4	3390.0	769.0	15750.0	4306.7	37.7	8644
Assam	2	1991	1149.4	3450.0	792.0	17090.0	4404.0	35.5	8724
Assam	2	1992	1143.8	3420.0	816.0	15570.0	4503.5	26.5	8448

Appendix 1.2 (Continued)

State	St ID	Year	Value of Output	Gross Area	Gross Irrigated Area	Rainfall	Agri-cultural Labour	Fertilizer	Tractors
Bihar	3	1970	1806.5	11026.0	2732.0	9406.2	14198.0	99.2	1568
Bihar	3	1971	1859.2	10684.0	2788.0	13128.8	14386.0	108.3	2352
Bihar	3	1972	1895.7	10383.0	2688.0	7636.5	14576.5	118.9	3607
Bihar	3	1973	1673.4	10767.0	2797.0	10932.9	14769.6	96.9	5488
Bihar	3	1974	1802.8	10530.0	3055.0	11287.9	14965.2	116.8	6972
Bihar	3	1975	1987.6	10990.0	3363.0	10615.8	15163.4	133.7	8142
Bihar	3	1976	1919.9	11020.0	3604.0	11404.7	15364.2	155.9	9199
Bihar	3	1977	2012.1	11250.0	3780.0	11164.1	15567.7	173.2	10607
Bihar	3	1978	2013.1	11090.0	3707.0	11303.4	15773.9	94.7	12001
Bihar	3	1979	1546.1	10130.0	3390.0	8576.7	15982.8	184.4	13670
Bihar	3	1980	2005.4	10850.0	3632.0	11319.0	16194.5	204.5	15336
Bihar	3	1981	1769.3	10360.0	3582.0	10277.5	16409.0	205.3	17593
Bihar	3	1982	1619.9	9360.0	3350.0	7650.3	16792.9	205.5	18793
Bihar	3	1983	2056.4	9970.0	3570.0	8931.5	17185.7	292.3	20355
Bihar	3	1984	2122.3	10040.0	3784.0	13085.5	17587.7	381.6	22590
Bihar	3	1985	2248.1	10250.0	3819.0	9946.3	17999.2	501.5	25999
Bihar	3	1986	2211.0	10170.0	3831.0	9700.1	18420.2	527.5	29912
Bihar	3	1987	2032.1	10070.0	4054.0	13555.5	18851.2	485.9	35818
Bihar	3	1988	2410.6	10250.0	4242.0	10916.2	19292.1	608.0	40835
Bihar	3	1989	2436.8	10170.0	4122.0	10546.2	19743.5	564.1	43993
Bihar	3	1990	2549.7	10230.0	4092.0	11533.1	20205.3	598.5	49430
Bihar	3	1991	2278.1	9880.0	4050.8	9539.3	20678.0	603.6	52442
Bihar	3	1992	1952.8	9010.0	4040.0	6986.7	21161.7	595.8	51385
Gujarat	4	1970	1996.3	10045.0	1307.0	12580.1	5409.1	164.6	18230
Gujarat	4	1971	2071.2	9933.0	1307.0	7523.5	5508.0	182.2	19302
Gujarat	4	1972	1084.0	9628.0	1549.0	4243.5	5608.7	178.3	20393
Gujarat	4	1973	1771.9	10130.0	1549.0	9051.8	5711.2	211.8	22392
Gujarat	4	1974	1098.0	7340.0	1488.0	3091.2	5815.7	135.0	24455
Gujarat	4	1975	2091.1	9060.0	1535.0	9290.8	5922.0	148.7	25915
Gujarat	4	1976	2051.3	8960.0	1373.0	11187.1	6030.2	202.4	27066
Gujarat	4	1977	2047.1	8970.0	1814.0	9324.1	6140.5	290.1	28096
Gujarat	4	1978	2237.1	9090.0	1936.0	6631.4	6252.7	293.7	30347
Gujarat	4	1979	2112.8	8880.0	1936.0	7175.0	6367.1	377.5	32937
Gujarat	4	1980	2175.4	8940.0	2334.0	7238.3	6483.5	356.9	37811
Gujarat	4	1981	2635.1	9370.0	2522.0	7800.0	6602.0	401.4	42595
Gujarat	4	1982	2245.6	9170.0	2614.0	4832.0	6724.5	363.0	46815
Gujarat	4	1983	2676.1	9440.0	2614.0	11213.3	6849.4	502.3	52759
Gujarat	4	1984	2696.4	9210.0	2797.0	7458.1	6976.5	504.6	60245
Gujarat	4	1985	1702.2	8460.0	2797.0	4145.2	7106.0	421.3	64966
Gujarat	4	1986	1781.2	8170.0	2710.0	3798.2	7237.9	402.3	66845
Gujarat	4	1987	827.6	5030.0	2381.0	3494.4	7372.2	442.3	69738
Gujarat	4	1988	3020.0	8560.0	2100.0	11710.8	7509.1	643.5	74333
Gujarat	4	1989	2724.3	9130.0	2100.0	7874.1	7648.4	695.4	78841
Gujarat	4	1990	2581.6	8650.0	2422.0	8917.8	7790.4	706.4	84270
Gujarat	4	1991	2096.7	9130.0	2501.6	7564.6	7935.0	733.3	92117
Gujarat	4	1992	3269.7	8650.0	3227.0	9545.5	8082.3	716.6	90966
Haryana	5	1970	1218.3	4941.0	2158.0	5383.0	1690.1	70	2877
Haryana	5	1971	1138.5	4957.0	2230.0	5599.0	1733.0	82.1	4315
Haryana	5	1972	1085.1	5048.0	2284.0	3528.0	1777.0	186.8	7236
Haryana	5	1973	1009.6	5188.0	2478.0	5631.0	1822.1	115.0	10068

Appendix 1.2 (Continued)

State	St ID	Year	Value of Output	Gross Area	Gross Irrigated Area	Rainfall	Agri- cultural Labour	Fertilizer	Tractors
Haryana	5	1974	958.6	5150.0	2584.0	2934.0	1868.4	75.5	14007
Haryana	5	1975	1327.2	4390.0	2396.0	6952.0	1915.9	96.9	18369
Haryana	5	1976	1366.8	4980.0	2742.0	7251.0	1964.5	137.3	23131
Haryana	5	1977	1455.5	4880.0	2698.0	6117.0	2014.4	188.7	29972
Haryana	5	1978	1611.5	5060.0	2776.0	6239.0	2065.6	204.0	39573
Haryana	5	1979	1200.3	5110.0	2979.0	2834.0	2118.0	215.6	50068
Haryana	5	1980	1459.8	4490.0	2979.0	6643.0	2171.8	230.8	59878
Haryana	5	1981	1464.3	5000.0	3309.0	3731.0	2227.0	251.6	71641
Haryana	5	1982	1569.3	5360.0	3455.0	3474.0	2272.6	271.9	81363
Haryana	5	1983	1587.4	4840.0	3559.0	4240.0	2319.1	326.0	90896
Haryana	5	1984	1632.7	5260.0	3594.0	6211.0	2366.5	336.6	100902
Haryana	5	1985	1899.1	5050.0	3504.0	10603.0	2414.9	372.2	109898
Haryana	5	1986	1834.4	5130.0	3678.0	5000.0	2464.4	414.8	119264
Haryana	5	1987	1511.5	5210.0	3912.0	3020.0	2514.8	394.0	129209
Haryana	5	1988	2275.6	4210.0	3883.0	9240.0	2566.2	509.2	140988
Haryana	5	1989	2140.7	5500.0	4074.0	3560.0	2618.7	535.5	153780
Haryana	5	1990	2429.8	5140.0	4253.0	6090.0	2672.3	586.3	167091
Haryana	5	1991	2462.9	5420.0	3880.7	3880.0	2727.0	638.2	179938
Haryana	5	1992	2496.3	5150.0	4472.0	4470.0	2782.8	608.6	175176
Karnataka	6	1970	1866.8	10867.0	1355.0	7066.1	6610.4	155.7	8482
Karnataka	6	1971	1983.2	10988.0	1598.0	5735.2	6790.0	166.8	8981
Karnataka	6	1972	1557.2	10410.0	1325.0	4966.7	6974.4	201.8	9515
Karnataka	6	1973	2121.3	10893.0	1422.0	6043.7	7163.9	195.2	10649
Karnataka	6	1974	2140.4	10140.0	1490.0	5374.0	7358.5	232.8	12098
Karnataka	6	1975	2256.8	10290.0	1707.0	7745.6	7558.4	218.7	14118
Karnataka	6	1976	1710.2	8640.0	1467.0	4815.7	7763.7	206.2	14723
Karnataka	6	1977	2410.5	10100.0	1699.0	5419.8	7974.6	269.0	15112
Karnataka	6	1978	2426.3	10610.0	1718.0	6423.3	8191.2	361.2	15626
Karnataka	6	1979	2410.6	10630.0	1718.0	6459.4	8413.7	366.4	16159
Karnataka	6	1980	2080.6	9550.0	1676.0	6021.6	8642.2	343.9	16978
Karnataka	6	1981	2428.8	10710.0	1801.0	6710.2	8877.0	383.6	18468
Karnataka	6	1982	2285.4	10550.0	1792.0	5196.8	9062.5	383.7	19846
Karnataka	6	1983	2585.9	10970.0	1945.0	9018.3	9251.8	487.2	21942
Karnataka	6	1984	2720.5	10680.0	2101.0	4733.2	9445.1	590.7	25392
Karnataka	6	1985	2316.0	10580.0	2012.0	6442.2	9642.4	555.6	28394
Karnataka	6	1986	2790.5	11240.0	2247.0	5302.6	9843.8	565.8	29219
Karnataka	6	1987	2665.4	11620.0	2296.0	4642.7	10049.5	558.4	30650
Karnataka	6	1988	2941.3	11170.0	2606.0	9290.4	10259.5	799.9	32964
Karnataka	6	1989	3050.2	11450.0	2580.0	8157.6	10473.8	779.1	35166
Karnataka	6	1990	2900.5	11080.0	2726.0	7221.2	10692.6	832.9	37138
Karnataka	6	1991	3499.6	11720.0	2883.0	8295.2	10916.0	905.7	40280
Karnataka	6	1992	3522.2	11390.0	2802.0	7772.7	11144.1	780.2	39675
Kerala	7	1970	1246.6	2916.0	589.0	17492.0	3035.6	56.6	1332
Kerala	7	1971	1305.5	2933.0	601.0	22036.0	3014.0	65.0	1410
Kerala	7	1972	1308.2	2958.0	612.0	15607.0	2992.5	75.4	1544
Kerala	7	1973	1287.1	2986.0	623.0	14016.0	2971.2	81.9	1752
Kerala	7	1974	1308.4	3000.0	638.0	21130.0	2950.0	67.4	1966
Kerala	7	1975	1237.5	2370.0	652.0	24426.0	2929.0	63.9	2323
Kerala	7	1976	1201.9	2310.0	274.0	12226.0	2908.1	69.3	2439
Kerala	7	1977	1134.0	2270.0	373.0	17049.0	2887.4	78.5	3940

Appendix 1.2 (Continued)

State	St ID	Year	Value of Output	Gross Area	Gross Irrigated Area	Rainfall	Agri-cultural Labour	Fertilizer	Tractors
Kerala	7	1978	1172.1	2190.0	354.0	19319.0	2866.8	99.9	4068
Kerala	7	1979	1169.3	2100.0	354.0	17559.0	2846.4	105.6	4266
Kerala	7	1980	1180.1	2120.0	354.0	19461.0	2826.1	97.5	4465
Kerala	7	1981	1181.1	2060.0	381.0	21580.0	2806.0	94.8	4625
Kerala	7	1982	1193.3	2100.0	383.0	15419.0	2837.4	104.3	4774
Kerala	7	1983	1084.7	2050.0	389.0	19727.0	2869.1	129.5	4955
Kerala	7	1984	1257.5	2020.0	396.0	14143.0	2901.2	127.6	5298
Kerala	7	1985	1251.0	2010.0	423.0	17099.0	2933.6	141.3	5654
Kerala	7	1986	1226.5	1980.0	399.0	13260.0	2966.4	151.4	5800
Kerala	7	1987	1254.1	1770.0	426.0	14810.0	2999.6	182.5	6030
Kerala	7	1988	1430.5	1970.0	393.0	20570.0	3033.1	213.9	6272
Kerala	7	1989	1486.0	2000.0	406.0	18430.0	3067.0	212.5	6467
Kerala	7	1990	1543.6	2020.0	397.0	15020.0	3101.3	244.4	6790
Kerala	7	1991	1531.0	2030.0	371.0	24360.0	3136.0	224.5	7008
Kerala	7	1992	1686.4	2060.0	376.0	24290.0	3171.1	203.0	6892
MP	8	1970	2409.1	20561.0	1523.0	11922.2	11872.1	80.5	1177
MP	8	1971	2623.2	20892.0	1705.0	11572.5	12147.0	118.3	1765
MP	8	1972	2438.7	20742.0	1762.0	8838.3	12428.3	139.9	2751
MP	8	1973	2383.5	21212.0	1733.0	12600.8	12716.1	141.3	4118
MP	8	1974	2432.7	19510.0	1701.0	8108.4	13010.6	99.4	6701
MP	8	1975	2795.2	20380.0	1896.0	11259.3	13311.9	108.5	8933
MP	8	1976	2205.2	19840.0	2050.0	10486.7	13620.2	136.6	11741
MP	8	1977	2599.4	20440.0	2238.0	10641.0	13935.6	159.1	13810
MP	8	1978	2640.2	20680.0	2413.0	11056.6	14258.3	192.3	15729
MP	8	1979	1777.6	19790.0	2413.0	6648.2	14588.5	159.7	18311
MP	8	1980	2753.4	20590.0	2453.0	11692.6	14926.3	196.8	21577
MP	8	1981	2865.3	20700.0	2510.0	9170.5	15272.0	236.2	25786
MP	8	1982	2809.6	21290.0	2744.0	10625.2	15590.0	240.0	28381
MP	8	1983	3495.6	21560.0	2867.0	11743.9	15914.6	315.0	32708
MP	8	1984	3090.8	21330.0	3105.0	9637.2	16246.0	372.6	38654
MP	8	1985	3416.5	21950.0	3088.0	8674.9	16584.2	437.1	44227
MP	8	1986	3088.8	21170.0	3456.0	10007.3	16929.5	493.5	49610
MP	8	1987	3416.3	21620.0	3437.0	8660.9	17282.1	508.1	56393
MP	8	1988	3801.1	21610.0	3785.0	9480.9	17641.9	684.1	65795
MP	8	1989	3549.4	21440.0	3739.0	8535.0	18009.2	674.7	74471
MP	8	1990	4245.4	22860.0	5051.0	12451.7	18384.2	812.4	82269
MP	8	1991	3697.3	22090.0	4880.0	9314.3	18767.0	809.7	93885
MP	8	1992	4224.7	22260.0	4918.0	9108.0	19157.8	793.0	91077
Maharashtra	9	1970	2001.5	18737.0	1656.0	10305.4	11656.3	199.3	10604
Maharashtra	9	1971	1823.8	18115.0	1566.0	7419.0	11930.0	241.4	11228
Maharashtra	9	1972	1392.6	16980.0	1468.0	5404.1	12210.1	199.9	12085
Maharashtra	9	1973	2309.0	19486.0	1764.0	8467.7	12496.7	260.7	13461
Maharashtra	9	1974	2747.9	18110.0	1933.0	6212.8	12790.1	303.3	15002
Maharashtra	9	1975	2853.1	18720.0	2171.0	10377.3	13090.4	265.0	16375
Maharashtra	9	1976	2996.7	18880.0	1801.0	8027.0	13397.7	290.0	18370
Maharashtra	9	1977	3241.2	19280.0	2306.0	7008.7	13712.3	360.0	20268
Maharashtra	9	1978	3183.6	19110.0	2306.0	7713.1	14034.2	380.0	22846
Maharashtra	9	1979	3279.6	19160.0	2306.0	7858.5	14363.7	421.1	25766
Maharashtra	9	1980	3199.9	19330.0	2516.0	8162.2	14700.9	421.0	29893
Maharashtra	9	1981	3633.0	19660.0	2415.0	8751.6	15046.0	529.1	34741

Appendix 1.2 (Continued)

State	St ID	Year	Value of Output	Gross Area	Gross Irrigated Area	Rainfall	Agri-cultural Labour	Fertilizer	Tractors
Maharashtra	9	1982	3444.6	18960.0	2686.0	6216.3	15358.9	501.0	37566
Maharashtra	9	1983	3579.1	20150.0	2686.0	11091.5	15678.4	642.0	41378
Maharashtra	9	1984	3501.6	19730.0	2518.0	5905.5	16004.4	581.3	44615
Maharashtra	9	1985	3249.9	19670.0	2462.0	6930.1	16337.3	668.0	48234
Maharashtra	9	1986	2682.7	19130.0	2462.0	6504.6	16677.1	656.2	50088
Maharashtra	9	1987	3705.2	19750.0	2381.0	5953.6	17023.9	740.3	52809
Maharashtra	9	1988	3872.0	20420.0	2381.0	11675.3	17378.0	891.1	56926
Maharashtra	9	1989	4673.1	20460.0	2381.0	9442.3	17739.4	1182.0	61123
Maharashtra	9	1990	4517.5	20770.0	3411.0	9901.3	18108.4	1317.4	66883
Maharashtra	9	1991	3311.7	18820.0	3090.0	8606.4	18485.0	1264.0	72788
Maharashtra	9	1992	4565.6	19700.0	3235.0	8495.2	18869.5	1132.0	70793
Orissa	10	1970	1113.7	6761.0	1391.0	11338.0	5202.3	27.9	530
Orissa	10	1971	990.2	6874.0	1149.0	11644.0	5305.0	49.8	562
Orissa	10	1972	1095.9	6936.0	1260.0	11136.0	5409.7	62.8	664
Orissa	10	1973	1180.2	7285.0	1188.0	12303.0	5516.5	63.2	780
Orissa	10	1974	970.9	6730.0	1276.0	7800.0	5625.3	49.4	914
Orissa	10	1975	1267.8	7290.0	1481.0	11424.0	5736.3	47.6	1041
Orissa	10	1976	976.5	6780.0	1383.0	10128.0	5849.6	62.0	1159
Orissa	10	1977	1294.8	7410.0	1449.0	11442.0	5965.0	63.9	1247
Orissa	10	1978	1410.8	7760.0	1586.0	10974.0	6082.7	71.8	1379
Orissa	10	1979	1005.3	7580.0	1647.0	9138.0	6202.8	67.4	1626
Orissa	10	1980	1511.5	8090.0	1711.0	12922.0	6325.2	76.4	2032
Orissa	10	1981	1489.3	7960.0	1779.0	10439.0	6450.0	82.0	2344
Orissa	10	1982	1290.3	7610.0	1851.0	11015.0	6554.5	95.2	2649
Orissa	10	1983	1813.0	8280.0	2006.0	12300.0	6660.8	103.0	2895
Orissa	10	1984	1603.6	7290.0	2030.0	11868.0	6768.7	114.0	3170
Orissa	10	1985	1904.5	8500.0	2159.0	11957.0	6878.4	140.5	3379
Orissa	10	1986	1739.0	8520.0	2088.0	12010.0	6989.9	151.7	3494
Orissa	10	1987	1535.0	8230.0	2062.0	7370.0	7103.2	151.5	3761
Orissa	10	1988	1893.2	8400.0	2350.0	10330.0	7218.3	161.7	4063
Orissa	10	1989	2072.4	8580.0	2350.0	11070.0	7335.3	204.7	4366
Orissa	10	1990	1939.1	8550.0	2415.0	9480.0	7454.2	192.6	4975
Orissa	10	1991	2103.6	8890.0	2511.0	11610.0	7575.0	196.0	5641
Orissa	10	1992	1603.7	8750.0	2471.0	10820.0	7697.8	203.0	5523
Punjab	11	1970	1660.0	4780.0	2888.6	5383.0	2414.5	213.1	42107
Punjab	11	1971	1791.6	4890.0	2955.0	5599.0	2452.0	289.8	44584
Punjab	11	1972	1809.6	5120.0	3041.0	3528.0	2490.0	322.9	48828
Punjab	11	1973	1889.1	5270.0	2976.0	5631.0	2528.7	333.0	53874
Punjab	11	1974	1926.5	5120.0	2891.3	2934.0	2567.9	271.0	59504
Punjab	11	1975	2087.5	5470.0	3121.0	6952.0	2607.7	311.3	66391
Punjab	11	1976	2090.1	5470.0	3194.0	7251.0	2648.2	371.0	72491
Punjab	11	1977	2321.3	5580.0	3286.0	6117.0	2689.2	453.0	82308
Punjab	11	1978	2532.8	5870.0	3262.0	6239.0	2730.9	593.7	97588
Punjab	11	1979	2438.6	5790.0	3217.5	2834.0	2773.3	682.2	114811
Punjab	11	1980	2454.4	5920.0	3382.0	6643.0	2816.3	753.6	136692
Punjab	11	1981	2737.9	6120.0	3408.0	3731.0	2860.0	820.5	159673
Punjab	11	1982	2829.1	6100.0	3550.0	3474.0	2907.3	891.6	179681
Punjab	11	1983	2793.0	6190.0	3609.0	4240.0	2955.4	991.7	199806
Punjab	11	1984	3158.7	6200.0	3621.0	6211.0	3004.3	1047.6	214684
Punjab	11	1985	3360.4	6330.0	3690.0	10603.0	3054.0	1098.2	229543

Appendix 1.2 (Continued)

State	St ID	Year	Value of Output	Gross Area	Gross Irrigated Area	Rainfall	Agri-cultural Labour	Fertilizer	Tractors
Punjab	11	1986	3274.6	6470.0	3717.0	5000.0	3104.5	1115.6	239405
Punjab	11	1987	3467.6	6340.0	3774.0	2790.0	3155.9	1111.5	256029
Punjab	11	1988	3521.6	6540.0	3776.0	9050.0	3208.1	1116.9	270727
Punjab	11	1989	3858.4	6290.0	3919.0	4290.0	3261.2	1144.9	287835
Punjab	11	1990	3774.4	6380.0	3975.4	6950.0	3315.2	1197.8	304696
Punjab	11	1991	4117.7	6400.0	3987.8	4090.0	3370.0	1244.7	322090
Punjab	11	1992	4070.6	6470.0	4031.5	4190.0	3425.8	1199.4	315990
Rajasthan	12	1970	2132.1	16729.0	2453.0	5105.1	5864.9	53.7	18820
Rajasthan	12	1971	1586.8	16773.0	2440.0	5173.1	5975.0	71.0	19927
Rajasthan	12	1972	1275.9	16097.0	2682.0	3264.9	6087.1	57.9	21492
Rajasthan	12	1973	1655.6	17886.0	2679.0	6619.1	6201.4	74.1	23586
Rajasthan	12	1974	1329.8	14290.0	3143.0	3349.2	6317.8	58.4	25663
Rajasthan	12	1975	1981.8	16170.0	2934.0	7243.6	6436.3	77.5	27803
Rajasthan	12	1976	2027.4	15920.0	2976.0	6121.6	6557.1	98.7	30088
Rajasthan	12	1977	2004.8	15810.0	3167.0	6609.9	6680.2	113.0	32963
Rajasthan	12	1978	2178.3	16400.0	3451.0	5584.1	6805.6	133.6	36810
Rajasthan	12	1979	1265.3	14680.0	4084.0	3154.3	6933.3	147.2	40753
Rajasthan	12	1980	1602.6	15880.0	3749.0	3674.6	7063.4	134.1	44837
Rajasthan	12	1981	1897.6	16620.0	3722.0	3816.6	7196.0	138.0	49474
Rajasthan	12	1982	2099.0	16690.0	4088.0	3499.8	7404.3	169.3	53355
Rajasthan	12	1983	2657.7	17590.0	4014.0	5411.2	7618.7	209.7	59070
Rajasthan	12	1984	2258.9	16170.0	3830.0	3891.6	7839.3	206.6	65487
Rajasthan	12	1985	2163.7	17080.0	3863.0	2908.6	8066.3	220.9	71456
Rajasthan	12	1986	1867.9	16610.0	4351.0	3784.7	8299.8	247.1	75104
Rajasthan	12	1987	1491.8	12600.0	3995.0	1977.6	8540.1	214.7	81963
Rajasthan	12	1988	3136.0	17660.0	4365.0	3598.3	8787.4	305.4	89851
Rajasthan	12	1989	2768.8	16800.0	4461.0	2974.4	9041.8	285.6	97023
Rajasthan	12	1990	3596.6	18510.0	5419.0	5204.1	9303.6	371.0	105425
Rajasthan	12	1991	2949.6	17100.0	5006.0	3112.2	9573.0	440.9	117984
Rajasthan	12	1992	3602.7	18740.0	5486.0	5472.1	9850.2	490.5	115699
Tamilnadu	13	1970	2226.2	6560.0	2465.9	3221.0	8879.9	259.0	2897
Tamilnadu	13	1971	2493.9	7210.0	2710.0	2944.0	9098.0	346.0	3067
Tamilnadu	13	1972	2410.2	7260.0	2815.0	2913.0	9321.4	324.3	3958
Tamilnadu	13	1973	2648.1	7190.0	2816.0	3111.0	9550.3	341.0	4995
Tamilnadu	13	1974	1955.1	6230.0	2440.3	3255.0	9784.9	257.5	6186
Tamilnadu	13	1975	2377.0	6810.0	2565.0	3936.0	10025.1	299.9	7380
Tamilnadu	13	1976	2238.6	6690.0	2330.0	3058.0	10271.3	277.5	8387
Tamilnadu	13	1977	2733.0	7300.0	2836.0	3174.0	10523.6	426.7	8904
Tamilnadu	13	1978	2693.6	7250.0	2873.0	2835.0	10782.0	493.0	9856
Tamilnadu	13	1979	2628.1	7290.0	2889.0	3242.0	11046.8	537.9	10824
Tamilnadu	13	1980	2180.1	5850.0	2570.0	1936.0	11318.1	491.3	12354
Tamilnadu	13	1981	2682.1	6670.0	2709.0	3849.0	11596.0	512.6	13794
Tamilnadu	13	1982	2044.6	5830.0	2255.0	1813.0	11778.9	471.9	15447
Tamilnadu	13	1983	2317.3	6610.0	2618.0	3932.0	11964.6	586.8	17085
Tamilnadu	13	1984	2733.9	6630.0	2640.0	3354.0	12153.3	690.5	20201
Tamilnadu	13	1985	2954.0	6610.0	2501.0	4297.0	12344.9	668.3	23430
Tamilnadu	13	1986	2807.4	5950.0	2356.0	2220.0	12539.6	674.4	25840
Tamilnadu	13	1987	3017.0	6400.0	2438.0	2530.0	12737.4	678.9	28462
Tamilnadu	13	1988	3018.8	6290.0	2375.0	4010.0	12938.2	768.6	30982
Tamilnadu	13	1989	3213.1	6320.0	2497.0	3740.0	13142.2	782.1	33602

Appendix 1.2 (Continued)

State	St ID	Year	Value of Output	Gross Area	Gross Irrigated Area	Rainfall	Agri-cultural Labour	Fertilizer	Tractors
Tamilnadu	13	1990	3147.7	5890.0	2327.1	2830.0	13349.5	830.9	37288
Tamilnadu	13	1991	3560.7	6280.0	2481.2	3840.0	13560.0	839.2	41313
Tamilnadu	13	1992	3551.3	6430.0	2540.5	3450.0	13773.8	799.5	40306
UP	14	1970	6049.9	23207.0	8363.0	8746.0	20873.8	410.4	23932
UP	14	1971	5313.9	23025.0	8090.0	11063.3	21151.0	478.0	25340
UP	14	1972	5700.3	22927.0	8511.0	5289.8	21431.9	518.8	32381
UP	14	1973	5233.8	23007.0	8492.0	8077.5	21716.5	465.3	39529
UP	14	1974	5620.0	24450.0	9190.0	8095.9	22005.0	409.7	46910
UP	14	1975	6106.9	24550.0	9231.0	11361.5	22297.2	480.1	52195
UP	14	1976	6188.6	24750.0	9741.0	9202.5	22593.3	729.4	59331
UP	14	1977	6697.7	24790.0	10009.0	8257.3	22893.4	859.8	68841
UP	14	1978	6734.3	27660.0	10575.0	10382.7	23197.4	1058.4	79391
UP	14	1979	4948.3	25130.0	11051.0	4534.6	23505.5	1009.1	91487
UP	14	1980	7157.8	26240.0	11371.0	13206.8	23817.7	1150.6	103985
UP	14	1981	7364.5	26410.0	11620.0	8654.3	24134.0	1269.6	125398
UP	14	1982	7702.9	25120.0	12125.0	8568.0	24653.6	1432.9	138073
UP	14	1983	8065.7	25250.0	12148.0	9029.0	25184.5	1642.8	152951
UP	14	1984	7990.4	24480.0	12731.0	10227.7	25726.7	1612.9	168789
UP	14	1985	8123.5	24570.0	12908.0	8886.1	26280.7	1709.0	187044
UP	14	1986	8326.9	24630.0	12908.0	7098.2	26846.6	1678.3	203378
UP	14	1987	8839.9	23670.0	13920.0	5966.1	27424.6	1596.3	223103
UP	14	1988	10206.3	24490.0	14113.0	8812.9	28015.1	2135.9	240964
UP	14	1989	9418.6	24650.0	14375.0	7833.2	28618.3	2091.7	265369
UP	14	1990	10016.5	24540.0	16055.0	9366.9	29234.5	2240.9	297156
UP	14	1991	10149.8	24060.0	15741.0	8700.0	29864.0	2248.6	329495
UP	14	1992	9910.4	24450.0	15996.0	7148.0	30507.0	2179.7	322359
W Bengal	15	1970	1563.6	7092.0	1147.0	14578.1	7112.1	72.8	5808
W Bengal	15	1971	1656.1	7271.0	1181.0	16154.8	7227.0	104.4	6150
W Bengal	15	1972	1449.6	7091.0	1216.0	11430.5	7343.7	92.0	6383
W Bengal	15	1973	1518.7	7462.0	1253.0	13838.4	7462.4	99.4	6753
W Bengal	15	1974	1681.4	7410.0	1291.0	12593.8	7582.9	126.9	7061
W Bengal	15	1975	1830.6	7600.0	1329.0	7811.2	7705.4	129.7	7351
W Bengal	15	1976	1669.8	7270.0	1369.0	7768.5	7829.9	152.5	7700
W Bengal	15	1977	1961.6	7510.0	1410.0	13767.9	7956.3	172.2	7994
W Bengal	15	1978	1870.4	7020.0	1453.0	15311.8	8084.9	243.4	8377
W Bengal	15	1979	1654.6	7520.0	1496.0	10626.2	8215.4	240.7	8979
W Bengal	15	1980	1877.3	7040.0	1541.0	12531.0	8348.2	282.8	9324
W Bengal	15	1981	1618.8	7030.0	1735.0	14234.3	8483.0	258.4	9445
W Bengal	15	1982	1543.1	6630.0	1834.0	9913.2	8698.4	268.2	9559
W Bengal	15	1983	2155.2	7300.0	1980.0	13842.2	8919.2	369.2	9729
W Bengal	15	1984	2199.7	7210.0	2079.0	16344.7	9145.6	405.7	10082
W Bengal	15	1985	2252.3	7290.0	2183.0	10480.1	9377.8	408.5	10082
W Bengal	15	1986	2317.9	7480.0	2292.0	13216.7	9615.9	499.6	10059
W Bengal	15	1987	2536.8	7620.0	2407.0	13736.9	9860.0	561.2	10532
W Bengal	15	1988	2761.4	7550.0	2527.0	13162.6	10110.3	635.0	11477
W Bengal	15	1989	2856.6	7620.0	2653.0	11407.4	10367.0	671.1	12413
W Bengal	15	1990	2797.7	7830.0	2786.0	12003.2	10630.1	753.0	13454
W Bengal	15	1991	3124.7	7870.0	2925.0	12779.2	10900.0	555.5	14376
W Bengal	15	1992	2986.1	7820.0	3072.0	10868.1	11176.7	731.3	14027

Notes:
1. The years are agricultural years for crop output and financial years for estimating inputs of fertilizer. In the case of labour, the estimates are based on Census figures on number of cultivators and agricultural labourers as main workers; Stock of tractors is derived based on annual data on tractor sales and the number of registered tractors at the beginning of 1980-81.
2. Value of output is derived based on crop output list in Appendix 1, in 1980-81 prices, Rs 10 million (crores).
3. Gross cropped area is in '000 hectares.
4. Gross irrigated area is in '000 hectares.
5. Rainfall data is for the period June-September in mms.
6. Fertilizer consumption is in nutrient terms (NPK) in '000 tonnes.
7. Tractors are in '000 numbers.
8. Data sources: Centre for Monitoring Indian Economy, NCAER data bank, Indian Agricultural Statistics, Census of India, Fertilizer Association of India.

Appendix 2

Model Equations: Specification

The econometric model developed in this study comprises of a variety of equations as is usually the case with such models. As described in the text in Chapters III, IV and V the equations in the model were estimated using different approaches: random coefficient modeling methods, ordinary least squares and generalized least squares suitable for the pooled cross section and time series data. Besides these econometrically estimated equations, the model also has definitional identities. Some of the econometrically estimated equations are 'link' equations in the sense that they provide the empirical link between two or more endogenous variables without explaining explicitly the nature of the linkage. In this appendix, we provide a comprehensive list of all the equations in the model developed in this study for easy reference to the reader interested in the specification of the model. The equations are arranged below in the order of their presentation in Chapters II, III and IV in the text. There are in all 265 equations in the model, some of which are identities. Table A2.1 given at the end of this Appendix provides a list of variables and coefficients with their brief description.

Notations

The relationships between variables in the model are specified as equations or identities below. The random error term in the equations is not indicated in the equations for convenience. The equations are presented with the same notation for coefficients such as a0, a1, a2, ..., etc. However, in the equations in the model, these coefficients differ across equations. The trend variable is indicated as 'T'. Exogenous variables are marked with '. Logarithmic operator 'Ln' is with the natural base 'e'. Lagged values of the variables are indicated by -1, -2 etc in the parentheses as (-1), (-2), etc. The first difference is shown using the symbol Δ. Although the variables are defined in the text, a separate list is provided in Table A1 in this Appendix.

I. Agricultural Output, Prices and Trade

I a. State Level Equations

$$\text{Ln } (VQ/GA)_j = ao^* \theta_j + a1 \text{ Ln } R_j + a2 \text{ Ln } (IA/GA)_j + a3 \text{Ln } (F/GA)_j$$
$$+ a4 \text{ Ln } (TR/GA)_j + a5 \text{ Ln } (LAB/GA)_j + a6 \text{ Ln } RWFG_j \qquad (1\text{-}15)$$

$$\text{Ln } ((\theta/(1-\theta)))_j = a0 + a1 \text{ Ln } (FGQ/NFGQ)_j + a2 \text{ DUMAG'}_j + a3 \text{ Ln FSZ'}_j$$
$$+ a4 \text{ Ln FSZ'}_j * \text{RURLIT'}_j + a5 (TSC'/POP')_j * \text{RURLIT'}_j$$
$$+ a6 \text{ T'} \qquad (16\text{-}30)$$

$$\Delta\text{Ln } (F/GA)j = a0 + a1\Delta (IA/GA)_j + a2 \text{ Ln } \Delta(PF/PA(-1)) + a3 \text{ Ln RNM'}_j$$
$$+ a4 \text{ Ln RNM'}_j * \Delta\text{Ln } (PF/PA(-1))$$
$$+ a5 (IA/GA)_j * \Delta\text{Ln } (PF/PA(-1)) \qquad (31\text{-}45)$$

$$\text{TRPUR}j = a0 + a1 \text{ D1'} + a2 \text{ Ln TPUR}(-1)_j + a3 (IA/GA) (-1)_j$$
$$+ a4 \text{ Ln } (PTR'/PA(-1))$$
$$+ a5 \text{ Ln FSZ'}_j + a6 \text{ Ln VQ}(-1) \qquad (46\text{-}60)$$

$$\text{TR}j = TR(-1)_j + \text{TPUR}_j \qquad (61)$$

$$(IA/IAS)_j = a0_j + a1_j (1/T') \qquad (62\text{-}75)$$

$$(IA/IAS)_{j=15} = 1 - \Sigma (IA/IAS)_{j=1,14} \qquad (76)$$

$$\text{Ln GA}_j = a0 + a1 \text{ Ln GA}(-1)_j + a2 \text{ Ln IA}_j + a3 \text{ Ln } (R'/RNM')_j \qquad (77\text{-}91)$$

$$\text{Ln RWFG}_j = a0 + a1 \text{ Ln RWFG}(-1)_j + a2 \text{ Ln } (PRW/PFG)(-1)$$
$$+ a3 \text{ Ln } (IA/GA)_j + a4 \text{ Ln R'}_j$$
$$+ a5 \text{ Ln RNM'}_j \qquad (92\text{-}106)$$

$$\text{Ln } (FGQ/NFGQ)_j = a0 + a1 \text{ Ln } (FGQ/NFGQ)(-1)_j + a2 \text{ Ln } (PFG/PNFG)(-1)$$
$$+ a3 \text{ Ln } (IA/GA)_j + a4 \text{ Ln } (R'/RNM')_j$$
$$+ a5 \text{ DUMFG}_j' \qquad (107\text{-}121)$$

$$\text{VQ}j = (VQ/GA)_j * GA_j \qquad (122\text{-}136)$$

$$\text{Ln GDP\_CROPS}_j = a0 + a1 \text{ Ln VQ}_j \qquad (137\text{-}151)$$

$$\text{Ln GDP\_LSTK}_j = a0 + a1 \text{ T} + a2 \text{ Ln GDPR} \qquad (152\text{-}166)$$

$$\text{Ln GDP\_FF}_j = a0 + a1 \text{ T} + a2 \text{ Ln VQ}_j \qquad (167\text{-}181)$$

$$\text{GDP\_ALD}_j = \text{GDP\_LSTK}_j + \text{GDP\_FF}_j \qquad (182\text{-}196)$$

I b. National Level Equations

$$\text{Ln } (IAS/GAS) = a0 + a1 \text{ Ln T'} + a2 \text{ Ln } (PUBINV'/GAS)$$
$$+ a3 \text{ Ln } (YLD * PA/ PM) \qquad (197)$$

$$IAS = \Sigma\ IAj=1,15 \tag{198}$$

$$GAS = \Sigma\ GAj=1,15 \tag{199}$$

$$\text{Ln PRW} = a0 + a1\ T' + a2\ \text{Ln PRW}(-1) + a3\ \text{Ln PP} + a4\ \text{Ln (QRW/GDPR)} \\ + a4\ \text{Ln (QRW/GDPR)}(-1) \tag{200}$$

$$\text{Ln POFG} = a0 + a1\ T' + a2\ \text{Ln PP} + a3\ \text{Ln QOFG} \\ + a4\ \text{Ln QOFG}(-1) \tag{201}$$

$$\text{Ln PFG} \equiv k1\ \text{PRW} + (1\text{-}k1)\ \text{POFG} \tag{202}$$

$$\text{Ln PNFG} = a0 + a1\ T' + a2\ \text{Ln PNFG}(-1) + a3\ \text{Ln (PNFG}(-2) + a4\ \text{Ln ER'} \\ + a5\ \text{Ln (M1/GDPR)} + a6\ \text{Ln (NFGQ/ GDPR)} \tag{203}$$

$$PA \equiv w1\ \text{PRW} + w2\ \text{POFG} + (1\text{-}w1\text{-}w2)\ \text{PNFG} \tag{204}$$

$$\text{Ln XQRICE} = a0 + a1\ \text{Ln XQRICE}(-1) + a2\ \text{Ln (FGST/POP)} \\ + a3\ \text{Ln (PRW/UVIXR')}(-1) \tag{205}$$

$$\text{Ln XQNFG} = a0 + a1\ T' + a2\ \text{DUM80'} \\ + a3\ \text{Ln (PNFG/UVIXN)}(-1) \tag{206}$$

$$\text{Ln MQWHT} = a0 + a1\ (\text{FGST/POP'}) + a2\ \text{Ln (PRW/UVIMW')}(-1) \tag{207}$$

$$\text{Ln MPUL} = a0 + a1\ T' + a2\ \text{QOFG}(-1) \tag{208}$$

$$\text{FGST} \equiv \text{FGST}(-1) + \text{PROC}(-1) - \text{DIST}(-1) - \text{XRICE}(-1) \\ + \text{MWHT}(-1) \tag{209}$$

$$\text{Ln PROC} = a0 + a1\ T' + a2\ \text{Ln (PP/PRW)} \tag{210}$$

$$\text{Ln DIST} = a0 + a1\ T' + a2\ \text{Ln FGQ} + a3\ \text{Ln (IP'/PRW)} \tag{211}$$

$$\text{Ln PP} = a0 + a1\ \text{Ln PP}(-1) + a2\ \text{Ln (FGST/POP)} \\ + a3\ \text{Ln (PRW/PM)}(-1) \tag{212}$$

$$VQ = \Sigma\ VQj \tag{213}$$

$$\text{GDP\_CROPS} = \Sigma\ \text{GDP\_CROPS}_j \tag{214}$$

$$\text{GDP\_ALD} = \Sigma\ \text{GDP\_ALD}_j \tag{215}$$

$$\text{GDP\_AGALD} = \text{GDP\_CROPS} + \text{GDP\_ALD} \tag{216}$$

II. Non-Agricultural Sector Output, Prices and Trade

II a. Manufacturing

$$\text{Ln (GVAD)}_t = a0_t + a1\text{Ln (K/LAB)}_t + a2t\ T'_t \tag{217}$$

$$a0t = a0^*\ \text{INTEFF}_t \tag{218}$$

$$a2_t = a2^*_t\ \text{TECEFF}_t \tag{219}$$

$$a0^* = \max\ (a0_t)\ \text{for}_t = 1, TT \tag{220}$$

$$a2^*_t = \max\ (a2_t)\ \text{for}_t = 1,_{,t} \tag{221}$$

$$
\begin{aligned}
\Delta\text{Ln INTEFF} = {} & a0 + a1\ \Delta\text{Ln INTEFF}(-1) + a2\ \Delta\text{Ln INTEFF}(-2) \\
& + a3\ (\text{STQ/Q})(-1) + a4\ (\text{STQ/Q})(-2) \\
& + a5\ [\text{Ln INTEFF} + a6\ (\text{STQ/Q}) + a7\ T'](-1)
\end{aligned} \tag{222}
$$

$$\text{Ln TECEFF} = a0 + a1\ \text{Ln INTEFF} \tag{223}$$

$$
\begin{aligned}
\text{Ln GFCF} = {} & a0 + a1\ \text{Ln GFCF}(-1) + a2\ \text{Ln Q}(-1) \\
& + a3\ (\text{NR'} - \text{INFLM}(-1))
\end{aligned} \tag{224}
$$

$$K \equiv (1 - \delta)\ K(-1) + \text{GFCF} \tag{225}$$

$$
\begin{aligned}
\text{Ln LAB} = {} & a0 + a1\ t + a2\ \text{Ln}\ [\text{Q}(-1)/\text{Q}(-2)] + a3\ \text{Ln NWt} \\
& + a4\ \text{Ln NW}(-1) + a5\ \text{Ln NW}(-2) + a6\ \text{INFLC} + a7\ \text{INFLC}(-1) \\
& + a8\ \text{INFLC}(-2) + a9\ \text{INFLC}(-3)
\end{aligned} \tag{226}
$$

$$\text{Ln NW} = a0 + a1\ \text{Ln NW}(-1) + a2\ \text{Ln Q} + a3\ \text{INFLC} \tag{227}$$

$$(\text{STQ/Q}) = a0 + a1\ t + a2\ \text{INFLM} + a3\ \text{Ln}\ (\text{Q/Q}(-1)) \tag{228}$$

$$
\begin{aligned}
\text{Ln Q} = {} & a0 + a1\ \text{Ln Q}(-1) + a2\ \text{Ln}\ (\text{Q}(-2) + a3\ \text{Ln}\ (\text{Q}(-3) \\
& + a4\ \text{Ln GVAD}
\end{aligned} \tag{229}
$$

$$
\begin{aligned}
\text{Ln GVAD\_UR} = {} & a0 + a1\ \text{Ln GVAD\_UR}(-1) + a2\ \text{Ln GVAD} \\
& + a3\ \text{Ln GVAD}(-1) + a4\ \text{Ln GVAD}(-2)
\end{aligned} \tag{230}
$$

$$
\begin{aligned}
\text{Ln PM} = {} & a0 + a1\ \text{Ln PM}(-1) + a2\ \text{Ln PM}(-2) + a3\ \text{Ln PFPL'} \\
& + a4\ [(\text{TAR'}^*\text{ER'})(-1) + \text{INDTX'}(-1)] + a5\ \text{Ln (M3/GDPR)}
\end{aligned} \tag{231}
$$

$$\text{Ln XMFG} = a0 + a1 \text{ Ln XMFG}(-1) + a2 \text{ Ln WGDP'}(-1)$$
$$+ a3 \text{ Ln (UVIXM*XSUB'/PM)}$$
$$+ a4 \text{ Ln (UVIXM*XSUB'/PM)}(-1) \tag{232}$$

$$\text{Ln MMFG} = a0 + a1 \text{ Ln MMFG}(-1) + a2 \text{ Ln GDPR}$$
$$+ a3 \text{ Ln (UVIMM'* (1+TAR')/PM)} \tag{233}$$

II b. Other Sectors

$$\text{Ln CONY} = a0 + a1 \text{ Ln CONY}(-1) + a2 \text{ Ln GDPR} \tag{234}$$

$$\text{Ln THRY} = a0 + a1 \text{ Ln THRY}(-1) + a2 \text{ Ln GDP1}$$
$$+ a3 \text{ Ln GDP1}(-1) \tag{235}$$

$$\text{GDP1} \equiv \text{GDP\_AGALD} + \text{GDP\_MFG} + \text{GDP\_PAD'} +$$
$$\text{GDP\_MNG'} \tag{236}$$

$$\text{Ln GDP\_OTHRS} = a0 + a1 \text{ Ln GDP\_OTHRS}(-1) + a2 \text{ Ln GDPR}$$
$$+ a3 \text{ Ln GDPR}(-1) \tag{237}$$

III. Macro Aggregates, Fiscal and Monetary Variables

$$\text{GDPR} \equiv \text{GDP1} + \text{CONY} + \text{THRY} + \text{GDP\_OTHRS} \tag{238}$$

$$\text{Ln GDPMP} = a0 + a1 \text{ Ln GDPR} \tag{239}$$

$$\text{Ln DEF\_FC} = a0 + a1 \text{ Ln CPI} \tag{240}$$

$$\text{Ln DEF\_MP} = a0 + a1 \text{ Ln CPI} \tag{241}$$

$$\text{Ln GTAX} = a0 + a1 \text{ T} + a2 \text{ Ln GTAX}(-1)$$
$$+ a3 \text{ Ln IIPM} + a4 \text{ Ln PM} + a5 \text{ Ln PM}(-1)$$
$$+ a6 \text{ Ln INDTR'} + a7 \text{ Ln INDTR'}(-1) \tag{242}$$

$$\text{GREV} \equiv \text{GTAX} + \text{GNTAX'} \tag{243}$$

$$\text{Ln (GEXP1/WPI)} = a0 + a1 \text{ Ln PADY'} \tag{244}$$

$$\text{Ln GINT} = a0 + a1 \text{ Ln GINT}(-1) + a2 \text{ Ln DEBT'} \tag{245}$$

$$\text{Ln (FTSB/F)} = a0 + a1 \text{ T'} + a2 \text{ Ln (PFPL'/PF')} \tag{246}$$

$$\text{Ln (FDSB/DIST)} = a0 + a1 \text{ T'} + a2 \text{ Ln (IP'/CPI(-1))}$$
$$+ a3 \text{ Ln (PP/PRW)} \tag{247}$$

$$\text{FTSB} \equiv \text{(FTSB/F) * F} \tag{248}$$

$$\text{FDSB} \equiv \text{(FDSB/DIST) * DIST} \tag{249}$$

$$\text{Ln OTHSB} = a0 + a1 \text{ T'} + a2 \text{ Ln OTHSB(-1)}$$
$$+ a3 \text{ Ln (PFPL'/CPI)} \tag{250}$$

$$\text{GEXP} \equiv \text{GINV'} + \text{GEXP1} + \text{GINT} + \text{FTSB} + \text{FDSB} + \text{OTHSB}$$
$$+ \text{OTHEXP'} \tag{251}$$

$$\text{GFISC} = \text{GEXP} - \text{GREV} \tag{252}$$

$$\text{OBUDG} = \text{GFISC} - \text{DBOR'} - \text{EBOR'} \tag{253}$$

$$\text{HM} \equiv \text{HM(-1)} + \text{OBUDG} + \Delta\text{FOREX} \tag{254}$$

$$\Delta\text{RM} = a0 + a1 \text{ T'} + a2 \, \Delta\text{HM} \tag{255}$$

$$\text{Ln M3} = a0 + a1 \text{ INFLC} + a2 \text{ Ln RM} \tag{256}$$

$$\text{Ln M1} = a0 + a1 \text{ Ln M3} \tag{257}$$

$$\text{Ln CPI} = a0 + a1 \text{ Ln (M1/GDPR)} + a3 \text{ Ln WPI} \tag{258}$$

$$\text{INFLC} \equiv \text{Ln CPI} - \text{Ln CPI(-1)} \tag{259}$$

$$\text{INFLM} \equiv \text{Ln PM} - \text{Ln PM(-1)} \tag{260}$$
$$\text{WPI} \equiv v1 \text{ PA} + v2 \text{ PFPL'} + v3 \text{ PM} \tag{261}$$

$$\text{Ln NMPOL} = a0 + a1 \text{ Ln NMPOL(-1)} + a2 \text{ Ln IIPM(-1)}$$
$$+ a3 \text{ Ln QPOL'} \tag{262}$$

$$\text{TDEF} = \text{MMFG * UVIMFG'} + \text{MWHT * UVIMWHT'} + \text{MPUL * UVIMPUL'}$$
$$+ \text{NMPOL * UVIPOL'} - \text{XRICE * UVIXR'}$$
$$- \text{XNFG * UVIXNFG'} - \text{XMFG * UVIMFG'} - \text{XOTHR'} \tag{263}$$

$$\text{CAD} \equiv \text{TDEF} + \text{INVDEF'} \tag{264}$$

$$\Delta\text{FOREX} \equiv \text{CAD} + \text{KINFL'} \tag{265}$$

Table A2.1   List of Coefficients and Variables in the Model Equations

List of Coefficients

Sl No.	Coefficient	Description
1	aj	Regression coefficients in various estimated equations
2	$a0^*$	Frontier Production Function coefficients for Registered Manufacturing
3	$a2^*_t$	Frontier Production Function coefficient for Registered Manufacturing
4	θ_j	Efficiency parameter in crop yield function
5	kj	Weights for aggregating food grain prices
6	vj	Weights for aggregating crop prices
7	wj	weights for aggregating WPI
8	δ	Rate of depreciation of capital stock in registered manufacturing

List of Variables

Sl No.	Variable	Description
1	CAD	Current account deficit (Rs)
2	CONY	GDP real from Construction
3	CPI	Consumer Price Index
4	D1'	Dummy Variable
5	DBOR'	Domestic borrowing by the Central government
6	DEBT'	Total debt of the Central government at the beginning of the year
7	DEF_FC	Deflator for GDP at factor cost
8	DEF_MP	Deflator for GDP at market prices
9	DIST	Distribution of food grain through Public Distribution System
10	DUM80'	Dummy variable
11	DUMAG'	Dummy variable
12	DUMFG'	Dummy variable
13	EBOR'	External borrowing by the Central government
14	ER'	Exchange rate of the rupee (rupees per US dollar)
15	F	Fertiliser consumption (NPK)
16	FDSB	Food subsidy payments by the Central government
17	FGQ	Food grain output
18	FGST	Stock of food grain with the government at the year's beginning
19	FOREX	Foreign exchange reserves of the Reserve Bank of India

List of Variables (Continued)

Sl No.	Variable	Description
20	FSZ'	Average size of farm holdings
21	FTSB	Fertiliser subsidy payments by the Central government
22	GA	Gross cropped area
23	GAS	Gross cropped area of all the major 15 states
24	GDP1	GDP real from selected sectors (real)
25	GDP_AGALD	GDP from agriculture and allied activities (real)
26	GDP_ALD	GDP from allied activities of agriculture (real)
27	GDP_FF	GDP from forestry and fisheries (real)
28	GDP_LSTK	GDP from livestock activities (real)
29	GDPMP	GDP at market prices (nominal)
30	GDPR	GDP at factor cost (real)
31	GDP_AGALD	GDP from agriculture and allied sectors (real)
32	GDP_MFG	GDP from manufacturing (real)
33	GDP_MNG'	GDP from mining and quarrying (real)
34	GDP_OTHRS	GDP from other services (real)
35	GDP_PAD'	GDP from Public Administration and Defense (real)
36	GEXP	Total expenditures of the Central government (nominal)
37	GEXP1	Salary and consumption expenditures of the Central government
38	GFCF	Gross fixed capital formation in registered manufacturing (real)
39	GFISC	Gross fiscal deficit of the Central government
40	GINT	Interest payment on Central government debt
41	GNTAX'	Non-tax revenues of the Central government
42	GREV	Gross revenue receipts of the Central government
43	GTAX	Tax receipts of the Central government
44	GVAD	Gross value added in registered manufacturing sector (real)
45	GVAD_UR	Gross value added in unregistered manufacturing sector (real)
46	HM	High powered money
47	IA	Irrigated area (gross)
48	IIPM	Index of Industrial Production for Manufacturing
49	INDTR'	Ratio of indirect tax revenue of the Central government to value of industrial output
50	INFLC	Inflation rate based on CPI
51	INFLM	Inflation rate based on manufactured products prices
52	INTEFF	General efficiency in manufacturing output
53	INVBAL'	Balance on invisibles external account
54	IP'	Issue price index for food grain distributed through PDS
55	K	Capital stock in registered manufacturing (real)

List of Variables (Continued)

Sl No.	Variable	Description
56	KINFL'	Net capital inflows in external account .
57	LAB	Labour in registered manufacturing
58	M1	Narrow money
59	M3	Broad money
60	MMFG	Imports of manufactured products
61	MPUL	Imports of pulses
62	MQWHT	Imports of wheat
63	NFGQ	Non food grain crop output
64	NMPOL	Net import of crude petroleum and products
65	NR'	Nominal lending rate
66	NW	Nominal wage rate in registered manufacturing sector
67	OBUDG	Overall budget deficit of the Central government
68	OTHEXP'	Other expenditures of the Central government
69	OTHSB	Other subsidies of the Central government
70	PA	Agricultural price index
71	PADY'	GDP from Public Administration and Defense (real)
72	PF	Price index of fertilizers
73	PFG	Price index of food grain
74	PFPL'	price index of energy products
75	PM	Price index of manufactured products
76	PNFG	Price index of non food grain crops
77	POFG	Price index of food grains other than rice and wheat
78	POP'	Population
79	PP	Index of procurement price for rice and wheat
80	PROC	Procurement of rice and wheat by the government
81	PRW	Price index of rice and wheat
82	PTR'	Price index of tractors
83	PUBINV'	Public investment in agriculture
84	Q	Gross output of registered manufacturing sector (real)
85	QOFG	Output of food grains other than rice and wheat
86	QPOL'	Output of petroleum sector
87	QRW	Output of rice and wheat
88	R	Rainfall
89	RM	Reserve money
90	RNM'	Mean rainfall
91	RURLIT'	Rural literacy rate %
92	$RWFG_j$	Ratio of rice and wheat output in good grain output
93	STQ	Inventory level in registered manufacturing
94	TAR'	Import tariff rate
95	TDEF	Trade deficit

List of Variables (Continued)

Sl No.	Variable	Description
96	TECEFF$_t$	Technical efficiency parameter in registered manufacturing
97	THRY	GDP from trade, hotels and restaurants (real)
98	TR	Stock of tractors
99	TRPUR	Purchase of tractors
100	TSC'	GDP from Transportation, storage and communication
101	T'	Time trend variable
102	UVIXMFG'	Unit value index of exports of manufactured products
103	UVIMM'	Unit value index of imports of manufactured products
104	UVIMPUL'	Unit value index of imports of pulses
105	UVIMWHT'	Unit value index of imports of wheat
106	UVIPOL'	Unit value index of imports of petroleum crude and products
107	UVIXNFG'	Unit value index of exports of crops other than foodgrain
108	UVIXR'	Unit value index of exports of rice
109	VQ	Value of gross output of crops (real)
110	WGDP'	World GDP (real)
111	WPI	Wholesale Price Index
112	XMFG	Exports of manufactured products
113	XOTHR'	Exports of other commodities
114	XQNFG	Exports of crops other than food grains
115	XQRICE	Exports of rice (quantity)
116	XRICE	Exports of rice (value)
117	XSUB	Subsidy on exports
118	YLD	Crop output per hectare of crop area

Note: Exogenous variables are marked'.

Appendix 3

Model Equations: Estimation Results

The model equations were presented in their algebraic form in Appendix 2. These equations are those selected from alternative estimates. As noted previously in Appendix 2, the estimation involved alternative approaches. The varying Coefficients Modelling methods outlined in Kalirajan and Shand (1994) formed the basis for estimating the 'mean output response' functions in the case of crop yield equations and the mean output response function in the case of registered manufacturing. From the estimated mean response equation, 'efficiency' estimates were obtained as described in Chapter II.

The pooled cross section and time series were used for estimating a number of equations relating to agriculture: general efficiency, fertilizer demand, demand for tractors, irrigation. In each case, while one overall or mean relationship is estimated, state level differences in intercept term were further estimated using the residuals of the mean relationship. In the cases where lagged dependent variables were present in an equation where 'pooled data' were used, we have chosen Instrumental Variables method of estimation taking lagged values of the independent variables and other 'exogenous' variables as the instrumental variables. All the pooled data estimation was carried out using Shazam 7.

In the case of regressions using time-series data, we first tested for order of integration of the variables. These results are not presented in the report. In majority of the cases, the variables were non-stationary and integrated of order 1. We adopted the Autoregressive Distributed Lag (ARDL) approach as the general estimation strategy as it provides for choice of optimal lag orders of dependent and independent variables in the regression. Microfit 3.1 was used for estimation of the national level equations. Major diagnostic test results were examined before a particular model was chosen. In general, the models pass through the tests for serial correlation, functional form, normality of residuals and heteroscedasticity. There are cases where some of the models do not pass all the four tests. However, we have retained the estimated equations in such cases if alternative models that are theoretically plausible also produced similar results.

In the case of 'link equations' that are used to relate some endogenous variables to others without explicitly specifying the underlying structure, either the ordinary least squares or the P-H methods were used when the ARDL approach was not satisfactory.

In this Appendix, we report the estimated equations along with details of estimation. Some of the state level link equations have not been presented. The structure of such equations can be seen in the more comprehensive list of equations given in Appendix 2. We also provide a list of variables with brief definitions in Appendix 2.

I. Agricultural Output, Prices and Trade

I.S State Level Equations

I.S1 Mean Output Response Function for Agricultural Output

$$\text{Ln (VQ/GA)}_j = 1.3008 + 0.2489 \text{ Ln R}_j + 0.1215 \text{ Ln (IA/GA)}_j + 0.2178 \text{ Ln (F/GA)}_j$$
$$\qquad (2.87^{***}) \quad (5.81^{***}) \quad (1.97^{**}) \qquad (7.12^{***})$$
$$+ 0.0731 \text{ Ln (TR/GA)}_j + 0.1244 \text{ Ln (LAB/GA)} + 0.2276 \text{ Ln RWFG}_j \qquad (1\text{-}15)$$
$$\quad (3.09^{***}) \qquad (2.19^{**}) \qquad (3.98^{***})$$

Method of estimation: Generalized Least Squares
Number of observations: 15 states * 23 years = 345 Mean square error: 0.0072
Breush-Pagan χ^2 test for RCM (Ho: No RCM) = 29.85***
(degrees of freedom = 6)

I.S2 Disembodied Efficiency in Crop Production

$$\text{Ln } (\theta/(1-\theta))_j = 139.9800 - 0.5215 \text{ Ln (FGQ/NFGQ)}_j + 0.5514 \text{ DUMAG'}_j$$
$$\qquad\qquad (16.45^{***}) \ (16.85^{***}) \qquad\qquad (15.13^{***})$$
$$- 0.7596 \text{ Ln FSZ'}_j + 0.0072 \text{ Ln FSZ'}_j * \text{ RURLIT'}_j + 0.00004 \text{ (TSC'/POP')}_j *$$
$$\text{RURLIT'}_j \ (5.41^{***}) \quad (2.51^{***}) \qquad\qquad (3.45^{***})$$
$$- 0.0687 \text{ T'}$$
$$(16.25^{***})$$

Method of estimation: Pooled data estimator Number of observations: 345
$R^2 = 0.6022$

I.S3 Fertilizer Consumption: $N+P_2O_5+K_2O$ kg per Hectare

$$\Delta\text{Ln (F/GA)}_j = 0.5356 + 1.3206 \ \Delta \text{ (IA/GA)}_j + 0.4638 \text{ Ln } \Delta(\text{PF/PA}(-1)) - 0.0996 \text{ Ln RNM'}_j$$
$$\qquad (9.41^{***}) \ (16.71^{***}) \qquad (6.96^{***}) \qquad\qquad (7.83^{***})$$
$$- 0.1108 \text{ Ln RNM'}_j * \Delta\text{Ln (PF/ PA}(-1)) + 0.3362 \text{ (IA/GA)}_j * \Delta\text{Ln (PF/PA}(-1))$$
$$\quad (16.06^{***}) \qquad\qquad\qquad (2.04^{**})$$

Method of estimation: Pooled data estimator Number of observations: 330
$R^2 = 0.7099$

I.S4 Tractors Purchased (Number)

$\text{TRPUR}_j = -1.2357 + 0.0854 \text{ D1'} + 0.7482 \text{ Ln TPUR}(-1)_j + 0.8582 \text{ (IA/ GA) }(-1)_j$
$\qquad (2.09^{**}) \quad (1.36) \qquad (7.88^{***}) \qquad\qquad (2.22^{**})$
$- 1.6820 \text{ Ln (PTR'/PA}(-1)) + 0.2517 \text{ Ln FSZ'}_j + 0.3599 \text{ Ln VQ}(-1)$
$(2.18^{**}) \qquad\qquad\qquad (2.76^{***}) \qquad\quad (2.57^{***})$

Method of estimation: Instrumental Variables Number of observations: 330
$R^2 = 0.7099$

I.S5 Gross Cropped Area

$\text{Ln GA}_j = -0.1981 + 0.9897 \text{ Ln GA}(-1)_j + 0.0213 \text{ Ln IA}_j + 0.0284 \text{ Ln (R'/RNM')}_j$
$\qquad\quad (2.44^{**}) \quad (93.83^{***}) \qquad\quad (2.13^{**}) \qquad\quad (3.40^{***})$

Method of estimation: Instrumental Variables Number of observations:
330 $R^2 = 0.9865$

I.S6 Composition of Food Grain Output (Proportion of Rice and Wheat in Total Food Grain Output)

$\text{Ln RWFG}_j = -3.7255 + 0.2889 \text{ Ln RWFG}(-1)_j + 0.3819 \text{ Ln (PRW/PFG)}(-1)$
$\qquad\qquad (20.07^{***}) \quad (10.60^{***}) \qquad\qquad (2.77^{***})$
$+ 0.3904 \text{ Ln (IA/GA)}_j - 0.3478 \text{ Ln R'}_j + 0.7779 \text{ Ln RNM'}_j$
$(25.14^{***}) \qquad\qquad (30.26^{***}) \qquad (31.75^{***})$

Method of estimation: Instrumental Variables Number of observations:
330 $R^2 = 0.7008$

I.S7 Composition of Crop Output (Ratio of Food Grain Output Index to Non-Food Grain Output Index)

$\text{Ln (FGQ/NFGQ)}_j = 0.0589 + 0.9709 \text{ Ln (FGQ/NFGQ)}(-1)_j + 0.1737 \text{ Ln (PFG/PNFG)}(-1)$
$\qquad\qquad\qquad (2.05^{**}) \quad (57.18^{***}) \qquad\qquad\qquad (1.87^{*})$
$+ 0.0189 \text{ Ln (IA/GA)}_j + 0.1472 \text{ Ln (R'/RNM')}_j - 0.0677 \text{ DUMFG}_j{'}$
$(1.05) \qquad\qquad (4.26^{***}) \qquad\qquad (2.27^{**})$

Method of estimation: Instrumental Variables Number of observations: 330
$R^2 = 0.9722$

I.N National Level Equations

I.N1 Irrigated Area as a Percentage of Gross Cropped Area

Ln (IAS/GAS) = -2.0205 + 0.0178 T' + 0.0584 Ln (PUBINV'/GAS)
         (7.50***) (13.38***) (2.85***)
+ 0.0958 Ln (YLD * PA/ PM)
  (1.75*)
Method of estimation: ARDL Number of observations: 23 R^2 = 0.9834

Diagnostic Tests	Statistic (χ^2)	Probability of Significance
Serial Correlation	0.1028	0.75
Functional Form	0.2062	0.65
Normality	0.7863	0.68
Heteroscedasticity	0.3486	0.56

I.N2 Price Index of Rice and Wheat (WPI)

Ln PRW = -5.7576 + 0.0072 T' + 0.2841 Ln PRW(-1) + 0.4867 Ln PP
         (2.12*) (0.65)   (1.78*)   (2.56**)
– 0.3234 Ln (QRW/GDPR) – 0.5907 Ln (QRW/GDPR)(-1)
  (1.17)   (2.07**)

Method of estimation: ARDL Number of observations: 23 R^2 = 0.9858 DW = 2.28

Diagnostic Tests	Statistic (χ^2)	Probability of Significance
Serial Correlation	0.93	0.34
Functional Form	1.44	0.23
Normality	14.58	0.00
Heteroscedasticity	2.33	0.13

I.N3 Price Index of Other Food Grains (WPI)

Ln POFG = 3.8924 + 0.0445 T' + 0.7646 Ln PP – 0.2053 Ln QOFG – 0.7705 Ln QOFG(-1)
         (2.00*) (2.19**)   (2.58**)   (0.63)   (2.51**)

Method of estimation: ARDL

Number of observations: 23 R^2 = 0.9666 DW = 1.73

Diagnostic Tests	Statistic (χ^2)	Probability of Significance
Serial Correlation	0.30	0.58
Functional Form	3.00	0.08
Normality	4.26	0.12
Heteroscedasticity	1.90	0.17

I.N4 Price Index of Non-Food Grain Crops (WPI)

Ln PNFG = 2.5942 + 0.0815 T' + 0.0631 Ln PNFG(-1) – 0.5697 Ln (PNFG(-2)
     (2.26**) (3.40***)   (0.36)   (3.91***)
+ 0.3566 Ln ER' + 0.1118 Ln (M1/GDPR) – 0.3720 Ln (NFGQ/ GDPR)
 (3.33***)   (0.61)   (1.44)

Method of estimation: ARDL Number of observations: 23 R^2 = 0.9950 DW = 1.82

Diagnostic Tests	Statistic (χ^2)	Probability of Significance
Serial Correlation	0.16	0.69
Functional Form	1.84	0.18
Normality	0.87	0.65
Heteroscedasticity	1.14	0.29

I.N5 Exports of Rice (Quantum)

Ln XQRICE = 8.1640 + 0.8465 Ln XQRICE(-1) + 0.5346 Ln (FGST/POP)
       (2.83***) (7.92***)   (2.00*)
-0.9670 Ln (PRW/UVIXR')(-1)
 (2.11*)

Method of estimation: ARDL Number of observations: 22 R^2 = 0.8306 DW = 1.41

Diagnostic Tests	Statistic (χ^2)	Probability of Significance
Serial Correlation	0.82	0.36
Functional Form	0.07	0.80
Normality	0.41	0.81
Heteroscedasticity	2.62	0.11

I.N6 Exports of Non-Food Grain Agricultural Commodities (Quantum Index)

Ln XQNFG = 5.5898 + 0.0109 T' + 0.9577 DUM80' − 0.1778 Ln (PNFG/UVIXN)(-1)
            (35.51***) (1.19)   (6.71***)   (1.40)

Method of estimation: ARDL Number of observations: 22 R^2 = 0.9218 DW = 1.75

Diagnostic Tests	Statistic (χ^2)	Probability of Significance
Serial Correlation	0.38	0.54
Functional Form	2.59	0.11
Normality	0.70	0.70
Heteroscedasticity	0.12	0.73

I.N7 Imports of Wheat (Quantum)

Ln MQWHT = -1.8979 − 1.8328 (FGST/POP') + 0.1860 Ln (PRW/UVIMW')(-1)
             (0.97)   (4.22***)   (0.91)

Method of estimation: ARDL Number of observations: 22 R^2 = 0.5172 DW = 2.00

Diagnostic Tests	Statistic (χ^2)	Probability of Significance
Serial Correlation	0.02	0.89
Functional Form	1.93	0.17
Normality	0.21	0.90
Heteroscedasticity	1.24	0.27

I.N8 Imports of Pulses (Quantum)

Ln MPUL = 0.3041 + 0.0476 T' − 0.1704 QOFG(-1)
           (0.34)   (2.74***)   (0.73)

Method of estimation: ARDL Number of observations: 22 R^2 = 0.3421 DW = 2.25

Diagnostic Tests	Statistic (χ^2)	Probability of Significance
Serial Correlation	0.33	0.57
Functional Form	0.02	0.89
Normality	7.56	0.02
Heteroscedasticity	3.41	0.07

I.N9 Procurement of Rice and Wheat (Quantum)

Ln PROC = 3.2727 + 0.8622 T' + 2.0097 Ln (PP/PRW)
            (2.64**) (2.96***)   (4.02***)

Method of estimation: ARDL Number of observations: 22 R^2 = 0.8861 DW = 1.54

Diagnostic Tests	Statistic (χ^2)	Probability of Significance
Serial Correlation	1.13	0.29
Functional Form	0.48	0.49
Normality	0.97	0.62
Heteroscedasticity	0.77	0.38

I.N10 Distribution of Rice and Wheat through Public Distribution System (Quantum)

Ln DIST = 3.50 + 0.0290 T' – 0.1857 Ln FGQ – 0.8154 Ln (IP'/PRW)
            (2.18**) (2.45**)   (0.51)   (1.94*)

Method of estimation: ARDL Number of observations: 22 R^2 = 0.8211 DW = 2.11

Diagnostic Tests	Statistic (χ^2)	Probability of Significance
Serial Correlation	0.42	0.52
Functional Form	2.22	0.14
Normality	1.34	0.51
Heteroscedasticity	.39	0.24

I.N11 Procurement Price of Rice and Wheat (Index)

Ln PP = –0.5034 + 1.0513 Ln PP(–1) – 0.0864 Ln (FGST/POP) –0.4135 a3 Ln (PRW/PM)(–1)
            (3.14***) (41.53***)   (3.60***)   (2.22**)

Method of estimation: ARDL Number of observations: 22 R^2 = 0.9914 DW = 1.43

Diagnostic Tests	Statistic (χ^2)	Probability of Significance
Serial Correlation	1.37	0.24
Functional Form	4.02	0.05
Normality	0.94	0.62
Heteroscedasticity	0.90	0.34

I.N12 Price of Tractors (WPI)

Ln PTR = -0.1035 + 0.5172 Ln PTR(-1) + 0.5083 PM
          (0.78)   (4.21***)   (3.71***)

Method of estimation: ARDL Number of observations: 22 R^2 = 0.9912 DW = 1.85

Diagnostic Tests	Statistic (χ^2)	Probability of Significance
Serial Correlation	0.01	0.92
Functional Form	4.46	0.04
Normality	0.13	0.94
Heteroscedasticity	2.93	0.09

II. Non-Agricultural Sector Output, Prices and Trade

IIA. Manufacturing Sector

II.A1 Mean Response of Manufacturing Output in the Registered Sector

Ln (GVAD) = –1.2076 + 0.4147Ln (K/LAB) + 0.0392 T'
            (31.09***) (8.90***)   (23.19***)

Method of Estimation: GLS MSE = 0.0136 Number of observations: 23
Breush-Pagan χ^2 test statistic for RCM (Ho: No RCM) = 4.15** (degrees of freedom 2)

II.A2 General Efficiency of Manufacturing Output in the Registered Sector

ΔLn INTEFF = –0.1937 + 0.7202 ΔLn INTEFF(–1) + 0.5004 ΔLn INTEFF(–2)
              (6.04***) (3.39***)   (3.54***)
+ 3.4321 (STQ/Q)(–1) + 1.4143 (STQ/Q)(–2)
 (3.46***)   (1.84*)
– 1.9721 [Ln INTEFF – 3.4300 (STQ/Q) + 0.0027 T'](–1)
 (6.65***)

Method of estimation: ARDL Number of observations: 22 R^2 = 0.8591 DW = 2.29

Diagnostic Tests	Statistic (χ^2)	Probability of Significance
Serial Correlation	1.21	0.27
Functional Form	0.14	0.70
Normality	1.17	0.41
Heteroscedasticity	0.16	0.69

II.A3 Technical Efficiency of Manufacturing Output in the Registered Sector

Ln TECEFF = 0.0010 + 0.1136 Ln INTEFF – 0.0106 D1
      (0.48)   (11.95***)   (2.71**)

Method of estimation: OLS Number of observations: 22 R^2 = 0.9114 DW = 2.04

Diagnostic Tests	Statistic (χ^2)	Probability of Significance
Serial Correlation	0.04	0.85
Functional Form	0.10	0.75
Normality	0.47	0.79
Heteroscedasticity	4.33	0.04

II.A4 Gross Fixed Capital Formation (Real) in the Registered Manufacturing Sector

Ln GFCF = -2.2179 + 0.4314 Ln GFCF(-1) + 0.4756 Ln Q(-1) - 0.0055 (NR'-INFLM(-1))
      (1.51)   (1.77*)   (2.11**)   (0.84)

Method of estimation: ARDL Number of observations: 22 R^2 = 0.8462 DW = 2.21

Diagnostic Tests	Statistic (χ^2)	Probability of Significance
Serial Correlation	0.83	0.36
Functional Form	1.51	0.22
Normality	1.17	0.56
Heteroscedasticity	0.26	0.61

II.A5 Demand for Labour in the Registered Manufacturing Sector (Labour Days)

Ln LAB = 13.3650 + 0.1276 T' + 0.1679 Ln [Q(-1)/Q(-2)] – 0.3436 Ln NW
      (42.38***) (14.82***) (1.37)   (2.45**)
0.4276 Ln NW(-1) – 0.6303 Ln NW(-2) + 0.3060 Ln NW(-3) – 0.3596 INFLC
(3.10***)   (3.62***)   (2.15*)   (2.31**)
+ 0.4747 INFLC(-1) + 0.5432 INFLC(-2) + 0.2064 INFLC(-3)
(3.19***)   (3.40***)   (1.85*)

Method of estimation: ARDL Number of observations: 22 R^2 = 0.9943 DW = 2.40

Diagnostic Tests	Statistic (χ^2)	Probability of Significance
Serial Correlation	2.49	0.11
Functional Form	2.10	0.15
Normality	1.30	0.52
Heteroscedasticity	3.23	0.07

II.A6 Nominal Wage Rate in the Registered Manufacturing Sector

Ln NW = -1.6068 + 0.5231 Ln NW(-1) + 0.3504 Ln NW(-1) + 0.1997 Ln Q + 0.8986 INFLC
    (1.90*) (2.82***)   (1.84*)   (1.79*)   (4.49***)

Method of estimation: ARDL Number of observations: 22 R^2 = 0.9940 DW = 2.30

Diagnostic Tests	Statistic (χ^2)	Probability of Significance
Serial Correlation	1.35	0.25
Functional Form	3.65	0.06
Normality	8.34	0.02
Heteroscedasticity	3.68	0.06

II.A7 Inventories in the Registered Manufacturing Sector

(STQ/Q) = 0.0088 – 0.0014 T' + 0.2239 INFLC + 0.1726 Ln (Q/Q(-1))
    (2.09**) (2.00*)   (3.08***)   (2.09**)

Method of estimation: ARDL Number of observations: 22 R^2 = 0.4742 DW = 1.94

Diagnostic Tests	Statistic (χ^2)	Probability of Significance
Serial Correlation	0.01	0.93
Functional Form	0.43	0.51
Normality	4.08	0.13
Heteroscedasticity	0.22	0.64

II.A8 Gross Value of Output in the Registered Manufacturing Sector

Ln Q = 0.7790 + 1.0209 Ln Q(-1) – 0.6887 Ln (Q(-2) + 0.4335 Ln (Q(-3) + 0.1976 Ln GVAD
    (2.04*) (4.25***)   (2.14**)   (2.14**)   (2.36**)

Method of estimation: ARDL Number of observations: 22 R^2 = 0.9923 DW = 1.46

Diagnostic Tests	Statistic (χ^2)	Probability of Significance
Serial Correlation	1.82	0.18
Functional Form	0.73	0.73
Normality	0.68	0.71
Heteroscedasticity	0.27	0.60

II.A9 Gross Value Added in the Unregistered Manufacturing Sector

Ln GVAD_UR = 0.7496 + 0.5260 Ln GVAD_UR(-1) + 0.6569 Ln GVAD
$\qquad$ (2.73***) (3.33***) $\qquad$ (4.43***)
− 0.5753 Ln GVAD(-1) + 0.2991 Ln GVAD(-2)
(2.75***) $\qquad$ (2.24**)

Method of estimation: ARDL Number of observations: 22 $R^2 = 0.9932$ DW = 2.01

Diagnostic Tests	Statistic (χ^2)	Probability of Significance
Serial Correlation	0.01	0.92
Functional Form	1.48	0.22
Normality	0.14	0.93
Heteroscedasticity	0.85	0.36

II.A10 Price of Manufactured Products (WPI)

Ln PM = 3.3441 + 0.3461 Ln PM(-1) − 0.4622 Ln PM(-2) + 0.4188 Ln PFPL'
$\qquad$ (7.27***) (1.79*) $\qquad$ (3.94***) $\qquad$ (3.43***)
+ 0.0002 [(TAR'*ER')(-1) + INDTX'(-1)] + 0.3102 Ln (M3/GDPR)
(3.74***) $\qquad$ (4.82***)

Method of estimation: ARDL Number of observations: 22 $R^2 = 0.9977$ DW = 1.77

Diagnostic Tests	Statistic (χ^2)	Probability of Significance
Serial Correlation	0.05	0.82
Functional Form	2.38	0.12
Normality	2.33	0.31
Heteroscedasticity	0.02	0.89

II.A11 Exports of Manufactured Products (Quantum Index)

Ln XMFG = -5.0739 + 0.4833 Ln XMFG(-1) + 1.9155 Ln WGDP'(-1)
         (2.31**) (3.23***)   (2.62**)
+ 0.3544 Ln (UVIXM*(1+XSUB')/PM) + 0.3241 Ln (UVIXM*(1+XSUB')/PM)(-1)
   (0.83)   (2.88**)

Method of estimation: ARDL Number of observations: 22 R^2 = 0.9928 DW = 1.50

Diagnostic Tests	Statistic (χ^2)	Probability of Significance
Serial Correlation	1.53	0.22
Functional Form	3.17	0.08
Normality	0.05	0.97
Heteroscedasticity	0.16	0.69

II.A12 Imports of Manufactured Products (Quantum Index)

Ln MMFG = -16.8342 + 0.2419 Ln MMFG(-1) + 2.1083 Ln GDPR
          (5.56***) (2.37**)   (6.49***)
- 0.5705 Ln (UVIMM'* (1+TAR')/PM)
   (7.86***)

Method of estimation: ARDL Number of observations: 22 R^2 = 0.9856 DW = 1.59

Diagnostic Tests	Statistic (χ^2)	Probability of Significance
Serial Correlation	0.35	0.56
Functional Form	0.45	0.50
Normality	0.73	0.73
Heteroscedasticity	0.18	0.18

II.B Other Sectors

II.B1 Real GDP from Construction

Ln CONY = -0.8281 + 0.5007 Ln CONY(-1) + 0.4422 Ln GDPR
          (2.50**) (4.33***)   (4.18***)

Method of estimation: ARDL Number of observations: 22 R^2 = 0.9843 DW = 1.50

Diagnostic Tests	Statistic (χ^2)	Probability of Significance
Serial Correlation	2.72	0.10
Functional Form	0.40	0.53
Normality	1.46	0.48
Heteroscedasticity	1.36	0.24

II.B2 Real GDP from Trade, Hotels and Restaurants (THR)

Ln THRY = -1.1045 + 0.7992 Ln THRY(-1) + 0.5552 Ln GDP1 - 0.2857 Ln GDP1(-1)
            (2.19**) (8.53***)   (7.09***)   (2.54**)

Method of estimation: ARDL Number of observations: 22 R^2 = 0.9986 DW = 1.57

Diagnostic Tests	Statistic (χ^2)	Probability of Significance
Serial Correlation	1.48	0.22
Functional Form	0.77	0.38
Normality	1.03	0.60
Heteroscedasticity	0.17	0.68

II.B3 Real GDP from Services Other Than THR, Public Administration and Defense, Transport, Storage and Communication

Ln GDP_OTHRS = -2.8059 + 0.6806 Ln GDP_OTHRS(-1) + 0.2721 Ln GDPR
                    (4.56***) (7.63***)   (2.91***)
+ 0.2413 Ln GDPR(-1)
 (2.00*)

Method of estimation: ARDL Number of observations: 22 R^2 = 0.9985 DW = 1.96

Diagnostic Tests	Statistic (χ^2)	Probability of Significance
Serial Correlation	0.00	0.95
Functional Form	2.28	0.13
Normality	1.14	0.57
Heteroscedasticity	0.00	0.99

III. Macro Aggregates, Fiscal and Monetary Variables

III.1 GDP at Market Prices (Real)

Ln GDPMP = 0.0006 + 1.0091 Ln GDPR
(0.10)   (184.48***)

Method of estimation: P-H Bartlett weights, trended case Number of observations: 22

III.2 Price Deflator for GDP at Factor Cost

Ln DEF_FC = 0.1383 + 1.0045 Ln CPI
(2.04**) (75.02***)

Method of estimation: P-H Bartlett weights, lag=3 Number of observations: 22

III.3 Price Deflator for GDP at Market Prices

Ln DEF_MP = 0.1078 + 1.0090 Ln CPI
(1.42)   (62.47***)

Method of estimation: P-H Bartlett weights, lag=3 Number of observations: 22

III.4 Gross Tax Revenues of the Centre

Ln GTAX = -1.1354 - 0.0274 T + 0.3855 Ln GTAX(-1) + 0.7903 Ln IIPM
        (1.74*) (2.11**) (3.93***)   (9.16***)
+ 0.0042 Ln PM + 0.3011 Ln PM(-1) + 0.8007 Ln INDTR' - 0.3063 Ln INDTR'(-1)
(0.07)   (4.61***)   (13.99***)   (3.87***)

Method of estimation: ARDL Number of observations: 22 R^2 = 0.9999 DW = 2.36

Diagnostic Tests	Statistic (χ^2)	Probability of Significance
Serial Correlation	1.54	0.21
Functional Form	1.68	0.20
Normality	0.54	0.76
Heteroscedasticity	0.00	0.98

III.5 Real Expenditures of the Central Government on Salaries and Consumption

Ln (GEXP1/WPI) = -4.9440 + 0.9985 Ln PADY'
                (7.79***) (15.12***)
Method of estimation: P-H Bartlett weights, Trended case Number of observations: 22

Ln GINT = -1.9814 + 0.6427 Ln GINT(-1) + 0.4608 Ln DEBT'
     (5.07***) (9.03***)   (5.24***)

Method of estimation: ARDL Number of observations: 22 R^2 = 0.9997 DW = 2.03

Diagnostic Tests	Statistic (χ^2)	Probability of Significance
Serial Correlation	0.01	0.90
Functional Form	2.61	0.11
Normality	8.46	0.02
Heteroscedasticity	2.65	0.10

III.6 Fertilizer Subsidy per Unit of Fertilizer Consumption

Ln (FTSB/F) = -4.0519 + 0.1056 T' + 1.9798 Ln (PFPL'/PF')
         (10.22***) (3.30***) (2.67**)

Method of estimation: ARDL Number of observations: 22 R^2 = 0.9245 DW = 1.43

Diagnostic Tests	Statistic (χ^2)	Probability of Significance
Serial Correlation	1.11	0.29
Functional Form	10.36	0.00
Normality	1.85	0.40
Heteroscedasticity	2.18	0.14

III.7 Food Subsidy by Central Government per Unit of Food Grain Distribution through PDS

Ln (FDSB/DIST) = 2.6603 + 0.1197 T' - 3.3569 Ln (IP'/CPI(-1)) + 3.8919 Ln (PP/PRW)
       (6.01***) (6.46***) (1.45)   (1.53)

Method of estimation: ARDL Number of observations: 22 R^2 = 0.8829 DW = 1.74

Diagnostic Tests	Statistic (χ^2)	Probability of Significance
Serial Correlation	0.07	0.80
Functional Form	0.44	0.51
Normality	0.58	0.75
Heteroscedasticity	2.64	0.10

III.8 Other Central Government Budgetary Subsidies

Ln OTHSB = 1.6674 + 0.0388 T' + 0.0702 Ln OTHSB(-1) - 0.6091 Ln (PFPL'/CPI)
       (1.88*) (1.76*)   (4.59***)   (1.06)

Method of estimation: ARDL Number of observations: 22 R^2 = 0.9372 DW = 1.55

Diagnostic Tests	Statistic (χ^2)	Probability of Significance
Serial Correlation	0.82	0.37
Functional Form	3.49	0.06
Normality	1.76	0.42
Heteroscedasticity	0.22	0.64

III.9 Reserve Money

ΔRM = 607.0137 + 0.4343 ΔRM + 0.5636 ΔHM
      (0.96)   (3.25***)   (7.95***)

Method of estimation: ARDL Number of observations: 22 R^2 = 0.9164 DW = 1.63

Diagnostic Tests	Statistic (χ^2)	Probability of Significance
Serial Correlation	1.46	0.23
Functional Form	0.16	0.69
Normality	4.48	0.11
Heteroscedasticity	0.15	0.70

III.10 Broad Money Stock

Ln M3 = 0.9515 - 6543 INFLC + 1.0237 Ln RM
     (6.56***) (2.63**)   (72.81***)
Method of estimation: P-H Bartlett weights, lag=3 Number of observations: 22

III.11 Narrow Money Stock

Ln M1 = 1.2884 + 0.8096 Ln M3
      (4.15***) (29.32***)

Method of estimation: P-H Bartlett weights, lag=3, Trended case Number of observations: 22

III.12 Consumer Price Index for Industrial Workers

Ln CPI = 2.9032 + 0.4779 Ln (M1/GDPR) + 0.5264 Ln WPI
     (3.90***) (4.05***)   (4.25***)

Method of estimation: P-H Bartlett weights, lag=3 Trended case Number of observations: 22

III.13 Net Imports of Crude and Petroleum Products (Quantum)

Ln NMPOL = -3.0142 + 0.6547 Ln NMPOL(-1) + 1.8839 Ln IIPM(-1) – 1.4262 Ln QPOL'
     (3.33***) (4.56***)   (3.11***)   (2.45**)

Method of estimation: ARDL Number of observations: 22 $R^2 = 0.9065$ DW = 2.09

Diagnostic Tests	Statistic (χ^2)	Probability of Significance
Serial Correlation	0.18	0.67
Functional Form	2.63	0.10
Normality	4.42	0.11
Heteroscedasticity	0.81	0.37

References

Ahluwalia, M.S. (2000) Economic Performance of States in Post-Reforms Period, *Economic and Political Weekly*, Vol. 35, No.19, May 6, pp. 1637-1648.

Aigner, D.J. Lovell, C.A.K. and P.Schmidt (1977) Formulation and Estimation of Stochastic Frontier Production Function Models, *Journal of Econometrics*, Vol. 6, pp. 21-37.

Balakrishnan, P. and K. Pushpangadan (1994) Total Factor Productivity Growth in Manufacturing Industry: Fresh Look, *Economic and Political Weekly*, Vol. 31, July 30, pp. 2028-2035.

Battese, G.E. and T. Coelli (1992) Frontier production Functions, Technical Efficiency and panel Data: with Application to Paddy Farmers in India, *Journal of Productivity Analysis*, Vol. 3, pp. 153-169.

Bhattacharya, B.B. (1984) *Public Expenditure, Inflation and Growth: A Macroeconomic Analysis for India*, Oxford University Press, New Delhi.

Bhide, S., Kalirajan, K.P. and R.T. Shand (1998) India's Agricultural Dynamics: Weak Link in Development, *Economic and Political Weekly*, Vol. 33, No. 39, Sept 27-Oct 2, pp. A118-127.

Cassen, R. and V. Joshi (1995) *India, the Future of Economic Reforms*, Oxford University Press, Oxford.

Chadha, R., Pohit, S., Stern, R. and A. Deardorff (1998) *The Impact of Trade and Domestic Policy Reforms in India: A CGE Modelling Approach*, The University of Michigan Press, Ann Arbor.

Central Statistical Organisation (2000) *National Accounts Statistics 2000*, Government of India, New Delhi.

Cornwell, C., Schmidt, P. and R.C. Sickles (1990) Production Frontiers with Cross Sectional and Time-Series Variation in Efficiency Levels, *Journal of Econometrics*, Vol. 46, pp. 185-200.

Dahiya, S.B. (ed.) (1982) *Development Planning Models, Volumes 1 & 2*, Inter India Publication, New Delhi.

Desai, M.J. (1972) Macroeconometric Models for India: A Survey, *Sankhya*, Series B, Vol. 3, Part 2, pp. 169-206.

Government of India (2002) *Economic Survey*, Ministry of Finance, New Delhi.

Greene, W. (1990) A Gamma-Distributed Stochastic Frontier Model, *Journal of Econometrics*, Vol. 46, pp. 141-163.

Hildreth, C. and J.P. Housck (1968) Some Estimators for a Linear Model with Random Coefficients, *Journal of American Statistical Association*, Vol. 63, pp. 584-95.

IEG-DSE Research Team (1999) Policies for Stability and Growth: Experiments with a comprehensive Structural Model for India, *Journal of Quantitative Economics*, Vol. 15, No.2, pp. 25-109.

Joshi, V. and I.M.D. Little (1996) *India's Economic Reforms, 1991-2001*, Oxford University Press, Oxford.

Kalirajan, K.P. and M.B. Obwana (1994) Frontier Production Function: A Stochastic Varying Coefficients Approach, *Oxford Bulletin of Economics and Statistics*, Vol. 56, pp. 85-94.

Kalirajan, K.P., Obwana, M.B. and S. Zhao (1996) A Decomposition of Total Factor Productivity Growth: the Case of Chinese Agricultural Growth Before and After Reforms, *American Journal of Agricultural Economics*, Vol. 78, pp. 331-338.

Kalirajan, K.P., Shand, R.T. and S. Bhide (2000) Economic Reforms and Convergence of Incomes Across Indian States: Benefits for the Poor, in *Economic Reforms for the Poor*, edited by S. Gangopadhyay and W. Wadhwa, Konark Publishers, New Delhi.

Kalirajan, K.P. and R.T. Shand (1994) *Economics in Disequilibrium, An Approach from the Frontier*, Macmillan India, Delhi.

Kalirajan, K.P. and R.T. Shand (1997) Sources of Output Growth in Indian Agriculture, *Indian Journal of Agricultural Economics*, Vol. 52, No.4, October-December, pp. 693-706.

Kalirajan, K.P. and R.T. Shand (1992) Causality between Technical and Allocative Efficiencies: An Empirical Testing, *Journal of Economic Studies*, Vol. 19, pp. 3-17.

Kalirajan, K.P. and R.T. Shand (1999) Frontier Production Function and Technical Efficiency Measures, *Journal of Economic Surveys*, Vol. 13, No.2, pp. 149-172.

Krishna, K.L., Krishnamurty, K., Pandit, V.N. and P.D. Sharma (1991) Macroeconomic Modelling in India: A Selective Review of Recent Research, in *Econometric Modelling and Forecasting in Asia*, Development Papers No. 9, ESCAP, United Nations, New York.

Krishnamurty, K. (2001) Macroeconometric Models for India: Past, Present and Prospects, Presidential Address, *37th Annual Conference of the Indian Econometric Society*, South Gujarat University, Surat, Gujarat.

Kumbhakar, S.C. (1990) Production Frontiers, Panel Data and Time Varying Technical Efficiency, *Journal of Econometrics*, Vol. 46, pp. 210-211.

Lumbhakar, S.C. and C.A.K. Lovell (2000) *Stochastic Frontier Analysis*, Cambridge University Press, Cambridge.

Lucas, R.E. (1981) *Studies in Business Cycle Theory*, MIT Press, Cambridge, Massachusetts.

Maddala, G.S. (1977) *Econometrics*, McGraw Hill, New York.

Maddison, A (2001) *The World Economy: A Millennial Perspective*; Development Centre of the Organisation for Economic Co-operation and Development, Geneva.

Marwah, K. (1991) Macroeconometric Modelling of South- East Asia: the Case of India, in *A History of Macroeconometric Model-Building*, edited by Bodkin, R.G., Klein, L.R., and K. Marwah, Edward Elgar, UK.

Meeusen, W. and J. Nanden Broeck (1977) Efficiency Estimation from Cobb-Dougles Production Functions with Composed Error, *International Economic Review*, Vol. 18, pp. 435-444.

NCAER (2001) *Economic and Policy Reforms in India*, National Council of Applied Economic Research, New Delhi.

NCAER (2002) *Development of a Macroeconomic Model to Assess the Impact of social sector spending in India*, Unpublished Project Report, National Council of Applied Economic Research, New Delhi.

Parikh, K.S., Narayana, N.S.S., Panda, M. and A.G. Kumar (1997) Agricultural Trade Liberalization: Growth, Welfare and Large Country Effects, *Agricultural Economics*, Vol. 17 (1).

Reserve Bank of India (2002) *Currency and Finance Report*, Mumbai.

Reynolds, P. (2001) Fiscal Adjustment and Growth Prospects in India, in *India at the Crossroads, Sustaining Growth and Reducing Poverty*, edited by Callen, T., Reynolds, P. and C. Towe, International Monetry Fund, Washington, D.C.

Romer, P.M. (1986) Increasing Returns and Long-Run Growth, *Journal of Political Economy*, Vol. 94, pp. 1002-1037.

Shand, R.T. and S. Bhide (2000) Sources of Economic Growth, Regional Dimensions of Reforms, *Economic and Political Weekly*, Vol. 35, No. 42, Oct 14, pp. 3747-3757.

Storm, S. (1993) *Macroeconomic Considerations in the Choice of an Agricultural Policy: A Study into Sectoral Interdependence with Reference to India*, Ashgate Publishing Group.

Subramanian, S. (1993) *Agricultural Trade Liberalisation and India*, Organization for Economic Cooperation and Development (OECD), Geneva.

Swamy, P.A.V.B. (1970) Efficient Inference in a Random Coefficient Regression Model, *Econometrica*, Vol. 38, pp. 311-323.

Index